LENIN

THE MACMILLAN COMPANY
NEW YORK · BOSTON · CHICAGO · DALLAS
ATLANTA · SAN FRANCISCO

MACMILLAN & CO., Limited
LONDON · BOMBAY · CALCUTTA
MELBOURNE

THE MACMILLAN CO. OF CANADA, Ltd.
TORONTO

LENIN

BY

VALERIU MARCU

TRANSLATED BY E. W. DICKES

New York

THE MACMILLAN COMPANY

1928

SET UP BY BROWN BROTHERS LINOTYPERS
PRINTED IN THE UNITED STATES OF AMERICA
BY THE STRATFORD PRESS

Der bräunliche Hirtenknabe David, der die Philister besiegen soll, wird von Samuel zum König, d.h. zum Feldherrn gesalbt. Der neunjährige Hannibal gelobt, ein ewiger Feind der Römer zu sein, und wird vor dem Altar des Baal zum Feldherrn geweiht. Zu Napoleon ist kein Hoherpriester gekommen. Er hat auch vor keinem Altar des Baal gestanden. Dennoch war bereits der korsische Knabe vom "feu sacré" durchglüht. Der Sohn der Revolution wird sich, ein zweiter Prometheus, das Feuer vom Himmel gestohlen haben.

(The bronzed shepherd-boy David, who was to conquer the Philistines, was anointed by Samuel as King; that is, army commander. The nine-year-old Hannibal swore eternal enmity to the Romans, and was consecrated to command before the altar of Baal. To Napoleon no high priest came. Nor did he stand before the altar of any Baal. Nevertheless, the Corsican boy glowed with the genuine *feu sacré*. The son of the Revolution must, like a second Prometheus, have stolen his fire from heaven.)

FIELD MARSHAL
COUNT ALFRED VON SCHLIEFFEN.

CONTENTS

LIST OF ILLUSTRATIONS

HERITAGE FROM
THE REVOLUTIONARY PAST

Wir suchen überall das Unbedingte und finden immer nur Dinge.

(We search everywhere for the absolute, and always we find only the concrete.)

Novalis.

THE HANGING OF ALEXANDER ULIANOV

SCARCELY a month had passed since Vladimir Ilyitch Ulianov left school at Simbirsk, furnished with all the certificates needed for admittance to a university, when his brother Alexander was sentenced by the courts of the "Emperor and Autocrat of all the Russias, Tsar of Poland, Grand Duke of Finland, etc., etc.," to death by hanging.

Before St. Petersburg awoke on the bitterly cold morning of March 8, 1887, five youths were passing along the banks of the Neva, under lock and key, escorted by a party of soldiers on horseback, on the final journey of their life. They were charged with attempted assassination of the Tsar. Their cage on wheels, constructed to hold a number of prisoners, was flung open like a cupboard at a forgotten and disused landing-stage. A small steamer awaited them. Soon it left the shore, conveying its freight of sinners to that realm in which, it is supposed, knowledge and truth are attained without effort and sacrifice. It bore the friends to the outlet of Lake Ladoga into the Neva. Here the greenish and iridescent water reminds the visitor of the lagoons of Venice. After four hours the journey's end was reached. The five friends—Alexander Ulianov, Genieralov, Osipanov, Andreyushkin and Shivyerev—could see, on the topmost spire of a white tower that broke the walled monotony, a gilded key. It was the oldest prison in Russia—Schlüsselburg. The first inmates of this fortress had stood in intimate touch with the throne.

There were two dozen political prisoners in this for-

tress when the five comrades arrived. The twenty-four
had, under the orders of the Tsar Alexander III, thirty
warders: each prisoner cost the State over five thousand
roubles a year. From their barred windows they would
be able to see the doomed boys in the prison courtyard.
If they would weep at the spectacle of the gallows they
would rejoice at the knowledge that outside in the giant
empire, where holy mother Russia lazily stretched herself, "a vodka flask in her coarse fist, her head bumping
the icy North Pole, and her feet kicking the Caucasus,"
there were men driven by privation, by ideals, or by
fanaticism, who at one point or another rebelled. The
prison officials told no secrets. The prisoners could only
watch the latest arrivals and their escort—the judges and
their servants the hangmen.

ALEXANDER ULIANOV, LAST OF A HEROIC EPOCH

After 1884 hope of successful rebellion had been abandoned by the youth of Russia. The active terrorists,
remembered with joy or loathing at every mention of
the Tsar, dwindled away. Hundreds of families be-
wailed their kin abandoned to the living death of fortress, lunatic asylum, hospital or Siberia. A flood had
passed over the country, sinking into the warm, dry soil;
the steppes, villages and towns had consumed these men.
There remained only their skeletons.

Nothing had been left untried. Every ideal, had it
but gathered two or three together in some forgotten
corner of the West, had had its martyrs in Russia. Every
Utopia had been preached, every dogma, every aphorism,
from neighbourly love to murder. And as effort had
been piled on effort, so now lethargy grew and spread.
Everywhere men buried themselves in the soft pillows of
indifferentism.

In their dressing-gown somnolescence they were visited by a daylight spook—mysticism. This is the comforter of post-revolutionary epochs in Russia, born of despair of all solutions of the social struggle. In the West, in periods of social reaction, the intellectuals turn to scepticism; in Russia they seek God. Social criticism in Russia was not an organic growth. The revolutionaries, now become Slavophils, were able to dismiss the West in favour of an imagined Romanov Utopia. Even Peter the Great, in their eyes, was an intriguer after modernity. Europe recognized the limits of pure reason, but by no means abandoned it; the Slavophils roundly pronounced it superfluous. They still nursed living embers of feudalism, fanned to white heat by the beginnings of capitalism around them. Their ideal was the economic system of the earliest Ruriks. Where formerly they had found refuge in conspirators' clubs, they now found it in the cool of Byzantine monasteries. If they let in the sun's rays on the dust of forgotten archives they imagined that they were embracing living wisdom. Lev Tykhimirov, who, after the assassination of Alexander II, had come into prominence as a terrorist leader, wrote a pamphlet entitled *Why I Am No Longer a Revolutionary*. "When the rope tightens too closely on our necks," wrote Mereshkovsky, "when we begin spasmodically writhing, it is tightened still further and we stiffen."

The irrationalities of this epoch were the product of the curiously romantic regret for so much unfulfilled aspiration, of the tears on the grave of abandoned ideals. They were, at all events, born of love of one's fellow-creatures. The men of this school felt the pains of burdened humanity, and sought in the gloom for twigs wherewith to light lamps to be set in their windows for guidance.

"The basis of their theories," writes Alexander Herzen, "was an inward conviction, an ingrained view of life which enabled them to perceive a living soul in the people. But their instinct served them better than their logical premises. They realized that, if Russia's condition was terrible, it was not a death agony, and where Tchaadayev saw gleams of hope for individuals and none for the people they despaired of individuals but had great hopes of the people. 'The way out,' said the slaves, 'is behind us: back to the days before Petersburg, back to the people.' "

The remaining followers of terrorism now became the plaything of the police. *Agents provocateurs* are ineradicable denizens of the haunts of conspiracy, are its officially appointed abettors. Now that enthusiasm was gone they were likely to sow a heavy crop of mistrust. No one knew whether his neighbour, even his friend, was not in the pay of the enemy. What was easier than to pass from professional conspirator to spy? The more unbroken the reign of law and order, the grimmer loomed the prisons and the more effective were threats and promises. The future was veiled and indeterminate; the prison cell was vividly present.

There were still groups of revolutionaries who endeavoured to keep alive the spirit of the terrorist past. Frequently still there were bomb explosions. But the influence exercised over society by the terrorists steadily diminished, and their organization steadily dwindled. Yet the political problems for which the past generation had had its confident solutions could not be ignored. The indifferentism of the intelligentzia cannot be attributed to individual pusillanimity any more than the acts of the terrorists were due purely to a Platonic ideal of courage. The intelligentzia were, after all, themselves only the reflection of the intellectual basis of the changing social conditions. Their seeming retreat was no more than a sign that opposition to Tsarism called for new methods.

Alexander Ulianov, who had attempted to assassinate the Tsar, had believed that the movement was suffering only from want of heroism; he had hoped to put fresh life into the old tradition. Accordingly, the attempt on the despot's life was to be made on the sixth anniversary of the assassination of Alexander II, at the same hour and in the same street. With Ulianov, Peter Shivyerev and Lugatchevsky were the soul of the conspiracy, to which fifteen men were privy. They had no organization at their back, but felt that something had got to be done. On the anniversary of the death of Alexander II, his namesake and successor always drove to the murdered Tsar's tomb. This time the youths hoped would be his last. They studied the Tsar's habits and daily arrangements, and assiduously worked at their bomb-making. On February 25, 1887, they held their last committee-meeting. Ulianov read to his friends and fellow-conspirators their social and political programme, to give them material for the speeches in court if they failed. The group then proceeded to the Nevsky Prospect for a rehearsal on the route which Alexander III had to take.

Meanwhile the attention of the police had been drawn to the group by a letter which had fallen into their hands. It was addressed to a student in Kharkov, and assured him that terroristic action was certainly going to be resumed. The Kharkov police arrested the recipient of the letter, and he disclosed the writer's name. The writer was soon noticed in the Nevsky Prospect, in company with five other men, and the group were watched. They were surreptitiously carrying something under their overcoats. On March 1, the day on which the bomb was to have exploded, the group of friends were arrested.

Alexander Ulianov, as their leader, made the speech in court in their defence. He tried hard to demonstrate to justices scarcely easy to convince the necessity for terrorist methods. He declared that he had no fear of death, and he prophesied, as did each of the fifteen, that others would come after him and would make an end of despotism. The court condemned all the conspirators to death, but recommended them to mercy. Ten had their sentences commuted to penal servitude; five had to die.

The fifteen had first met together only shortly before the attempt to carry out their idea. They were divided on many other things, and united only by their belief in the necessity of terrorism.

General Shebekov, who had been responsible for the investigations, reported at length to Alexander III on the proceedings in court, pointed out the importance of his discovery, and, like the leader of the conspiracy, prophesied, but in the contrary sense. The terrorists, he declared, had now no organization; the last of them, the few determined men around Alexander Ulianov, had been foredoomed to failure; Russia would in a little while be the only country in Europe with no foothold for Socialism, no room for revolution!

LENIN'S BOYHOOD

The Volga has no interest in the way the crow flies. It winds and doubles, as though it knew all about the thirst of the steppe for moisture, along a course of two thousand three hundred miles through the very heart of Russia. On its banks, southwards from Kazan, lies Simbirsk, now renamed Leninsk in honour of one of its sons. The town rises in terrace formation on the picturesque hilly right bank, which drops steeply to the river like lakeside crags. Only here do the curving trails of distant villages catch and please the eye; over on the other side there stretches the desolate steppe. Far off on the horizon, scarcely visible, is the tiny molehill of a forgotten village.

Ilya Nikolayevitch Ulianov, the son of lower middle-class people from Astrakhan, born at Nijni-Novgorod, came to Simbirsk as an inspector of schools. He named the son who was born to him on April 10, 1870, Vladimir

Ilyitch. As a privilege of his rank his boy was able in due time to enter the public school at Simbirsk.

The small circle of the provincial upper class consisted of landowners or officials. It was a fundamental rule of Tsarism, initiated by Peter the Great, to be lavish with the parchment and seal of rank and status. Complicated tables defining fourteen degrees in the social order were protected by sixteen hundred Articles dealing with grades and official positions.

The privileges of the upper class were not associated, as, for instance, those of the French Order of St. Michael, solely with a general lustre of nobility. Those significant and longed-for privileges were conferred, not by the ownership of land, but by any inherited or acquired office. And the cosy corner in a Government department, the quiet seat in front of piles of official documents, was open to all grades. Whoever had the good fortune to possess a State inkpot belonged to the upper class. Tsarism aimed at using this petty nobility, born in plebeian homes in town or country, to cement its autocratic rule. These lower orders of the upper class were mostly the children of impoverished landowners, born in country farmhouses and bound up with the soil. Their dream was the same one as the peasant's: a bit of land all their own. But they were better able to express it, in more definite terms and with clearer ideas of what they wanted.

In the small towns these proud, poverty-stricken people felt at one with the ragged sons of the soil. But they drew a few poor drops of official salary, and the slightest sign of revolutionary thinking would have lost them all the creature comforts of their position. To compensate for their suppressed aspirations, they read the books that the West produced. They felt every day how for them the times were out of joint, and under the trees in their tiny properties they spoke to their childen of achievable Utopias.

Vissarion Grigorievitch Belinsky was their constant

solace. Ulianov's father must have shown Belinsky's books to his sons—Belinsky's literary essays, the epitome of their age: "Heaven forbid," he writes, "that I should rest content with this everyday life of ours."

Such sons of the impoverished gentility of officialdom as the Ulianovs had but to go to the window to see the peasant. They formed the class of dissatisfied intellectuals, suffering in some degree from the play of the sanctified order of the State. The coat of arms of such a household was quartered with sedition. Sons and daughters alike felt its influence. Their earliest environment, their first friendships, reinforced it. The police, concerned, if not for the material, at all events for the moral welfare of the Tsar's subjects, would keep a watchful eye on the Ulianov family.

The father died at the beginning of 1886. The mother, in the years that followed, had often to think anxiously of her imprisoned children.

After his brother's execution, Vladimir Ilyitch was his mother's favourite child. Many times in years to come she was to wait for him in prison visiting-rooms. In the prison cell every sign of affection from home and friends and the great public is worth more even than better food. It gives strength in melancholy, conjures up pictures of the world outside, and peoples the narrow, closely watched cell. If a mother's tears and reproaches do not pile an added weight of invisible shackles on the prisoner, a hand-clasp in front of the warders, as though in challenge, brings relief for long hours to follow.

Ulianov's sister tells us of his industry as a child. Perhaps the quiet of a country town of something like 30,000 inhabitants, without many diversions, without a flow of passing trivialities, is the best school for thoroughness. What determines taste and inclinations as youth unfolds? Why does a boy take from the proffered dish of motley opinions one and not another? He acquires feelings, ideas, errors, principles, criteria, almost as he assimilated the sounds around him as a child. The process is, indeed, less mechanical than the child's: character implies something done with the impressions received. Nowhere does more depend on inflexible effort and nowhere less on gifts from without than in the formation of character.

"I recall," writes Lenin's sister, "how when I was living in the country Vladimir Ilyitch went every morning after tea to an out-of-the-way summer-house, laden with dictionaries and text-books, bent on study. Here he passed most of the day over his text-books. Vladimir Ilyitch not only knew how one should read, but how to study; he made voluminous notes and extracts. I used at that time to go over to his corner of the garden to learn foreign languages with him. I was still only a child, but even then I was struck with the tenacity and conscientiousness with which Vladimir Ilyitch carried through to the end whatever he took up. Even at that time his example had so powerful an influence over me that, without any other urging, I was ready to do anything in the world if I could satisfy him and earn his approval. He sat over his books the whole day through."

His adolescence was uninfluenced by any outstanding event in Russian history. The voice of the discontented no longer disturbed, as it had done, the leisurely conversation of the satisfied. For this very reason—no period is confined to efforts in one direction—there were budding silently and in isolation in scattered dreamy hamlets, close to the peasant, in the corridors of the universities, in growing industrial centres, the elements of opposition to the general and, as it seemed, unchallengeable lethargy of the revolutionaries.

Ulianov had left the school at Simbirsk, thanks to his passion for accuracy and attention to detail, in his seventeenth year with the best reports in every subject. His head master, the father of the future Prime Minister, Kerensky, wrote on his certificate: "Very gifted; consistently painstaking and regular in his attendance."

THE EXILED STUDENT

From school Vladimir Ilyitch went to the University of Kazan to study law. The university was founded at the beginning of the nineteenth century with a definite general programme. The ukase governing it declared that the world began with the Christian antiquities; that the professors must expound from reliable sources the wisdom and endurance of the martyrs, the dazzling and unspotted purity of the hermits, and demonstrate that true saints are only to be found in the ranks of the advisers of the Throne and the commanders of its armies. All that was counted for wisdom and virtue in pagan history was but a spiritual arrogance that blenched before the majesty of the simple Cross.

Among the students in Kazan this programme went short from the first of its due respect. Its hearers had since changed in social position, in aspirations and hopes and ideas. For the unclassed—the impoverished upper class and the intelligentzia outside that class—learning constantly became a more expensive luxury. The nobles, true to the example of their forefathers, had no taste for strict religious disciplines, and spent their student days on horseback in the military riding-schools. The audience were now mainly merchants' sons. *The Day,* one of the newspapers of the time, complained towards the end of the last century:

"Nowadays money has to be paid out for everything: annual fees for school attendance, matriculation fees, college fees, money for educational books and equipment, to say nothing of maintenance at college. Every student has to spend at least four hundred roubles a year. The students of the theological seminaries are shut out from access to the higher secular educational institutions, and only a few of them, sons of the better situated clergy, are able to pass through the public schools and on to the university. Yet there is all this pressure for admittance to the universities and institutes and technical high schools. What is the explanation?"

The narrower grew the patrimony which they would one day inherit, the more the sons of the officials and of the poorer section of the upper classs saw in study the one essential for the only possible career—as officials. They came from all the surrounding provinces, and especially the twelve counties of the *gubernia* (province) of Kazan; they read with one book between three, lived five in a room, made speeches on academic freedom, and ended by agitating for the abolition of the death penalty. In the traditional gatherings in the long corridors, where the walls were covered with notices of old books and clothes for sale, apartments to let, or offers of coaching-lessons, where the floor was slippery from constant spitting, the windows closed and the air heavy with smoke, discussion went on early and late. Most of the faces were emaciated, the cheeks unrosy, the clothes misfits. Nerves were in constant tension, and not only from absorption in study. Feverish, a little distorted, strained or exultant were the faces; the figures spare and ascetic: a flock of lean kine.

Into this circle came Vladimir Ilyitch Ulianov. He brought with him a testimonial not very welcome to the governors: the brother of a would-be assassin of the Tsar. They had not to watch his steps for long. There was no need for him to talk any louder or more emphatically than his comrades to win for himself, barely thirty days after his arrival at Kazan, banishment to the village of Kokushkino. At seventeen he suffered his first penalty at the hands of the State.

Sentences inflicted on boys for their opinions are pregnant with dangers that their judges wot not of. Conviction as a political offender reveals to the boy that, young as he is, he is not of no account; he is almost of importance. As his consciousness unfolds he sees himself at first as one of a multitude; he looks with wonderment and curiosity at anyone who comes into public notice. That he should himself come into the dock seems hardly imaginable. At his first appearance in court he glows with immense excitement. The conviction carries in itself the danger that it may be made use of as a distinction, and vaingloriously paraded in the market-place of lesser or high politics. Ulianov, however, had the advantage of his education, of the stern realities of his early life and the circumstances of his growth to adolescence. During two years of seclusion, buried in the heart of the country, he studied the turns and twists of the crushed peasants— the agrarian question; he learned jurisprudence; and he read the Book of his group of friends—Karl Marx's *Kapital*.

He must have learnt first of Marx from his brother. A few months before the attempt on the Tsar's life, Alexander Ulianov had been trying to produce a periodical review, and he had translated an article of Hegel's.

Youth always hunts ideas in packs, applauds, gossips or condemns. What can a seventeen-year-old or eighteen-year-old understand of Marx? He is impressed by the monumental scale and the close consistency of the German philosopher's system. But his verdict is generally determined by the reading of a single dazzling sentence. The system of Marxian dialectic spreads over the things of this world a shadow of its own forming, and draws over everything a thin veil which blurs secondary things, while bringing into prominence the main forms of social structure. It connects and divides sharply, so that the young reader, who always loves a generalization and a clear-cut issue, finds set out before him in ideal clarity two world narratives—that of the rulers and that of the ruled. Such over-simplification either sharpens or weakens the vision. Either the eye grows accustomed to the familiar phraseology of the first admired pages, or else it arms itself for microscopic examination of particular features. Later on, perhaps, it is realized that there are not two world histories, that there is no dividing fence, that the roots are intertwined however much the tree may seem to stand in a melancholy self-sufficiency that asks nothing from man or Nature for its growth.

The circle in which Ulianov found himself was seeking the new way, like all the rest, friend and foe alike. He defined the general purpose, applying it objectively to himself, when, as his sister relates, after his brother's execution he said, "No, we shall get nowhere along this road; it is not the right one."

All the feverish reading of foreign authors was to yield a new answer. Industriously and with keen interest their pages were scanned. The dispersed intellectual energies, lacking a common purpose, waited only for an event that should enable them to concentrate on a single goal.

THE CATASTROPHE OF 1891

Even the little that they had could be taken away from the peasantry; what the Tsar left, Nature could take. From time to time the drops yielded by their fount of life could be dried up by the sun.

The countryman weaves cloth from the plants in his own field. In autumn and spring the mud colours the village; in summer dust blows about it; in winter the peasant creeps away from the snow, which mounts up above his small, low windows, right up to the eaves of his one-roomed cottage. One third of the interior is taken up by a big stove, which provides heat for cooking, baking bread, washing clothes and bathing. Here breathing becomes a torture; the smoke bites into the eyes, for the stove has no chimney. Vermin do not trouble the peasant. In 10 per cent. of the farmhouses in the government of Voronesh there were no cockroaches, owing to food shortage and cold. And cockroaches are much more careless of comfort, much more plebeian in taste than bugs. The man who has bugs is the envy of his neighbours. They are the outward sign and ornament of prosperity and comfort. The peasant eats meat on great saints' days, perhaps twenty days in the year. For the rest of the year he lives on watery soup coloured with a few drops of milk, with pickled cabbage-leaves swimming in it. Cucumber is the seasoning of the meal. He crosses himself at table, in gratitude to God for these delicacies.

When drought comes it dries up the countryman along with the grass in the meadows. But men take longer to die than stalks, and do not droop so quickly. First they become skin-clothed skeletons, light as feathers; or they swell monstrously, grotesquely. The children lose their voices; the grown-ups are as sparing of words as if they were crumbs. The times when there was bread, cabbage, cucumber seem fairy-tales of a former life. Ragged unfortunates, wild and brutish, with a wandering gaze that tells of the ultimate despairing hunger for life, leave their villages and creep along the main roads: corpses in search of graves.

Such was the famine which struck down forty million souls at the beginning of 1891.

Then came typhus and cholera.

Tsar and court, officers of the guards, secret police, governors were shaken by chill dread. They suddenly found that they too were mortal. They feared that the Death who was playing with forty million souls might cross the threshold of their own carefully closed houses. They lived apart from the forty millions, they had no fear of hunger though half the nation starved, they had never felt the hardships of the poor; were they now suddenly to have their diseases? They were seized with rage against the ulcers of the mob; the dirt of the incoming tramp threatened to reach them. No diet, no disinfectant, no ointment promised safety. The police were

their only bulwark, and were ordered out against cholera,
typhus and starvation. The quarantining of the villages
and small towns went on endlessly. The cholera became
a source of business profit for its fighters. Sergeant-majors, gendarmes, subordinate officers set up as diagnosti-
cians. Drunkards reeling along the streets were brought
into hospital; when they had peacefully slept off their
debauch and wanted to get out, they found they had tips
to pay first. Suspected cases were locked in in the infirm-
aries. Those who escaped from the houses of death or
from the barricaded villages spread fantastic tales of the
ill-will of the sanitary authorities. The measures adopted
only mystified the mass of the people. As all evil things
came from the Government, they imagined that it had
invented the cholera. Many declared roundly that it
had no existence. In many places hospitals were stormed,
ambulance cars destroyed, moribund patients pulled out
of bed and told they were free to go, doctors beaten.

In the provincial towns the population, in its blind
superstition, went daily in procession through the streets
with ikons of the saints, with flag and candle and song;
they kneeled for hours at a time before the altars in impotent terror, waiting for a miracle. After their devo-
tions they beat the heretical. The burning candles and
the pious intonation of hymns and litanies produced fantastic visions of a world dying in sin. Tortures of conscience drove the provincials from their homes. In their
despair they had visions of the last judgment; they saw
the earth covered with falling stars, clothed by them, as
in autumn by withered leaves. The firmament hung
down in rags; companies of angels passed like Cossacks
through the doomed streets of the dying world, and
sought for the just in inns and tabernacles. "Popes" [1] in
the last stages of gloomy intoxication came to the doctors
and nursing sisters, to read at them in shaky voices the
words of Christ: "Without me ye can do nothing. If

[1] Parish priests.

a man abide not in me, he is cast forth as a branch and is withered; and men gather them and cast them into the fire, and they are burned."

Just sixty years before, Russia's capital had been in the throes of a similar rebellion of visionaries and those in contact with cholera victims. Famine, then as now, had been the precursor of epidemic. The mob had murdered a doctor and threatened to storm the hospitals. Then Tsar Nicholas I had appeared before the crowd and hurled menaces at it, ordered it to come closer and addressed it, standing up in the imperial coach: "Come closer, come closer; I fear no one. Down on your knees, cross yourselves, pray!" The crowd knelt before the Tsar as before the altar. He, too, made the sign of the cross; then, shaking his right forefinger at them, he shouted angrily: "What did you do yesterday? You disgraced me before all the world. Are you Frenchmen, Poles? You killed a doctor—is that the way Russians behave? I'll make it hot for you, banish you. Remember what I say, I fear no one." The kneeling crowd kissed the dust, the bearded children sobbed and begged for their father's blessing. The Tsar gave it and drove away.

Now, in the autumn of 1891, when the sun once more, in its impartiality, was parching rye and wheat, oats and millet, men, women and children, the superstitious religiosity and the incalculable emotions of the masses were unchanged, but in the six decades the figure of the Tsar had dwindled. The ruling powers feared not only cholera, but popular movements: the epidemic of neighbourly love among the intellectuals, who until now had been too timid to assert themselves. Leo Tolstoy wrote his manifesto of sympathy, and preached salvation by repentance. The might of penitence was to tear down every barrier between cultured and simple, poor and rich, and fuse the mass with the élite. The roads alive with misery, the gasping villages, the beleaguered towns produced in the ranks of those who could realize and think, in the

ALEXANDER ULIANOV, LENIN'S BROTHER

LENIN'S BIRTHPLACE

PEASANTS IN WINTER CLOTHING

thousands of chapels of various creeds and confessions, a thrilled energy of mutual aid. Metaphysics, mysticism, speculative subtleties, idle whims were set aside, interrupted by the death-rattle of the forty millions. The dispersed forces now had a single aim; passive yawning in front of blazing fires had given place to the brisk activity of associated service.

Scarcely had the whirlwind of death been stilled when disunion came among the helpers.

The theories of personal rule remained unchanged, as a thousand years before; the same prayers went up to God, the same thin candles of poor sinners and thick candles of rich ones burned before the same altars; but the function of the towns in economic life had changed. Just before the catastrophe the very class which during the famine had possessed the wherewithal for the exercise of philanthropy, and had saved lives by gifts from their superfluity, had been discussing economic problems in the business pages of the newspapers, without metaphysics, honestly and with clear heads. The propertied intelligentzia was occupied by, and divided over, the question of protective duties. The farmers were up in arms against them. Thus the *Russkiya Vyedomosti* wrote:

"Anyone who compares present conditions in agriculture and in industry will find it inconceivable that the former should be required to make sacrifices for the latter. Is there anyone who is not aware that for a decade past our agriculturists have been in the throes of one long crisis? . . . This year the farmers' losses have been substantially added to by the rise in the paper rouble. And it is suggested that the farmer's meagre income should yet further be reduced in the interest of the industrialist! . . . Company reports make no secret of the big profits of the industrialists—profits not infrequently reaching 20, 30, and 40 per cent. of capital. A fraction of these figures would certainly make a happy man of the most exacting landowner."

To this the protectionists replied:

"No doubt some people think that the growth of industry is no blessing, that it brings with it exploitation of labour, the creation of a proletariat, the impoverishment of the masses, the concentration of enormous wealth, the triumph of the Jews and the middle class, and a general lowering, in consequence, of the standard of public life. However much truth there may be in this picture, which is presented already in some of the industrial districts in Russia, there is no escaping the period of industrialism or capitalist production in the history of any people, and it is impossible to enjoy the fruits of so-called 'civilization,' the cheapening of the means of transport and of industrial products, if we are to cling to primitive, patriarchal forms of social organization. However unpleasant it may be, one must keep up with the times."

After the joy of mutual aid came the relapse into egotism. After the common efforts called forth by the famine, the most varied private interests pushed their way forward, the most urgent demands were pressed. Social classes, unlike individuals, cannot sacrifice their own existence in the interest of an ideal harmony. From these issues flowed all the talk, the formulæ and the postulates, the definitions of history, the tears of joy over supposed progress, the melancholy laments over decay, the expositions of the spirit of the times; these were the reservoir of the billions of words in countless discussions in banks, in Court circles, in prison cells and police barracks. Tsar, administrator, terrorist, student, "pope" and high priest, all until now had offered sacrifice on the altar of declamation to one ideal type—the little peasant. The question now gained concreteness. Slowly the image of the *mujik* [1] disappeared. There were too many dead bodies on the roads. Among the awakening intelligentzia, in banking circles and in financial and commercial journalism, reality was taking on sharper outlines.

---

[1] Small peasant.

In the last three years Ulianov had moved in a circle
of friends who were sceptical of the idealized little peasant. In Samara, where he had been most of the time,
famine had raged even more terribly than elsewhere.
Here, when he looked up from his books, the student
could see the facts of existence. It was then that he read
Marx's *Kapital,* and became convinced that the doctrine
of this book "can lead the Russian people to freedom."

The young man determined to meet other people who
shared this view. It was the moment in which a man puts
away childish things, shuts up his books at times and
looks around him. Though it may seem a wretched
world, it opens wide to him.

It must have been the longing for activity which led
him to Samara—the diffident ardour of two-and-twenty,
of the youth who in all modesty is harbouring infinite
aspirations. Life was beginning to take on visible shape.
Until now it had flowed quietly along in a backwater;
now he pushed out into mid-stream. Things read were
corrected by things seen, and he began to discover that
no theory produced in the minds of any two men conclusions that entirely harmonized. He was making his first
decisions, and it may be that they demanded the daring
of a general going into battle.

Ulianov had just been through the external examination in the Faculty of Law at the University of St. Petersburg. If he looked curiously at his brand-new diploma,
he could see the legal mountains he had traversed. Before
him stood all manner of official posts, pleasant conditions,
rural or urban districts to control, subordinates, chiefs,
social circles in which one may be merry or witty, the
opened career of a lawyer, activity, the opportunity of
softening the impact of hard laws, the attraction of freedom in the obscurity of an office. Alongside these there
were fantasies of a half-divined mission, faith in himself,
radiations of the fascination of great things read in books
and of things experienced—the great temptation to pass

by all that pointed to settled security. The temptation overcame him. Perhaps no small part of it was the memory of his brother, whose *nom de guerre* LENIN he adopted. Above all, he was influenced by the terrible experiences of the year 1891. He did not hesitate long. Already the storm-clouds of the future threw their first shadows over him.

He was twenty-four years old when he set off for St. Petersburg in the definite search for men of his own sort.

As he gazed at the desert steppes of his native province, the young man, whose ideas and resolves were already formed and fixed, was filled with illimitable thoughts, illimitable as Russia herself.

THE BIRTH OF A CLASS AND THE WILL OF ITS LEADER

Die harte Schule dreissigjähriger Erfahrungen änderte seine Ansicht über die Mittel, wie dieses Ziel zu erreichen sei; das Ziel blieb ihm dasselbe in den Zeiten hoffnungsloser Erniedrigung wie unbegrenzter Machtvollkommenheit, in den Zeiten, wo er als Demagoge und Verschworener auf dunklen Wegen zu ihm hinschlich, wie da er als Mitinhaber der höchsten Gewalt und sodann als Monarch vor den Augen einer Welt im vollen Sonnenschein an seinem Werke schuf.

(The hard school of thirty years' experience altered his view of the means of attaining this end. But the end remained for him the same in times of hopeless abasement as of boundless power, when he crept towards it by dark ways as demagogue and conspirator as when, first in joint possession of supreme power and then sole monarch, he worked at his task in broad daylight before the eyes of all the world.)
                                    Mommsen on Julius Cæsar.

LENIN'S HOPE OF INDUSTRIAL DEVELOP-
MENT AND CONTROVERSIES
WITH ITS OPPONENTS

EVEN before Vladimir Ilyitch Ulianov, as a young man of twenty-four, definitely settled in St. Petersburg, he had sent from Samara to the Moscow *Legal News* his first work on a considerable scale, "The New Economic Movement Among the Peasantry," the result of statistical studies. It did not appear. But the secret police, keen to add to their reference library, saved the article from the grave in which those unpublished works lie which are written under the impulse of a spirit of bold questioning —the grave of first essays. For the police not only narrowly watched the printed line, they also loved unpublished manuscripts. Three decades passed before Ulianov's scientific essay was released from its archive prison.

The young man in Samara had found that his carefully unravelled statistics pointed in the direction in which he himself meant to go: towards the capital. The figures for 1894 showed that in fifty governments of European Russia there was work with plough, sickle or scythe for 13½ million peasants. There were 15½ million peasants seeking work. Two millions must migrate. Most of these went to increase the population of the industrial zones, of which they formed one quarter. The rest wandered at random, seeking fertile soil as gold-diggers search for veins. They only knew that their masters' kingdom was wide. The wanderers pushed on as far as the ocean, hoping against hope to find somewhere the six or eight dessiatines [1] of their dreams. The peasant is in love with the soil. When he drives his spade into the soft mould he believes that the earth rejoices. For him the crown and completion of existence lies in association with the mother of all things. These living, breathing clods went out to the farthest boundaries of the empire which their forefathers had set. If they missed the way, if they got lost in green prairies or in forests, along trails of their own devising, one of them who could write had to send in their name to St. Petersburg, where the Tsar lives, this or some such letter: "We set off, your Excellency, for Asiatic Europe, a place well known to your Excellency, but we can't find it nohow."

Ulianov examined the causes of this migration, and found them not in any fanciful spirit of adventure, not in the lure of infinite space, but in class changes in the village, where the rich man has no need of the help of the police, but edges out the poor man purely through his better resources in livestock and equipment, and takes his land away from him.

The hanged boy's brother knew the common people that inundate the towns, watching the factory gates in anxious wretchedness, and hiding the shame of their poverty in the suburbs.

Ulianov was led to statistics by a passion for accuracy. He followed the statistics closely, and saw how the town comes into being. He had prepared himself for St. Petersburg with the same thoroughness as for his legal examination, had deliberately made for the centre of the empire. Ulianov never wrote a poem in lyric exaltation, but when he had figures in front of him he became a realist poet, seeing poignant visions of the ugly realities they stood for. From his twenty-second year he had had a passion for these thick statistical volumes, with or without commentary; in them he saw how the creative years of the individual worker are brought, by the shortening

[1] A dessiatine is 1.09 hectare or about 1¾ acres.

of his life, into the right relations to it for the extraction of the average profit.

No one can say with the exactitude of a mathematical solution why the eye so develops that one sees and selects certain things, excluding all else as not of interest to him. As a man with a map follows the course of the rivers, so the statistician in the distant Volga province had followed the slow, hesitating course of the herd that approached St. Petersburg, almost as though beaten forward. He sought their dimly conceived goal, the factory.

As though the machinery—whose hurrying wheels seemed to be undisturbed by any impulse from without— had built its own dwellings, there continually grew up in the farther suburbs of the capital, in the district of Peters- dorf, near the railway, an unending succession of new walls. In barely ten years the Putilov works had taken in twelve new streets. Houses of many storeys, shops and factories were built in a few months, emulating the booths that spring up in a night at a fair. Nearer the city, not only would the ground have been dearer, but there would have been sanitary restrictions to comply with. That would never do. Houses of quite fantastic construction shot up in the midst of dirt and offal.

Along the Schlüsselburg Avenue forty tile factories were at work, without drain pipes; the waste water was run out into the open space at the entrance to the work- men's dwellings; all kinds of filth accumulated here. In a paper factory the vertical pipe which served for trans- mitting pulp three storeys up was cleaned by living brooms. A woman, entirely naked, had to slip down the pipe in a sack, her body thus wiping down the walls. An engineer, correspondent of a cotton-spinning mill, wrote in 1896:

"The new arrival is struck at once by two contradictory things—the cleanliness and order in the factory, the bright machinery, the warm, dry air, an occupation so light that women and children can carry it on with no undue expen-

diture of energy; and over against all this the appearance
of the workers.   They are skinny and undeveloped, all
their limbs seem undergrown.   They look like old children or young dotards.   The workers of all the cotton
mills are just the same.   It is the permanent temperature
of 70 degrees or thereabouts that tears at their vitality."

The factory chimneys of Schlüsselburg Avenue loved
greyness; they were determined to throw over everything
the mantle of their smoke.   Even the inhabitants of neighbouring villages, who asked no better air than the reek
of their cottages, moved away.   It was impossible to
open a window in the neighbourhood of the factories.
Their smoke oppressed every living being; vapours and
soot destroyed plants and domestic animals, and blackened
every metal object.   The pestilent atmosphere would still
be slowly spreading out over the suburbs when dawn
came; one had to go far out along the great main road
before the air became clear.

The price of the soil thus fertilized rose in two decades
from a few kopeks to forty roubles the square metre.   The
cheap servants, the proletarianized peasants, needed room
to stretch their bodies; their limbs must have a certain
length to rest in.   But the lord of the site calculated in
advance every movement of his subject, added the results
together, and saw what expense the room required would
run him into.   Accordingly, he crammed them together.
In most districts the workers' dwellings were managed
as follows: A woman made beds out of boards, which
she leaned against the walls, and began to trade in them.
The workers could not expect mattresses, or, as a rule,
pillows.   In the morning they went to work tired, worn
out at the outset.   A room would hold more people than
might be supposed.   Old women, young girls, half-grown
youths, old men, would lodge together.   In one room a
mother was living with her consort, who had a grown-up
daughter; on another bedplace a girl slept between men
and women.   "In inspecting workmen's dwellings in St.

Petersburg," wrote a woman doctor, "we found rooms with less than a hundred cubic feet of air to each occupant.[1] A single room would often be found to be occupied by five to nine persons, and a single bed by three to five."

The average price of a room was six roubles a month. Each sleeping-place cost about 2 roubles 30 kopeks. But the occupants had no great objection to overcrowding, for the more the lodgers the less each one had to pay.

Anyone who had a place next to the window in these rooms could find relief by pressing his forehead against the cool glass. If he looked out he could see men and women moving about in the gloom, losing their idle hours in dull nothingness. The forms of the passers-by were indistinct. Through the unwashed glass each individual seemed undersized, forlorn, poverty-stricken, blind, hardly recognizable as a human being. They were restricted in every possibility of self-development, at the mercy of sterile emotions and inchoate thought.

And yet St. Petersburg could be beautiful. It was not entirely made up of dismal walls out of which human beings flocked through black gates, to disappear soon into rows of houses like coffins. The city had golden islands, architectural landscapes. Bridges had been built, marshes drained, streets paved, parks laid out. The Neva flows between embankments of red granite. In June the bright daylight is without end. The river reflects like a silver dish. The roofs of the palaces, the domes of the churches, stand out against a sky of purple and amethyst. Minute by minute the horizon changes in shade. The light varies its tone, paints incredible pictures; endless new compositions succeed one another; one thinks of the Apocalypse, of the Sahara, of crumbling cities. Not till eleven o'clock does night come, the clouds fade away, the enchanted pictures disappear. By two

---

[1] The normal accommodation allowed for clerical workers in British Government offices is 600 cubic feet.

in the morning no star twinkles; the rosy veils of a new dawn are lifting.

In St. Petersburg, the chief cultural centre of the country, the Mecca of so many thirsters after knowledge, there was a group of intellectuals who named their movement "Inheritance." They were journalists who had adopted ideas of former decades, ardently attacking serfdom and advocating the traditional local autonomy of the past. They believed that the abolition of rural slavery would be the precursor of universal happiness. These men sought under the skies of St. Petersburg the harmony of cosmic laws; they echoed Fichte's dictum: "No grain of seed that I sow is lost in the moral world. On the day of the sheaves I shall behold their fruit and weave of it for myself undying wreaths."

To these seekers after beauty, if not the earth at least the universe was perfect. That our planet did not collide with other worlds and flatten the noses of the teeming and industriously increasing multitudes, was evidence to them of the utmost conceivable perfection. The disharmony between things, between the St. Petersburg of the palaces and of Schlüsselburg Avenue, produced in them a sensibility that found expression in heavy sentiment, daydreaming and rhetoric. They saw the fount of all evil in the spread of industry, whose chimneys clouded their prospect of universal happiness. Industry, in the view of these critics—they were called Narodniki (Populists)— only impoverished the nation. They saw in the rural co-operative association, the Artel, the expression of the native character of Russian economic life, and a means of existence without any sort of industrialism. These scrutineers of industrial life reported:

"Industry has not improved Russia's economic condition. On the contrary, through the union between factory and landowner, it has brought the worker down to entire misery. In ten out of the twelve industrial provinces the mortality is heavier than in the worst quarters of London, inhabited only by beggars and thieves. It is enough to turn the brain of a patriot! The division of labour which enables the proletarian to increase his productivity tenfold, is for him the source of hunger and destitution, the cause of so high a rate of mortality that in three of the twelve industrial provinces the population is decreasing."

But the spirit of history, which lives in conflict with itself, and is formed out of the mosaic of all circumstances, takes little account of human beings; its food is the life-blood of all. It seems to say to the nation's poor at the end of their day's work: "You have failed to learn to read and write. Your rough hands are good for nothing but manual labour. You may be offering the slow sacrifice of your life, but it is an offering of little importance."

Ulianov's method of enquiry, too, showed him Russia as a Golgotha wrapped in the blackness of night. But he was in love with the conception of inevitable laws. He dismissed from his analysis the ideas of Right and Wrong. He did not want to see the laws of economic change obeyed because they conferred satisfactions, but simply because they were laws; just as anyone obeys his superior, not out of love for him, but because he is his superior. The spirit, however, rebels against the insoluble. Thus the existing state of things was for him only the lamentable prior condition of a better state. His system, too, had windows with a hopeful prospect. He plunged into controversy with the Narodniki, who regarded capitalism in Russia as a step backwards; he declared that these disciples of dead heroes were dismal pessimists, as the view they upheld amounted to this—that the farther things pursued their own course the more difficult it would be to solve the problems so raised. The Narodnik fights from his romantic standpoint, throws to the winds all historic realism and is always comparing existing facts with idealized pre-industrial conditions. Ulianov himself saw "the pledge of a better future solely in the complete evolution of warring tendencies." The Narodniki, the heirs of the dead and buried terrorists, "see no necessity," he wrote, "for applying to Russian conditions the conceptions of different social classes and their conflicts which are the stock-in-trade of modern science. The peasant community they regarded as something of a higher and better order than capitalism. In this conception of the peasantry the discords implicit in all manufacture and exchange of goods, and all capitalist trade and industry, are ignored or glossed over; the identity of these primal discords with their advanced form in capitalist industry and agriculture is denied."

The conflicts of interest which had developed, in short, represented the opposite poles, the opposing forces, tendencies, personalities, institutions of the age. Seen from this point of view, every breath of perfume can be represented by a chemical formula; life proliferates into innumerable species. Every form, however, either serves or disserves the ultimate purpose. In the life of society everything fluctuates. These fluctuations have to be measured. Only that human voice is of importance which recognizes that capitalist change is along these same lines of inevitability. The other individuals are dreamily exchanging idle thoughts with the stars.

Ulianov, now twenty-five, was analysing himself and what the Russians call the intelligentzia, carrying on specially sharp polemics against people of his own sort, against the view that history can be arbitrarily side-tracked in a desired direction, and challenging the "ignoring of the helplessness of the intelligentzia in face of the material interests of particular classes of society."

These and similar ideas gave to the young Ulianov confidence of victory. The ice-capped mountains of opposition could not turn him from his course; he was sure that he knew, in broad, general lines, the course of coming change. Continually he studied statistics and agrarian history, and endeavoured to discover the general

direction of movement at the moment. He became tough
and tenacious, like his bride Necessity; he sought out
crucified humanity, studied its every face and form, in
order to be able to whisper into its ear secret promises
of deliverance.

LENIN'S VISIT TO PLEKHANOV

To the Russians of the towns the birds that migrated
across their country in the spring brought fancies of
unknown, longed-for skies. The vastness of their own
homeland oppressed their minds. The dwellers in palaces
fled from the tedium of their halls; they locked their
garden gates and went westwards. There, among the
upper ten thousand, they felt themselves to be the first
hundred. The rich, busy merchant left his counting-
house for scenes where life has a different *tempo*. The
student abandoned the dim light of his lamp for foreign
universities, to see celebrities whose fame had reached
him at home. The revolutionary—where he was not fleeing helter-skelter from the police, never turning his head
till he had got across the frontier—took up his staff for
a voluntary pilgrimage, to swing the censer of adoration
before the leader of his school of thought, usually in
some foreign country.

Vladimir Ilyitch Ulianov, too, travelled to Berlin and
Geneva, before his first imprisonment, to greet the Master,
George Plekhanov.

In those days Germany, for the young Russian Marxists, was the Promised Land. There they saw one of
their dreams fulfilled: the organization of the working
masses. This this-worldly apotheosis had in their eyes
something of the joyful radiance of the world to come.
In all their programmes, manifestos, pamphlets they
pointed to the example of Germany. As early as 1892
the eight hundred May-day celebrants in St. Petersburg

held their festival amid proud references to the workers of the Empire across the border. "One-fifth of the people of Germany," exultantly declared the propagandist Igor Afanasev, "is on the side of the workers and under their influence. They have 104 newspapers with 600,000 subscribers. The common funds amounted last year to 390,000 marks." To this proletarian of St. Petersburg and his fellow-workers, for whom a talk with twenty comrades was a risky adventure, and a polyautographed appeal would be menacingly suggestive of the thunder of Cossack cavalry, these figures from a foreign country must have been like a report from the statistical department of Paradise. The leaders could not speak in public, they could not safely consult in private. To avoid waking the nodding detective in their midst, they declaimed in a whisper. To them the thought of the meetings of the Berliners in the open at Treptow was a dream of ancient Athens.

The young men who read so much German philosophy in their rooms in St. Petersburg felt that in the streets of Berlin they saw the closing chapter of their favourite authors. They would have liked to ask the first policeman by the Spree, "Are you a Kantian or do you like Fichte best? But, seriously, only Hegel matters." Why, the very branch secretaries there took courses in classical philosophy; they spent their whole time studying the higher criticism.

No other Socialist party at that time could show the success achieved by the Germans. Yet, in view of the active governmental hostility to the Social Democrats, every vote cast for them had the flash of a rebel's lance; no one dreamed of the coming complications of growth and greatness.

Ulianov, too, on his journey, saw the German Labour movement irradiated by these legendary revolutionary anticipations. Ulianov, who never rested content with generalities, was out to observe men, to compare them

with the men in his northern organization; he attended
meetings, listened to speeches, and dreamed of himself
being able, some day, to venture to speak in freedom to a
crowd of hearers.

Then he went straight to Geneva, to Plekhanov.

The whole of the "Labour Liberation Party" could
have found room on the silk cushions of a single wandering gondola—to listen, perhaps, to flute-players on the
far shore of the Lake of Geneva. Four people had
founded the organization in 1883—George Plekhanov,
Axelrod, Vera Sassulitch and Deutsch.

So far as a party is ever one man's idea, this party was
Plekhanov's. He stands on the threshold of events in
Russia as Voltaire stood on the threshold of the French
Revolution; he was Lenin's teacher as Jean Jacques
Rousseau was Robespierre's. The personal career of this
man, a critic of Lessing's calibre, was tragic. Plekhanov
came to his end, before his death, in utter obscurity. No
song brought victory over his last sufferings. The man
whose theories were, through his disciples, to endow a
party with the nucleus of ideas and the vast flow of words
that make a revolution, after forty years in exile had no
means of publishing a single leaflet, had not as many as a
hundred followers, not three friends. In the silence of his
last weeks of life, in Petrograd in 1918, Plekhanov might
have repeated the words written by a Frenchman in
the seventeenth century: "The reward of virtue has its
seasons, like the fruits of the earth."

George Plekhanov made his first public speech on
December 6, 1876, at the first virginal appearance in the
streets of St. Petersburg of the red flag—a bit of bunting
that has heralded the ideas and emotions of revolt in many
forms. On this occasion it was fanned by the breezes only
for a short quarter of an hour. The police saw in amaze-
ment colours that were not Tsarist, and made a little
cavalry charge. The speaker, however, had had time for
a speech on "Land and Freedom." Like all the rebels of

his generation, he came from the ranks of the Narodniki.
Plekhanov, however, had stood out against assassination;
in his view the momentary triumphs of terrorism were
paid for by too many sacrifices, and the same cause could
be served much more fruitfully in other ways. He fled
abroad, and later wrote the first Social Democratic
pamphlet, little dreaming of the thunderous *Walkürenritt*
of its innumerable successors. He wrote that some years'
experience of the West had changed his views; and that
even if he were stoned with his dogmas of the past he
would not be dismayed. After all, every new idea is a
betrayal.

Plekhanov wanted to bring the revolutionary movement
in his own country into line with the European movement. He described how the production and reproduc-
tion of wealth alter the relations between men in the
process of their common employment and lead to the formation of classes. After this, individuals with particular
interests to serve try to influence the State, or even to rule
it as dictators. Sometimes they succeed, sometimes they
fail in the attempt. Their daily work brings them into
conflict with Autocracy, which has gradually to be modi-
fied in the direction of a wider national basis. First
political and economic needs force Tsarism to support
the bourgeoisie, but soon this class turns against personal
rule, and in the pride of their possessions the lords of
production demand certain freedoms, guaranteed by the
letters of a Constitution, which they call Eternal Rights
of Man. This effort deserves the support of the proletariat, which need have no fear of the development of
the economic power of the bourgeoisie, for it is this
development that first makes it possible for "the struggle
for liberty in Russia to succeed—as a labour movement
or not at all."

The relation between master and man (continues
Plekhanov) is changing, if not in substance, at all events

in form. The simplest types of economic dependence, originally naked and unashamed, begin only at later stages, amid the growing interconnexions of society, to be cloaked by the façades and refinements of an advanced civilization. New methods of production drag along in their wake the ideas of the old methods, as barefooted *burlaki* the Volga boats. Inherited conceptions veil the latest economic forces: traditional forms, through their familiarity, are much more noticeable than those just coming into existence at any period.

This is why many schools of Tsarist and anti-Tsarist thought declared that unorganized domestic industries were the dominant form in Russia and not industrial labour. It is true that until serfdom was abolished it was more advantageous for the manufacturers "to give out raw materials to the peasants for working up at home than to build workshops of their own. The rural labour was cheaper. Different villages specialized, moreover, in particular goods." Plekhanov investigated the conditions among these cottage industries. He showed his followers how a home worker is unable to meet the competition of the big capitalist, and how the industrial work of a peasant family is evidence only of their poverty and not, as has been contended, of their good fortune. It was the dream of these poor people to become factory workers. Most of them lived in huts with sodden roofs; the rain coming through was their bond with nature. The little room grew slightly larger if the walls bent dangerously outwards, not infrequently, in the end, to collapse altogether. For political reasons the Government was interested in helping this class, but there was little that it could do for it, except lavish praises on its genuinely national character.

Plekhanov was the first Russian opposition writer to investigate these conditions; and he had no more fear of capitalism than the capitalist himself. Both waited eagerly to see what would come out of the machinery halls, the critic with his eyes on the human beings, the owner with his on the goods.

The masses were assembled; only the leaders had still to come.

Ulianov had been spreading these ideas for more than half a decade. He had interpreted them in small pamphlets to his oppressed countrymen, and had sought to confirm the conclusions arrived at in substantial critical works of his own. Now he came to the Master from St. Petersburg.

Lenin was greeted in the Master's room in Geneva by the golden letters of familiar books. They seemed to be speaking in chorus with the great teacher. Pages came to life, chapters spoke up. The disciple bowed himself for the first time before the long-desired, loved the theory in the man and the man in the theory. He was happy in telling his tale to the teacher, describing days and nights of effort in Russia. The ripened scholar overcame his shyness in the fire of his story, and narrated things experienced as though to himself.

Plekhanov, now for a decade and more an exile, looked tensely into the distance, trying to picture a group of unknown faces. Looking out from his room, he saw, far beyond Lake Geneva, a strange landscape: the Idea made flesh and touching the earth, softly as a delicate veil touches a woman's shoulders. In a room in Switzerland, twelve years before, a nameless fugitive, living on little earthly bread but much from heaven, had given birth to ideas. A decade had passed, and the thoughts of that unknown man now possessed the souls and the wills of a few hundreds. It needed but an event, an occasion, and these ideas, popularized, watered down, perhaps distorted, at all events simplified, would let loose in a whole class forces that might be creative in space and time.

As yet, for the émigrés and for those still coming out

of Russia, the light was spread uniformly over all things. They saw the same picture. The reasoning powers of the disciple were the circulating life-blood of the new movement. In his brain, to which fine nerves led from palace and factory, brothel, inn and college, from the lives of those who cried out in comfort and those who dumbly faded, insight was strengthened and enriched.

To attain clearness and master the complicated mass of data, he had to narrow his field of attention. His intelligence accordingly registered primarily the general impulses, the stirrings of a section of humanity that was at that moment constituting itself a class.

The play of what men call chance had brought to the front in the hour of the birth of the proletariat a man who grew with it, who responded sensitively to its every pulsation, and in responding influenced the mass. At other periods in history classes have often passed long years in the wilderness before they found the predestined leader. Sometimes they have sought him in vain, groped blindly and painfully, to be led in the end by another, who was in others' service.

Ulianov had not the opportunity of giving direction to the stirring multitudes at his own discretion, but he was able to bring the leading ideas and movements into association; he found a definite and continually widening circle of influence. His was the intelligence that reacted creatively to the feelings of the masses.

Plekhanov and his friends valued in Lenin the one thing that they had not—his ingrained realism. Many exiles of their school came to them, but in every one they detected shortcomings, even when the pilgrim's intellect was perhaps more dazzling than Lenin's. Either the disciples came to Lake Geneva with industriously learnt, monotonous texts; or else, to escape from the regimentation inherent in any school, they built up doctrines on arbitrary aphorisms. Even "snobbism," dandyism, preciousness, like everything that exists, have their segment of reality. The world was not made by a party leader, and even these weaker brethren have the justification of their origin; but they are ineffective, they are not a force in the world, they do not get things done, they do not change humanity. There could be no common ground between an individual of this type and Lenin or his teachers. Their god was The Thing Achievable, and any scoffer or doubter they would have crucified.

Between Plekhanov and his friends Axelrod and Martov there was entire unity. They looked on their pupil as hopefully as he at that time reverently looked up to them. Ulianov took over the liaison with individual supporters, watched over everyday business, tested theories of the Master in factory life and in general investigations. The way was now smoothed. Martov, Plekhanov's friend of many years, said in Geneva:

"Plekhanov and I propagated our Marxist ideas for a long time without meeting with any response. And the supporters whom we slowly gained, those young Social Democrats who came abroad from Russia and visited us, were a continual disappointment in their political helplessness. Not until we met Ulianov did we at last breathe freely. Now at last, we said to one another, we can feel at rest; the cause of the Russian Social Democracy is in good hands. It has found a practical leader worthy of it."

And Axelrod, the joint founder of the party, said:

"I felt that I had in front of me a man who would be the leader of the Russian Revolution. He was not only a cultured Marxist—of these there were many—but he knew what he intended to do and how it was to be done. There was in him something of kinship with the soil of Russia. . . . When I read his first pamphlet I was at once convinced that he was of the stuff out of which leaders are made."

Such were the words of men who, later, were Lenin's bitter enemies in the field of the common faith.

WORKERS AND INTELLECTUALS
IN THE MILITANT UNIONS

The discontented are prone to wander in the valley of their desire. Here whole cities spring up, and in Jerusalem there is no room for the evil one. All that they find wrong with the world is banned. Consequently what is seen in the valley of desire is mostly abstraction, idea, generality.

Ulianov, in his constantly renewed strife with the Narodniki, fought against every arbitrary assumption. His fancy was controlled by reality. He saw the world unveiled. Yet he did not flee into the solitudes of the woods. His general theory saved him from that. The strength of his teaching, the secret of its power, its source of life, its colour, its effectiveness lay in his ability to see reality without despair. Lenin's fundamentalness, his habit of going to the root of things, saved him from thinking in terms of books. He saw the worker Ivan, the peasant Peter, the small tradesman Nikolayevitch, and was continually testing the doctrine which he had adopted by the touchstone of such men's relations with the community. His eye saw through the four walls around the men he observed. He knew how Ivan went in the early morning to the factory, and he could see Ivan's flat hand take his wages on Saturday. His love of clear outlines had in it a bold rejection of romance.

But how to arrive at the achievement of aspirations and ideas?

It was more difficult to move these men than to open a book on German philosophy from the dumb shelves of the library. The most complicated of all writings is still a monologue; a conversation with the most primitive of souls is a dialogue moving in contradictions. The way from writing-desk to fellow-man is much longer than the mere distance. To many it seems to meander away into the void. The path to my neighbour's brain has many vexations, surprises, monotonies to overcome.

The objects of Ulianov's concern were spiritual as well as bodily serfs. They were the sons of serfs. It was only three decades since in the villages the "popes" in their pulpits had announced to the peasant that in future he could no longer be staked by his lord at the gaming-table, given as a present to his lord's mistress, or bought and sold in the restaurants of Paris and St. Petersburg. Freedom then began. Each one had to look around for a job for himself. But the customs of half a thousand years did not vanish with the imperial proclamation of emancipation; they continued to regulate existence, to control the relations between man and man. Corporal punishment was with the peasant from his cradle to the hour in which, as the legend goes, God took his wandering soul to Himself and, instead of entering him in the celestial ledgers, lit a little candle by His throne.

A whip is easier to make than the fortress of Peter and Paul. The countryman, the worker, the shopkeeper could wield the knout like his betters. He might not rule a people, but he ruled wife, sons, daughters, dog and cat. He aped his master and beat them all. For every Ivan this was a sign of his superiority. And who does not want to be superior? In time corporal punishment came to have no significance left, no more reality than the other-worldly unpleasantnesses invoked in a curse, a "go-to-the-devil," have for the addressee. The following custom ruled almost throughout Russia: when a newly married couple had their first child, if the unfortunate little creature were a girl the father was visited next day, out of pure friendship and by way of a joke, with a beating, often continued until he lay on the ground streaming with blood. In the factories a casual exchange of words would lead to a fierce scuffle, and the combatants would part with teeth knocked out and ribs broken. Everyone was beaten by his superior—the schoolmaster by the head, the believer by the "pope," the police officer by the governor, the heir to the throne by the Tsar. The victims of the punishment agreed with the peasant in Turgenyev's hunting stories:

"I deserved it, little father, I deserved it. No one in our country is punished without good reason."

Not only physical chastisement was adopted in turn by the slaves, as though to prove that they too were somebody; the "sweet dumpling," the tip, associated with every office, was the pride of the small as of the great. The new arrival in the factory had to stand a bottle of brandy for luck; if he failed, at the end of the day's work he was beaten black and blue; and presents had to be made to the foreman, just as though he were an important Government official. A few of these workers, who could live on next to nothing, would earn a little more than most. They would enjoy their Sunday off. On that day life spread its magic carpet. They bought themselves patent boots with high heels, shirts resplendent in blazing colours, the brightest of sashes, and a mouth-organ for the soul's melancholy.

At the first breath of ideas of revolt the bulk of this multitude would feel discomfort, would scent an intruder. A worker who found consolation in any sort of vision of change wanted, in his neighbour's opinion, a beating. Shapovalov, who later became prominent in the Bolshevik dictatorship, relates how he first heard the words Revolution and Socialism. He was a lad of fourteen or fifteen. Early one morning he was lighting the smithery fire in a cutlery works. An old comrade sighed: "Ah, if only the Revolution would come along at last!" The others paled. "Stop your jaw," said one, "you're mad." Shapovalov recalls the day of the assassination of the Tsar—March 1, 1881. He was then an apprentice. "Why," he asked his mother, "have they sent us home so soon? Why are all the shops closed?" The old woman answered, in horror, "They have murdered the Tsar—

the cursed, godless Socialists have done to death our little father the Tsar."

But the machine, which was so quick in forming material things, was to form also these refugees from the soil, these semi-serfs. The intelligence of wheels and gearing matured their servants. Specialized industries need men of some sort of capacity, however primitive.

The man at the machine, who saw the results of just lifting his hand, began in time to have confidence in the law of cause and effect, began to differ from the sceptical British philosophy that taught that that law was only a pragmatic assumption. The uniform, vibrating hum of these gargantuan tools dulled the senses of most, but in some it engendered thought. What these men then felt seemed to them unprecedented, and their new ambition wildly unattainable.

The comfort offered by the crucifix waned and disappeared; the light of new religions, the glory of new sacrifices, streamed abroad. The book was the new altar. Ivan bowed down before it with the same humility as he had done before dumb, and for that reason all-vouchsafing, ikons. The heavy day's work was followed by nights devoted to reading. What these people called Science now brought to tired brains the delight that formerly had come from a long pilgrimage to Kiev.

The eye brightened at the printed page, the lip quivered with desire to preach the new faith. In the first speeches in the lives of workers of St. Petersburg one feels these welling impulses, one sees traces of a realization of new possibilities in life. Leaflets which reproduced a speech made by a worker—Bogdanov—in 1892 contain this declaration:

"Comrades, our faith must be firm in our victory, only we must arm ourselves with a powerful weapon. This weapon is the knowledge of the historic laws of human progress. Only with this weapon shall we defeat the enemy all along the line."

Another worker, Feodor Afanaov, declared in the same year:

"When we examine our position we find that all our sufferings are the result of the existing economic system. Consequently, if we are to improve our position, we must work for the destruction of the existing economic system."

The first May-day proclamation, of 1890—conscientiously preserved in St. Petersburg in the archives of the police—contained this promise:

"In recent decades the class consciousness of the Russian proletariat has so developed that we may hope for our First of May in no very distant future. Let us only be prudent, and wait until our organizations have members enough to enable us to begin action in earnest.

"This is the FIRST proclamation of the FIRST association of Russian workers opposed to the Government, written and printed, under very difficult conditions, in a single night. The association now has eight hundred members. Brothers! Workers! We shall meet again!"

The thrill of hope in this declaration of a will to live is akin to that of the songs which beguiled the long waiting in prison and Siberian exile:

> Up, brothers, to freedom,
> Up to the light of the sun!

The new religion of supposed science had smaller temples than the Saviour. The churches were never so full that there was not room to be found somewhere. But the thirsters after knowledge had not room enough. The *Novoye Vremya,* which was certainly not filled with dreams of new worlds born in radiant ecstasy, wrote:

"Early in 1891, St. Petersburg will possess three free public libraries. . . . Not three, but more like thirty-three free reading-rooms are needed to satisfy the enormous passion for reading among the poor, common people. . . . The reading public is recruited mainly from factory and other workers, artisans, and their

children. Very often admittance is refused for lack of
room. The late arrivals are those who come from farthest
off. They hardly ever go away, but wait patiently. Frequently, however, it happens that there is no room up to
closing time."

After the peasant disturbances Tsarism had been moved
to appoint voluntary officials from among the few of the
rural population who could read and write. The villages
were granted self-government; the village mayors were
now petty officials in the State hierarchy; they were
separated from the millions of illiterates, given a baton
and official paper and the glory of petty command. Now
the central power felt that the time had come to prepare some of the more intelligent among the proletarians
of the staple industries to become officials, spies or
"popes."

Such was the purpose of the evening and Sunday schools
opened by the Government.

For the revolutionaries of all schools these institutions
were a ready-sown field for gathering in their recruits.
Here they could find the finest fruits, teach the most
receptive minds.

Ulianov felt that now at last he had found a home, a
field of activity. He watched the schools, got together
the teachers, spoke to them for hours at a time on the
best methods of instruction, asked what progress they
were making, compared his system of general propaganda
with their special systems. Among these teachers he
secured many subsequent supporters of Social Democratic
propaganda and organization.

The paths followed by these pupils must have been an
absorbing study for him. For not every man left his
bench in the classes to join the company of political
workers. Some were content to become factory foremen,
others became flakes in the winter of Tsarist oppression,
yet others became prisoners of their primitive culture.
Under the oil-lamps in their living-rooms they patiently

learned astronomy or botany or studied the peculiarities
of the subsoil. The pages read and underlined, evidence
of industry spurred on by a hunger, alienated them from
their comrades in daily work. They imagined themselves
superior to the common herd, saw in its occasional political efforts only a crying folly.

Lenin watched the results of this education, aiming at
improving the fruit of his daily labours.

He spoke to workmen's clubs in St. Petersburg. He
tried to imbue a small number of men with many ideas.
He did not merely give learned or enthusiastic addresses
and, at the end of a short half-hour, go away again: in the
latter part of the evening he asked his listeners to tell him
about themselves, about their factory life, about the
general attitude of their comrades. It was for them, not
him, to tell the tale of their sufferings. In the first part
of the evening they had learnt from him; now he learned
from them. He accumulated details, impressed these
men's narratives on his memory. Those who told them
became an imperishable part of his consciousness and
accompanied him throughout his existence.

He drank in these character studies, heard apprehension, perceived the kaleidoscopic stir of contradictory
hopes, listened more devoutly than the pupils, sought to
give visible form to the abstract, sought to show that his
Theory was nothing but the ordered assembling of realities. Everything communicated to him by the students
became a ray in the sun of his system.

In the narrow room for which the police were seeking,
the Theory grew as naturally, as inevitably as the dawn.
When those who had come thus into contact with him
went home, they did not go as from an evening's amusement. Their steps were surer, firmer. In their fancy
the sanctuaries of the existing order were in flames.

Ulianov spoke always in his hearers' own language,
without high-flown metaphor, at most making use of a
peasant fairy-tale or simile. The teacher had no more

rhetoric than the man in the street; he could have used the same language behind the plough or at the lathe, without passing either for a crazy literary person or for a stupid peasant. In the dozen clubs of St. Petersburg this young man's audiences grew rapidly.

So always movements begin if they are to grip the masses, so thought takes human shape. The Socialist theory of the West grew on the stones of St. Petersburg into the meeting-place of the people. It did not come into being in the stillness of the study from a process of textual criticism. It reflected the face of suffering. Hope, privation, discontent wove invisible threads which clothed men in the hypotheses that were accepted as true. So it was that the theory remained present in men's thoughts, that it became a symbol, became a banner.

Ulianov, to avoid being spoken of in that name, known to the police of the district from his identity papers, used the name of Lenin from the beginning of his activity in St. Petersburg. His method of lecturing brought him more and more open supporters in the propaganda circles. He was their leader, organized districts into groups, and carried on a guerilla war against the faithful, vigilant police.

With the same closeness with which he observed men, he now watched the streets, called attention to technical needs, to the need for stratagem, taught dodges, told of dwellings with double exits. As the chief among the conspirators, he recognized the potential significance of the incidental on the road to the goal, the importance of small details in the contest of opposing forces.

The circles had to be extended, intercommunication, look-outs, hiding-places had to-day acquired the importance that theory had yesterday. The winding streets, the façades of the houses, were alive in his eyes. He found the trick wanted at the moment, saw the loophole of escape.

At the beginning of 1895, Ulianov's group were already

called the "old" ones. He worked to organize them as a unified body, aimed no more at imbuing a few with many ideas, but many with particular watchwords.

A newspaper must be brought out, a secret printing-press set up.

In a room in a suburb, with no communication with the world outside, some men lived the life of hermits—must never leave the room, must breathe lead-dust day and night. The neighbours must suspect nothing: the men put on the most commonplace, highly respectable air. Parcels containing paper had secretly to be dragged into the room, newspapers slipped with equal secrecy into the streets, without a sound, without a single unconsidered gesture. Lenin saw every line attentively through, knew the difficulties of every letter.

Men had to be found—men who knew how to slip past the police on illegal errands, who had done it already.

For the building of the new organization there was also old scaffolding that could be borrowed. The general commanding the secluded lurking-places in St. Petersburg, who already was in touch in many directions with the conspirators of other cities, called to mind the old groups of Narodniki. Lenin had derided their theories, but, he now said, that had nothing to do with the individual believer in terrorism; far from it—he held in honour their forerunners who had cheerfully faced the gallows; only he did not want to see the inheritance preserved as a curator might an old document; he wanted to see renewed personal activity. A group of Narodovoltzy joined up with his organization. So, at the beginning of 1896, was formed the "Militant Union for the Liberation of the Working Class."

Compared with the circles, the Union had an extended, broader, more complicated task in programme and leadership.

Party officials were coming into being. Ulianov taught his helpers, not how to shake the world, but new secret codes, the use of chemical inks, and the art of the dexterous use of false beards.

His company of spies and sentries were intellectuals, not proletarians. The workers remained in the adult education circles, went on spelling out the bases of the Social Democratic programme, endeavoured to collect fighting funds, watched mainly over the economic interests of the movement.

Lenin generally read his pamphlets to the leaders— hectographed sheets. He had written a small book of a hundred and fifty pages: *Who are the People's Friends, and how they Fight the Social Democrats.* This second work, like his first, found neither printer nor publisher. He could not see the book in the shop windows or have the gratification of seeing his name in print; he felt the irksomeness of the bonds drawn so tightly round him.

The work had been written for hundreds of thousands. Instead of that, two hundred and fifty copies were pulled off primitive machines by men who had always to be ready to flee at any moment. His writings had always the same circle of readers. The pamphlets had not the opportunity of circulation in masses as had Lassalle's in Germany; they remained in obscurity, confined to the uniform, monotonous applause of the same men. That is why his booklet also declared that its readers were called to greatness. They took comfort, perhaps, for the impossibility of saying everything to the whole nation by emphasizing the value of the *élite,* the leaders.

In his little book he already spoke of the hegemony of the proletariat, of the way which would open out into the victorious Communist Revolution.

The very cradle of the idea was shadowed by the characteristic element in the organization of revolution in Russia, a fundamental element in its later development: Technical direction was easier for the intellectuals to learn and carry out than for the workers. They were more tenacious, they remained the leaders, they provided the supporters in the circles with a stock of ideas. The mass of followers went on learning and merely exercised a general influence through their attitude, whether of enthusiasm or despair, on the students, lawyers, doctors, college professors, writers and journalists.

After three years' activity in St. Petersburg, Vladimir Ilyitch Ulianov was already called "Good Old Lenin" by those who saw him or heard of him daily, intellectuals and workers alike. The nickname arose neither from his years nor from any sort of shoulder-patting intimacy, nor even from his insight into affairs, but from the personal impression that he created.

Followers love their leaders in consequence of their own inadequacy and weakness. They discover in them qualities which the chosen sometimes do not possess at all, sometimes only half possess, still more seldom possess wholly. The man of the rank and file feels these qualities to be indispensable to his personal or to the common happiness. He himself may despair, may stumble, may have moments of fright; morning lures him, evening promises, the twilight brings wills-o'-the-wisp; earthly ambitions alternate with pleasure. Yet he may love the Cause, even though he does not live in it every waking and sleeping moment like a fish in water. He is ready to allow himself many an indulgence. "Our leader," he thinks to himself, "is looking after things! He does not despair or stumble, he never hears harmonies from the labyrinth in which the voice of Reality is wedded to that of Illusion; he is never cast down or lured away."

Amid such expectations the style of Ulianov's personal life was formed.

He had always lived in modest circumstances in Samara as a child; as a student in Kazan and Simbirsk he had never had the opportunity of setting eyes on luxury or magnificence. His interests saved him from the allure-ments that fill a passing hour. Now, in St. Petersburg, he was the prisoner of his environment. He had to take thought for the means of living, to bring his needs down to the minimum. For the whole of his life, from then on, clothing was a mere shell, food simply the means of further activity. In face of the purpose which he had set before him, Ulianov lost the sense of the decorative in life. He was so hardened that he might perhaps have understood weakness in others, never in himself.

All this came to him naturally, not as the result of prolonged thought. Nature had provided him in generous measure with a manna on which he could live cheaply anywhere: a purpose in the wilderness of distractions. His was no deliberate asceticism, he made of it no programme for himself or rule for others. He knew that Puritanism can only be of nature; that an out-at-heels life on thin water-soup is no temptation to anyone for its own sake; that torn trousers are no gospel.

A system of renunciation would have been a sophism, a side-issue, a playground for vanity. The next question would have been, "Who can go longest without eating and endure most?" Poverty was not the characteristic thing in Lenin. Perhaps it was necessary in Russia that a leader of plebeians and slaves, in constant touch with them, should live as they lived. His Puritanism made it easier for him to concentrate his passion uninterruptedly from earliest youth on a single object, imposed on his determination the confidence and definiteness that marked the character of Vladimir Ilyitch Ulianov at six-and-twenty.

His intelligence had its own optical laws; he saw the goal at close quarters. Nevertheless, he knew thoroughly well how long was the road to it.

Lenin perceived during his time in St. Petersburg how the organs of a class develop, how its mechanism comes into being, and he saw growth. In the hothouse air of industry, which oppresses so many, his lungs opened wide.

LENIN IN SIBERIA

GEORGE PLEKHANOV

THE FIRST STRIKES OF THE LABOUR MOVEMENT

It was said of the Tsars that people had no idea how little there is that the all-powerful can do. The acts of the Autocrats of all the Russias had this in common with those of ordinary people, in whose presence no one took oaths—that it was impossible to guess exactly what their consequences would be. Subsequent determinants of destiny, elements still to come, made no threat with outstretched finger, but slumbered in concealment in days yet unborn, and few could divine the coming lamentation.

The autocratic rulers had whipped the workers into the very insight and perception for the spread of which rebels had toiled for decades. The revolutionary greeted the towers of the fortress to which he was dedicated, and hailed the man in the factory almost as a redeemer. The humble workers understood nothing of all this; they continued to send their fellows as suppliants to the Tsar, to stammer out their desires in whining phrases. Workers' delegates were sent even to Alexander I, to hand him most humble petitions. They were arrested, and the trustful and confiding workers in the factory were soundly whipped. Next year there were fresh deputations and fresh public knoutings, because the complaints showed a want of proper submissiveness.

The proletarians brought their great trustfulness with them from the country. For a century past the façades of the Winter Palace had been growing hoary with the plebeians' affection for its inhabitants. From Alexander the First to Nicholas the Last they had made the pilgrimage to the Emperor, taking their ikons as spokesmen. The knoutings that they got hurt no more than their daily life; they howled, and returned to the doctrine of the hereditary monarchy.

The factory owners petitioned for help against the

introduction of State factory and workshop inspection, contended that the setting up of the inspectorate would destroy every bond between the masters and men and so work for evil instead of good, open the way to abuses and increase the volume of complaints.

The workers once more hoisted the standard of trust, and themselves swarmed round the imperial palace; but even under their slavery to tradition they showed a new tenacity. As the peasants had risen always in the name of the Tsar, so now did the workers. Tolstoy, Minister of the Interior, said in a note to Bunge, Finance Minister:

"The impossibility of suppressing the strike movement otherwise than by force of arms is proof enough of the unavoidable necessity of elaborating regulations which will do something to set limits to the arbitrary power of the factory owners."

None the less, armed force remained the obvious argument against the proletariat.

On the right bank of the Neva is Toruton's weaving shed. The other mills are across the river. The fever fumes of the chimneys meet over the water. Towards the end of 1895 sparks were falling from the doors and windows of this weaving shed.

In its first years of existence the proletariat is like an army unwillingly learning to fight. It finds its organization ready made, independently of its own initiative, through the factory system, within the framework of the organization of the works. So in the shops at Toruton's the weavers stood through the day elbow to elbow; the individual was lost. They were a compact mass, which slowly acquired the momentum of its numbers. They got into communication with those in service in other mills. When the evening siren hooted, the sky paled, and the machinery seemed sated, the individuals did not return to their solitude. They met in secret, observed one another, noted that they all looked alike. The more sensitive among them took up their neighbours' burdens.

There came a day when they realized the dull level of their existence, raised their arms in protest and struck work. The decision had nothing to do with politics. The mother could no longer complain as she had done when her son went off to attend meetings, nor the father beat him before the turn of the police came. The son was, indeed, striking also on their behalf.

The strike began on November 5, 1895.

On the 10th the workers in Laferme's cigarette factory also made an end of their wonted docility. Women who had been beaten by the overseers broke the windows, destroyed tools and equipment, threw their finished work into the Neva.

At this time Lenin's Militant Union counted a single workman only to every ten intellectuals. The proletarian supporters remained in the self-education circles, which were only loosely connected with the Union. But the workers from the idle factories found in the Union supporters and advocates, and in their turn brought life into its lotus islands of politics. The thralls who had struck could neither read nor write. At once every duplicating machine, every hand-printing press, was mobilized; appeals were read aloud; speakers, nervously expectant, were sent to the strikers. A manifesto was brought out containing the workers' demands, and bringing the news of the events along the Neva to distant industrial areas in St. Petersburg.

Ulianov wrote a pamphlet attacking the system of fines. He had listened to complaints from every worker of the absence of regulations governing the calculation of wages; even, too, when the basis of payment had been settled, a struggle would begin between employers and workers over delays in payment.

"Almost all factories," wrote Pakhitnov, "pay wages monthly in arrear, and even then the pay office keeps half a month's wages in hand. . . . Much more frequently payment is made only on great feast-days, eight times, six, five, even only four times in the year. . . . The vagaries of the notices given on discharge are one of the main causes of the unhappy situation of the workers. In other factories they only receive their wages at the expiration of the period of their contract. Anyone who has seen the workers, in their rags, beg cap in hand for the wages that belong to them, will understand why they have not been able to improve their conditions of life over those of penitents of bygone days. . . . In several factories a whole month's wages is stopped if a workman •voluntarily gives up his employment. . . . The regulation in the Schlippe chemical works runs: 'If the workman leave the factory before the end of his period of service, he receives only half of the stipulated wages.' In the cotton mill of Balin & Co., Makarov, the rule is: 'Workers and foremen who enter the factory at Easter must remain here till October, otherwise the whole of their wages is confiscated.' In the workshops of the Volga-Tver Shipping Company the following contract has to be signed: 'I undertake to leave one-tenth of my monthly wages always in the hands of the pay office . . . this tenth I lose if I am punished for any sort of offence.'

"Article 107 of the Trades and Industries Act declares penalties to be only permissible if workers deliberately lose time or cause loss to the employer. The manufacturers, however, have their own laws."

The most varied grounds of punishment were invented: for going out of the gates during the day, for plaguing the employer by asking for money, for arriving a quarter of an hour after the siren had stopped, for inattention, for disturbing the workers.

Ulianov's pamphlet, which gave all these facts, was in his characteristic style. This differed from that of his forerunners in pre-revolutionary France, from that of the Encyclopædist, and not only in his facts being taken mostly from unpublished sources. His style was also determined by his propagandist purpose. He had always in view the readers for whom the pamphlet on fines was written. Ulianov's intention was to make his pamphlet result in action on its readers' part. He aimed at continually reproducing the same words, tones, reflections, treatment and ideas. He had the monotony of a teaching method for primitives, and repeated himself deliberately a thousand times over. Whether Lenin was writing about hot water, in advocacy of free tea in the factory, about the dictatorship of the proletariat, against Kant or in favour of Hegel, he always wrote for the peasant. He assumed no knowledge in the reader. Free from vanity as Lenin was in life, he remained so at the writing-desk. He left his books as bare of efforts after style as he left himself. While writing he always had his reader with him, at his side; he never polished. Exposition in itself brought him no joy. He wanted, it is true, to tell of another world, another outlook; but not in his own language, but in that of the multitude.

His pamphlet was read to the strikers, and gave substance to the words of these groups of men and women. So the bond was knit between the Militant Union and the workers. After long years of endurance they came to the same conclusions as the leader of the organization, who had been intent on reaching the workers, spoke always of the proletariat, but up to now had only been in touch at most with five to six hundred of the men and women at the machine. They had felt abandoned by all the world, and here were the outstretched hands of unknown men. They met together in the strikes as at a rendezvous. Before the gates of one factory and another, in which the workers were inarticulately voicing their grievances, there appeared propagandists of the Union, speaking of the path to be trodden, of deliverance and of new shrines.

After the strikes of the weavers and the cigarette makers, a strike was declared in the shoe factories. The directors were caught napping; the garrison commander in St. Petersburg was speechless with astonishment. A few concessions were made; they worked like magic on the proletarians of the capital.

On December 9, Lenin was arrested. The police authorities guessed, with amazing discernment, that Vladimir Ilyitch Ulianov was the author of the leaflets that were to be found everywhere in the factory entrances, like puddles after rain. The Militant Union decided to attempt to divert suspicion from its leader by issuing, while he was actually under arrest, an appeal describing the general aims of the organization. Lenin himself now reaped the benefit of the thought he had given to devices for eluding prison warders. He was able, from his cell, himself to carry them into practice. In very few days he had regained touch with the Union, and was writing letters with such precise recommendations that the recipients continued to work under his control. Books were sent in to him to read. When he returned them, they had inconspicuous dots over occasional letters in the pages. These were patiently sought out, and made up sentences. He sent and received messages written with milk instead of ink.

He was not long under arrest. The very first days of freedom were to bring to him and to his friends of the Union, to the police chiefs in St. Petersburg, and to the Tsar Nicholas II, then just crowned in Moscow, some surprises.

In an open-air meeting, three hundred weavers and spinning operatives declared a general strike in their industry. They represented *thirty-five thousand* proletarians of the capital; they had formed a secret council of delegates of all the works affected; they demanded that the working day should be reduced from thirteen hours to ten and a half. The weavers had preserved their secret for many weeks before the stoppage. It had been whispered among thirty-five thousand, but neither the police nor Lenin's Militant Union had learnt anything.

The example of the Toruton works of the year before

had had its effect. For a year the spinning operatives had dreamed of this event, had met in self-formed groups and discussed the detailed events of the previous stoppage. This had provided a constant topic of their conversation. They got into touch with the colleagues who had had experience of a strike, admired the work, promised to follow the same path. A wave of excitement passed through the industrial population. The Militant Union, ignorant of all details, was constantly being asked for more leaflets and pamphlets. The old duplicating apparatus began to be inadequate. They longed for a machine which would enable them to bring a thousand words and more to many thousands of men and women.

The Militant Union now succeeded in placing itself at the head of the biggest Russian mass movement that had so far come into existence. Suddenly a hundred speakers had an army. They could not lead the army whithersoever they chose, could not realize their whole programme; none the less, increasing numbers brought their story to them, more and more joined them, more and more listened willingly to them; from their newly acquired knowledge they could elaborate further plans, making use of political ideas that had long awaited the moment of practical application.

A manifesto of Ulianov's described what had happened:

"In various towns a series of strikes have broken out . . . the majority of the strikes were failures only in appearance. . . . We have given plenty of occupation to the gentlemen in St. Petersburg. The weavers' strike at Toruton's, the cigarette makers' at Laferme's, the spinners' at Lebedov's, the strike in the machine-made shoe factory, the workers' agitations at König's, Vordnin's, and at the docks, have shown that we are no longer passive sufferers.

"As is well known, workers from many factories and works have formed the Militant Union for the Liberation of the Working Class. . . . The Union issues leaflets. It is not the leaflets that threaten the gentlemen, but the possibility of our mass action."

The weavers' strike lasted a month.

Ulianov's association provided the men and women for the laborious detail work. Some crept as in felt slippers into the excellently guarded works, and the workers found in the morning on the cold iron of their tools a manifesto. Others hurried from district to district, collecting news of the progress of the strike. Yet others carried news to the farthest corners of the industrial area, and called meetings together.

The extent of the strike, its duration, its orderliness, had attracted general attention to the workers of St. Petersburg.

The intelligentzia were astonished to observe a steadfastness new in Russia. In curiosity they asked who was leading the strike, and what were its aims. What Lenin had been heralding for two years past—the new language of the coming nameless hosts—seemed now to have come to pass. *So the strike broke through the narrow limits of the movement.* Classes that until then had stood aloof lifted the Union out of the silence of underground existence. This school of thought, though new for Russia, was able triumphantly to show that the metal was hot enough for casting; its leader wrote of a human tide flowing in from home and factory; the Union attracted faith; and—the principal thing in any movement—prophecies began to allure.

A newspaper of moderate democratic views wrote:

"The faces lit with intelligence and enthusiasm, this manlier tone coming from people whom one had been accustomed to regard as docile labourers, this protest, raised only by the workers amid the general silence, all these things speak of the birth and growth of the cause of freedom."

The police tried to collect strikers and force them back

into the workshops, arrested as many as they possibly could; the Government issued a manifesto breathing paternal benevolence. Witte, the Minister of Finance, made a public statement promising reduced working hours, but insisted that there could be no negotiations while the strike lasted. The weavers had no money, no strike fund; Lenin's Union had only a few thousand roubles. On June 18, 1896, the workers, amid the best of assurances from the Finance Minister, went back to the old machines that had been waiting four weeks for their servants.

By the end of a few months, however, the supreme authorities had forgotten the assurance they had given. On January 2, 1897, the weavers struck again, and attained their purpose: the working day was reduced by law to eleven and a half hours.

This victory made the name of the Militant Union widely known. Its reverberations spread throughout the empire.

During the strike more than a thousand workers were arrested; many of them were deported, or kept months and even years in the remand prison. This treatment, for those who underwent it, was a convincing demonstration of the soundness of the doctrine that Ulianov had taught in the evening courses. Everyday life may rub away the bright colours of a definite opinion; the prison cell protects faith's canvas from the damp. When, in the garment of an involuntary penitent, one wanders round a hermetically sealed room—why have the pains for nothing, why not commit the sin? Many of those who were arrested became ardent supporters of the Militant Union.

The agitation among the weavers, purely economic in origin, became in the end, through the ingrained characteristics of Tsarist policy, political. Lenin saw what he had hoped for—the widened arena for his activities, and the opening highway made for him and his fellow-workers by the juggernaut wheels of industrial development.

Ulianov saw avenues driven through the primeval jungle of Russian history, giving room for the movement of organized marching masses. He quoted his teacher, Karl Marx: "The more sweeping the processes of history grow, the more multitudinous will be the masses carrying them on." The disciple added his own comment, saying to himself and others:

"In these words there lies one of the deepest and most significant of truths. . . . With the broadening and deepening of the historic action of men and women will come an increase in the size of the mass of population consciously co-operating in the making of history."

LENIN IN SIBERIA

To cross oneself before any other mystery than that ordained by the Holy Synod was to have the Tsar's rope about one's neck. Those who were so tempted sowed anathemas and reaped long years of despair. "Such persons," writes Leo Tolstoy, "were treated like fishes caught with the draw-net; everything that fell in was tipped out on the shore, and the big fishes wanted were picked out, without troubling what became of the groundlings, who perished miserably on the strand."

To Siberia went all who vexed the Government:

The general who stole beyond the accepted conventional limit, without, it might be from an exaggerated sense of honour, sharing the booty with his superiors; the tramp who hawked from village to village without a pass; the old lady who entered into competition with the State, distilled schnapps and so made a hole in the monopoly; sectarians whose sign of the cross was not made the "pope's" way; peasants of the Odessa district who preferred to be buried alive rather than let their heads be counted by the authorities for statistical purposes; men and women who desired a Constitution, moderate or advanced, and those who desired an ideal system of anarchy.

Lenin, too, took the inescapable journey across the Urals. He was arrested in the midst of the strike wave in St. Petersburg and banished to the village of Shushenskoye, in the government of Yeniseisk, in Central Siberia. The district of Minusinsk, in which the place of his three years' exile lay, is on the border of Mongolia. The mountain slopes of the Sayan range form a deserted area in which villages mapped by no geographer lived as they had lived two thousand years before. The inhabitants shed no tears over their solitude. As the administrative authorities of St. Petersburg had not yet discovered them, they paid no taxes and furnished no conscripts. Mongol nomads often had no means of telling where Peking's realm ended, and got lost in Russian territory. The frontier was undefined; if peasants and gold-diggers passed on, they stretched the Tsar's realm in the process. Strategy had not yet discovered along this frontier the connexion between crags and national honour, but the many herds of cattle and sheep compensated for this moral loss by filling the bellies of the peasantry.

The legal experts who examined Vladimir Ilyitch Ulianov's views, activities and mode of life found nothing very damaging. They were used to worse, and had visited punishment in their time on greater sins against the light that radiated from the domes of autocracy. He was condemned and sentenced none the less—for people of such or kindred views were simply got out of the way and laid on ice in Siberia. The judges knew that individuals of this sort, if set free to-day, would have to be run to earth to-morrow, and were anxious to save the minor officials from unnecessary trouble.

The exiled man was nearing his twenty-eighth birthday. He was born in the same decade as most of his friends and co-religionists in the proletarian faith. All of them had the same fate—put off childish things in the prison cell and there grew into men. Every one of them, even if he were lucky enough to have many a hairbreadth escape, got into prison at least once before he was thirty. That was where the new generation in Russia greeted the earlier generation actually dying in the prisons and undergoing much severer sentences—the terrorists. The young men coming in reopened the past in the minds of these prematurely ageing victims.

Lenin had the good fortune neither to lose his reason in his country's prisons nor to become a cripple or tuberculous. His fate in the days that were now to follow depended, even more than that of other Russians, on the whims of minor officials. He depended now no longer on the attitude of the lawyers, Ministers, governors or judges, but of gendarmes, district officers or village mayors. When these instruments of power were not bored or anxious for distinction, and could expect tips, the captive had only to guard against the melancholy of peasant life in remote Siberia, against the temptations of solitude in relative freedom, against schnapps, lethargy, the wind and the ice-cold nights, against the howling of homeless dogs and against the many consolations offered by suicide.

Lenin's route lay along the narrow-gauge railway line that worms its way through the primeval forests like an unending labyrinthine tunnel through the mountains. Then at last came the open country of Siberia.

During long decades of desperate struggle, after streams of protests at sufferings which they had inflicted on themselves, the political prisoners had wrung from the authorities certain rights which had become customary. Until these conditions had been secured, the battle fought in prison must have been fiercer, more frightful than the struggle outside in freedom. In exile and in the prisons the politicals had had themselves to outdo the sufferings inflicted on them, had had to give themselves wounds which could horrify warders, prison governors, commandants, governors of provinces, Ministers. Some women and men had burned their living bodies; others had hunger-struck for weeks on end; yet others, in a fury of desperation, had attacked the warders and been strangled. Thus newcomers felt bound in honour to take the utmost care of the acquired scraps of decency, if only not to squander the heritage left by the predecessors who had died in those cells. In the Russian prisons, naked, powerless men and women creeping about their tombs had tamed the watchers over their martyrdom entirely by the spirit of their resolution.

Through their sufferings Lenin was able, in a hamlet at the end of the world, to enjoy certain freedoms.

He lived in a peasant's house. In a few weeks the walls of his clean little room were lined with books. In one corner there stood a broad bed. In the middle of the room lay a wooden slab on four logs; it threatened to collapse beneath the piled weight of the printed word. The little window looked out on the spellbound steppes, which no footfall, not a sound brought to life. The far mountains of Mongolia were a shimmering white, and seemed on winter mornings and summer days to suffer from excess of light. The Siberian farmhouses of this region had two roomy, bright rooms; in the kitchen there glowed a giant stove; the floor shone, covered only by some straw mats. On the farther side of the yard was the stock: the stalls and the barns with corn, flour and farming implements.

The streets were melancholy; they seemed made rather for the geese, ducks and pigs, out in search of puddles, than for human beings.

Lenin's wife, Nadeshda Konstantinovna Krupskaya, and her mother came with the exile into the valley of his seclusion. He had met them in the evening schools of the proletarians of St. Petersburg. Nadeshda Konstantinovna often saw him at the little private gatherings which Ulianov arranged to secure propagandists. She had the kindly, attractive face, the tranquil nature, the lofty brow, the special beauty of simple homeliness which some, though not many, of the Russian women revolutionaries possess. Nadeshda Konstantinovna was not one of those women agitators who are up in arms primarily against their sex, whose every sentence is accompanied by jerky, excited gestures, so that their advocacy, however much to the point, is spoiled by the general air of hysteria. Nadeshda Konstantinovna was to have throughout her life the qualities of a decent constitutional monarch, the single quality, indeed, that a king and, almost always, a woman need for the splendour of their majesty: to listen with interest and attentively keep silence. Most of the marriages of Russian revolutionaries were made in the same way. Finding that they thought alike in politics, they formed themselves into a party group, argued together till the moon went down and the two speechmakers suddenly discovered that they were man and woman.

The day did not begin encouragingly for Ulianov. Such a village in the morning, for the first half-hour after waking, is inviting as a freshly swept room. For a few moments one sees only the light, and rejoices in its waves that bathe everything in new life. Then, when in ten minutes one has walked right through, the last houses, standing at the foot of the steppe like stones at the water's edge, seem to be the end of the world. The unending plain gives the effect of a wall; slowly one is buried in the wilderness.

How many exiles had not been strangled here by the spectre of the heavy hours, sought in wild desperation any way out, and fled, only to lose themselves in forest and mountain. They shivered at the slow crawl of the days. The void must at all costs be filled. In the glimmering stillness of the night, in its inviting peace, it is easy to get to work; but in the eternal gloom and never-broken silence faces appear out of the unknown depths. One's head sinks in horror, thought dies out, the pen falls from the shaking hand; the most distant sound comes as a message of deliverance. Ulianov overcame the hypnotizing undulation of Siberian infinity, disciplined himself, organized his day, and rejoiced in the comfort of his work.

Above all, he listened tensely for the news that trickled so slowly through from Russia; in the underworld there, shortly after his banishment, there had been big events.

In the town of Minsk, in the middle of March 1898, a secret Social Democratic Workers' Congress had met —the first on Russian soil. After years of effort, the Militant Unions of St. Petersburg, Moscow and Kiev had met through their representatives, had constituted themselves a party. The envoys sent to Minsk appointed themselves a committee, and entrusted Peter Struve with the drafting of a manifesto, to proclaim the formation of the party and to explain its objects.

The total number of delegates assembled was nine. On the final evening the participants celebrated the event, and sent the resolutions adopted to Plekhanov at Geneva with their greetings. The discussions at Minsk had had this much of importance, that the meeting had shown how the workers, clamant in unison, had, after purely local efforts in their struggle with opposing powers, arrived at the stage when they could make a start on different lines which, from the standpoint of the members of the congress, were generally agreed to represent progress. A party always has its origin in this way—not out of brilliant programmes swamped in metaphor, but out of the common experience of many seekers after the same goal.

Nine days after this mainly theoretical stroke, made with an eye to the future, of the united Socialists against the rulers of the State, the Government succeeded in a practical one: five hundred members of the new party were arrested, and the central organization destroyed. The crisis, however, which now came was not the consequence of this successful police work, but of an internal disagreement. Long speeches and yet fuller replies seemed to show that, in the narrow circle of the intellectuals who were doing their thinking in the name of the proletariat, important questions of nation-wide scope were under discussion. Various opposing interests were anxious to secure the approving smile of Theory, and were seeking it in the works, crowned with laurels by his disciples, of Karl Marx.

The intelligentzia, who wrote manifestos, led Militant organizations and worked secret duplicating machines, read in the Master's books that industrial development was inescapable. Why, then, they asked, fight against it? "Let us admit our ignorance and sit at the feet of capitalism," was the advice of the draftsman of the first manifesto of the Socialist Party, Peter Struve. A few years later he was to write, as leader of the only true faith of the bourgeoisie:

"We, who live in the age of the complete clarification of evolutionist thought, know very well that the social revolution is an ideological monstrosity, and that Socialism is a synthesis of ideals which in the world of reality can only be broadly approximated to by particular social reforms."

The influence of Marxism has everywhere been in the direction of the development of the State, and especially so in agricultural countries; in these it served for general orientation, formed the theoretical basis of the next stage in their evolution. Many of the Socialists who spoke in the language of rebels were really pioneers, not of the proletariat, but of the bourgeoisie, which had not yet attained power. This modern theory of capitalism was used in their analysis by the theoreticians of two classes. It served the lords and the serving-men of the machine, *who were growing up together,* for the deduction of political formulæ from existing realities. In agrarian barbarism it is the Socialists themselves who advocate a form of society which springs from capitalism and obeys its laws.

Peter Struve and his friends faced life with a deep desire to liberate their country from oppressive relics of Asiatic conditions, from patriarchal relations between man and man. They believed, however, that insistent dwelling on purely proletarian demands could only dry up the sources of common effort, as it must strengthen the link between the lords of production and Tsarism.

The prophets of this next phase, of bourgeois predominance, Peter Struve and his friends, came into the workers' clubs for another reason: because only the lowest grades of society were showing readiness to act. That these Economists were anything but captains of industry, were themselves persecuted beggars, whose possessions consisted of books for which they had not paid and very little underclothing, made no difference to their importance to society.

Struve and his friends repudiated political action, declared that there was only a loose and indefinite connexion between the aspirations of the workers at the machine and general revolutionary, democratic effort. The new disciples were for a *purely economic movement,* were continually pointing out the independence of the workers in the past period of strikes, and declared that the intellectuals merely wanted to make use of the men in the workshop. The enthusiasts for politics, they argued, only wanted to be able to talk undisturbed in the cornfield, while naked reapers, working away in the blazing sun, were thirsting for water.

A programme of demands, richly provided with arguments, was drawn up and entitled "Credo." However, this bold beginning of party activity spoiled nobody's evenings. So much of the original theory as remained was still regarded as too seditious to pursue.

Only in Plekhanov's little room and in Lenin's peasant's cottage did the news of this defacement of the statue of

Truth as originally conceived come with the shock of an elemental catastrophe. The one could only gaze on the shores of Lake Geneva, the other on the ice-clad peaks of the Mongolian frontier. To the two exiles the life had been taken out of the Idea; for scepticism of the necessity of the Revolution amounted to disowning the idea of a Messianic mission of the proletariat, beginning with the temporary phase of dictatorship, and leading finally to the libertarian Paradise.

His friends in neighbouring colonies of exiles were summoned by Lenin to meet in a farmhouse in the village of Yermakoveskoye. In a talk with them he attacked the "Credo" of the Economists. This attempt to divert proletarian energies saw, he said, only the conflict between Capital and Labour, only the problems of this struggle, and ignored the continually spreading popular opposition to Tsarism. It closed its eyes to all the wounds inflicted by the Tsarist system, to its effects on peasant life and on the intellectuals; ignored the hydra-headed hierarchy, the passionate fanaticism of the sectarians driven underground, the pale multitudes of so many discontents; its advocates confined their attention to the chances of squeezing an extra kopek out of the employers.

Ulianov was striving for a very different goal.

The smallest hint of any opposition to the Régime had to be linked up with the bread-and-butter struggle of the factory workers, until the voice of the whole nation rang loud in confident rebellion; his party was to be the temple of fate in which proletarians, peasants and the masses that move between town and country would unite in Socialism. As later on, once it attained power, the organization would be all-commanding as God, so now it must be able to lead those who as yet were only half rebels. The coming dominance aimed at depended on the principle that there was nothing on Russian soil or along Russia's frontiers that did not interest political Socialism.

LENIN IN 1903

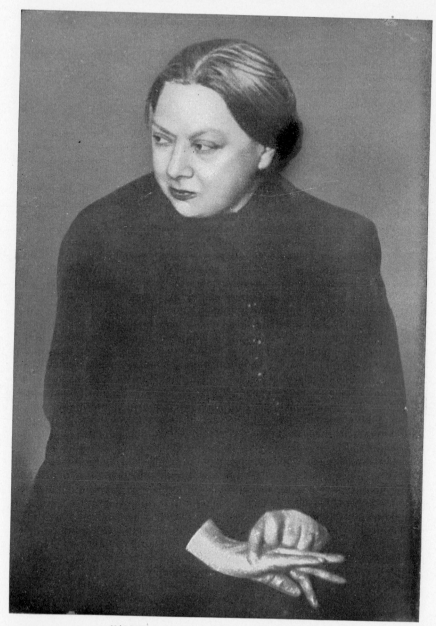

NADESHDA KONSTANTINOVNA, LENIN'S WIFE

"Through strike committees, clubs and mutual aid societies alone," he wrote, "the working class will never succeed in accomplishing the great historic task allotted to it, the task of its own liberation and the liberation of the whole of the Russian people."

The rebel, who could visualize the welcome to his words in so many distant faces, turned against the childish utterances of the new group and its setting up of rival leaders, and continued:

"No class has attained dominance in history without first singling out its chosen leaders, its representatives, men capable of organizing and leading the movement. The Russian working class has already shown that it is able to throw up such leaders. The extended struggle of the past five or six years has shown the enormous array of revolutionary forces latent in the working class."

A resolution was signed against the "Credo." Ulianov wanted to add to it a condemnation of the Reformism of Eduard Bernstein, as he felt that the ideas of the Russian Economists and the new current in Social Democracy in Germany were related. But his friends at Yermakoveskoye objected that respect for the great party of their faith should rule out any bitter polemics. Ulianov did not then know Bernstein's book, *Die Voraussetzungen des Sozialismus* [1] ("The Principles of Socialism"), and had only read some of his *Frankfurter Zeitung* articles, but already believed that he detected in them dangerous symptoms of capitulation to bourgeois notions.

Lenin was following the developments in events at home and in Europe as closely as if he were already in the seat of power and controlling men's destinies.

He played at organization and politics with ten exile friends, as a banished flute-player might tootle on his loved instrument in this Mongolian hermitage. Ulianov tried to form a Ministry out of a handful of men and

---

[1] English edition published in the Socialist Library under the title of *Evolutionary Socialism* (translated by Edith C. Harvey).

women, drafted resolutions with them, conducted sittings, was active, overworked, avoided relaxation. He tells of his childhood that "when I was still at school I became passionately fond of skating. But it made me very tired and I slept too much, so that I found myself compelled to give up the sport for the sake of my work." Similarly, even in Siberia, he would keep at bay passionate interests which might have gained too strong a hold over him. Lenin was devoted to chess, and could win simultaneous games against a number of opponents. This amusement, too, he cut down, and permitted himself to enjoy it only on the long Siberian journeys. "Lenin was bright and cheerful and full of energy," wrote one of the exiles, "and played a game of chess throughout the journey against three opponents. He played, too, from memory. The board over which his opponents consulted was in the other droshky."

He was passionately fond of shooting, too, but even here he was less afraid of losing the hares than the hours.

On the other hand, discussion would often last three days. Not only the Economists, but Peter Struve, had at long range to be consigned to the lowest spheres of the fallen angels.

Not only Lenin, but all the less recent exiles, had been withdrawn from the influence of the Economists, which bore heavily on nearly all who were active at home. They were saved from the labour and stress of standing out against the opinions of those around them. Ulianov strengthened them in his faith, gave the scattered exiles in the various villages something to do, started collections for the friends in Siberia, tried to lure each one into reading. In his own village there lived a Finnish workman and a Polish weaver. Ulianov at once became their teacher, gave them lessons, tried to lighten for them the difficulties of constructive economic study.

It may be that it was here that Lenin himself acquired the methodical habits of his later life. When newspapers came from home he did not allow himself to be tempted by the pile; he divided them into daily rations, and went on writing what became one of his principal works—a four-hundred-page description of the development of capitalism in Russia.

His liberation from the petty everyday details of a struggle against confused and undecided humanity and very clear and decided material obstacles gave him the opportunity for criticism on a broader and more fundamental basis. The years of intent observation and feverish work in St. Petersburg were necessary for realization of the pettinesses and limitations amid which the struggle went on. The period in the Siberian steppe rounded off his acquaintance with many actual lives of men. The general, the abstract, continually gained concreteness. He felt himself to be necessary, perhaps more necessary than before, and acquired the sense of his own significance needed if he was to dare to entertain his dream of the future. Amid the Mongolian mountain valleys, surmounted always by clouds like thronged angels, the Theory grew continually more all-comprehending.

"Once," relates one of his friends in exile, "we had a talk with Lenin high up on a mountain peak. The sun was going down, the atmosphere unusually clear. Far south, behind the climbing foothills, which might have been the gigantic waves of a suddenly frozen ocean, there stood out on the horizon the dazzling white outlines of the Sayan range. I was unable to turn my eyes away from these snow-clad giants, while I listened to Lenin declaring that science was on the side of us workers . . . that there was . . . no obstacle that could bar the progress of the all-conquering force of human reason. As I listened to all this I seemed to see, far off, visions of the great future. Vladimir Ilyitch left the village of Tessin. Friend Baramsin declared that he had never in his life heard so glowing a description of Marxian fundamentals."

To this rebel, too, humanity seemed to cry out for deliverance. Humanity is an abstraction, a moral conception difficult to define. All philosophic materialists become mystics when they speak of it. But it gives the strength that an individual needs for aims above the average. If one knew all the oaths that have already been sworn in its name, there would perhaps be no fresh adventuring. His obliviousness to them gave Lenin, too, the driving force to carry out his mission.

Everyone has a different impression of the deity called Humanity. The pilgrim Ulianov believed that it called for sacrifice.

The familiar scenes of the docks and factories slowly faded into the background of Lenin's consciousness. They became dwarfed amid the vastness of his plans. Their breath was lost in the breath of history.

Sharp, merciless, arbitrary as those frontier crags stood out in his consciousness the enslavement of the Russian people. In this mood he approached the last day of exile.

At the end of March, 1900, the road was clear for return to St. Petersburg.

On the first day of captivity all memories hang their heads; in the hours of re-won freedom they sing aloud. In the sleigh that took him, with Krupskaya and her mother, along the still frozen river, he felt no cold, threw his furs over the other two. Silently he drove three hundred leagues along the Yenisei. Soon they had crossed the Urals again.

FROM THE "ISKRA" CONTROVERSY TO THE FIGHT FOR THE KREMLIN

Les hommes que Dieu prend pour instruments de ses grands desseins sont pleins de contradiction et de mystère: il mêle et unit en eux, dans des proportions profondément cachées, les qualités et les défauts, les vertus et les vices, les lumières et les erreurs, les grandeurs et les faiblesses; et après avoir rempli leur temps de l'éclat de leurs actions et de leur destinée, ils demeurent eux-mêmes obscurs au sein de leur gloire, encensés et maudits tour à tour par le monde qui ne les connaît pas.

(The men whom God takes as instruments for His great purposes are full of contradictions and mystery. He mixes and unites in them, in proportions deeply concealed, qualities and defects, virtues and vices, enlightenment and error, greatness and weakness; when they have fulfilled their time with the splendour of their deeds and their destiny, they themselves remain hidden in the depth of their fame, admired and abused in turn by the world that knows them not.)

Guizot on Cromwell.

"THE SPARK"

THE exaltation of his wanderings over the Mongolian mountains, where the goal seemed enchantingly clear, soon deserted Ulianov. Party fractions and groups received him with the banners of their strife. There was endless speech-making, talk of all things. Only in views was there some definition; except for this, all suffered from the devastating desultoriness which comes from the desire to do much combined with the inability to choose a starting-point through the very profusion of tasks and opportunities. In comparison with his friends, who received every returning exile with a wild torrent of welcoming words, the thirty-year-old Lenin was more than a little cool and matter of fact. Often a characteristic smile played around his lips; only the eyes betrayed a man suffering in this environment. No gendarme would have dreamed of arresting him in the still-sleeping streets after an all-night sitting with these conspirators; for he had no liking for the customary uniform of a revolutionary. Nothing in him, neither a mop of hair nor a stuffed portfolio, neither a flowing cloak nor any sort of foible of crankdom, distinguished him from the average respectable citizen. To look at his face he might be just an ordinary countryman, typically Russian.

After his imprisonment in St. Petersburg and compulsory residence on the border of China, it would have been impossible for him to return to work in the capital. Ulianov felt, too, that in any case the oppressive atmosphere of a narrow range of ideas, even the necessary detail work in a room with a score of proletarians, at the doors of which a curious listener would have heard

77

unending whispers, no longer offered him a field of activity. When Ulianov thought in Siberia of the past he felt like one who looks in the looking-glass after a sleepless night and is shocked to observe his pallor. Lenin writes without heroics of his attitude at the time. "I was at work in a group who set before themselves very far-reaching and comprehensive tasks—and all of us, all the members of this group, had to suffer from the painful, torturing consciousness that we were *dilettanti*."

George Plekhanov had sent Vera Sassulitch from Geneva to Russia on a secret mission. She bore in her hands the Master's ointment of reconciliation; her face was lit up with heroic enthusiasm. It was her task to unite the warring groups, to harmonize their discordant interpretations of life, to make the resolutions of the Minsk Congress prevail, make dispersed efforts flow, purling, into a single stream. The Teacher in Geneva had expressly chosen Lenin for the honour of representing him at the proposed new congress. Lenin went to Moscow to set the matter in motion. It was easier, however, for the police to prevent a congress from meeting than for Plekhanov and Lenin to get their friends together. The leaders of the Militant Unions were arrested in a whole series of towns, and the congress had to be adjourned *sine die*.

Lenin now sketched a new plan, of which he had constantly dreamed while in Siberia. He proposed to start a newspaper, as the nucleus of a central organization. It was to be the general staff, to watch over the movement, guide it, give it a marching route, shine upon the local Unions like the moon in the happy valleys.

But such an organization, to be able to do any thinking, must be free from anxieties. If it was to fulfil its destiny and bring down the mightiest hierarchy in the world, at whose head stood a despot with two million bayonets and command of the telegraph wires, it could not be at the mercy of every spy, of the policeman at the next street-corner. Once freed from pitfalls, denunciations, chance mishaps, its members would not have to stand every moment in fear of the scornful, triumphant smile of the investigating judge. There was only one possible way to manage this: to leave the country and work abroad. As the organization could not be unconquerable, it must at least be undiscoverable. These plans had often been evolved by rebels; and they had, time after time, no difficulty in bringing out the first three issues of their paper. Then, however, their country vanished in distant mists; so soon did they lose touch with events at home.

Lenin wanted more than a simple propaganda sheet. He aimed at a home organization from which it could receive regular news, at means of circulation, at clubs in which it could be read, at correspondents in the *guberny* (provinces), at a first-hand Russian basis. As no house, not even a tent in the steppes, could offer security, the paper must be printed abroad, but it must have the effect of coming out in St. Petersburg. Even before he set out for the conference at which it was decided to start a paper, Ulianov tried to gain reliable friends for this foreign enterprise, satisfied himself as to directions in which the paper could penetrate, and discussed methods of secret circulation.

The conference met at Pskov, and approved the purposes and the name of the paper. It was to be called *Iskra, "The Spark."* Its motto was to be no secret: every number was to bear the line from Pushkin, "From the spark shall spring the flame."

Lenin soon left Pskov for St. Petersburg with the fruits of this resolution, to make final preparations for departure with his friend Martov. But Ulianov had not had time in St. Petersburg to recover from the weariness of travel before he was arrested. In the station searchroom the innermost of pockets soon holds no further secrets from the police; Lenin's yielded at once two thousand roubles, intended for the first needs of the enterprise, and a number of documents written in invisible ink. But the cautious conspirator had covered these potentially fatal sheets with ordinary laundry lists and other scrawled items for the entertainment of the public prosecutor. He was only detained under remand for a week, after which he stayed a further week in the capital, and then went, with the forged passport that had become a matter of course, via Prague to Munich.

The negotiations with the rest of the editorial committee—George Plekhanov, Vera Sassulitch, Potressov, Axelrod and Martov—as to the plan of publication of the *Iskra* dragged on. Already, unnoticed by Lenin and his five friends, there was developing the first breach. For his comrades the one joy longed for in their precarious existence was the opportunity, without let or hindrance, to write, and then, within at most a week, to see their thoughts in print, and to be able so to speak out without thereby heading straight for destruction.

The persecuted rebel who can use a pen, when he thinks of revenge, thinks of himself not as a crowned Cæsar, but as captain of the written word. The rebels' trade is often their whole life, their solace in gloom. They are writers before all else—did they not become revolutionaries because the white sheet of paper held out promises even in their childhood, because indignation brought the richest flow of words and ideas? In any other walk of life they would have had less to say. For Martov, especially, the sun only shone on the day which was passed in an unbroken flow of conversation. He always had an endless tale to tell. When his friend sought wearily the homeward way, Martov remained good company for himself; every day, reinvigorated by fresh ideas, he covered many fresh sheets of paper.

For Ulianov this literary creativeness was a thing of little account, and that not because Martov could be wittier, Plekhanov deeper, Sassulitch more meticulous, Axelrod more European than he in spinning words out of ideas and weaving ideas into words. To him the newspaper meant a political instrument, the head and centre of a movement in his homeland. From this difference of outlook came the rival proposals as to place of publication. The others wanted a city honoured with the presence of as many émigrés as possible; they could not bear separation from the environment to which they had grown used in the course of years. Ulianov had no love for the idea of working in the midst of the uprooted; he would best have liked not to meet a single Russian, in order to breathe with less distraction the air of his own country, to escape the influence on heart and mind of the casual talk of people with too much spare time, to be free from the puppet life around him.

At last, in Stuttgart, and afterwards in Munich, secret printing facilities were found. At the end of 1900, in the capital of Bavaria, there came out the first number of the *Iskra*.

Members of the German Social Democracy, notably Dr. Lehmann, Herr Dietz, Adolf Braun and Clara Zetkin, assisted in the work of smuggling the paper over the frontier. In double-bottomed trunks and in all manner of innocent-looking wrappings the *Iskra* reached its destinations.

The Russian censorship had at that very moment prohibited the mention of one thousand eight hundred and ninety-six matters. The State press supervisors used printers' ink by the ton to conceal from the wondering citizen everything that they found objectionable, even in foreign papers.

The secret newspaper stalls of the Munich organ grew more and more into centres of the organization, formed opinions, spread slogans. Secret printing-presses set to work also on Russian soil, issuing manifestos in the name of the *Iskra* and discussing matters of urgent local importance. All the threads of the organization led to Lenin's wife, who deciphered letters, answered questions, spread warnings, kept news files, supplied news and information to the various Militant Unions, and so quietly enabled Ulianov to control an apparatus as live as it was complicated.

Lenin had been living under the name of Meier, with a Social Democratic innkeeper. His study window opened on a court bounded by melancholy and oppressively ugly walls. Screaming children played there, and busy housewives gave noisy evidence of their presence as they worked with brawny competence. The innkeeper, Herr Rittmaier, would dry his hands and come away every now and then from his foaming beer-mugs, to tell Ulianov how scarce was money, how hard the times, how heavy was competition and how necessary was Socialism.

When Krupskaya arrived from Russia, the pseudo-Meier gave notice to Herr Rittmaier, and moved, without a furniture van, into a tenement dwelling in Schwabing. As they had auctioned the whole of their goods and chattels for twelve marks, the removal was an easy and pleasant stroll.

"WHERE TO BEGIN?"

How does any régime die? Must not the marble pillars of the palaces, the joyful acclamations of kneeling crowds, the majesty of things as they are, the pomp and circumstance that surround power at all times, condemn all its servitors to languish eternally?

And who are the rebels?

Lucian, the Roman-Semitic satirist, described them about the middle of the second century after Christ. They waste their days, run from Roman inn to inn, and imagine that they are achieving great things in treating their friends to child's fairy-tales. In the squares where they all shout the same thing in the same way, they are eaten up with envy. From their dirt, their lousiness, their mendacity they argue with conviction that they are called to redeem the world. To him, to the cultured Lucian, these Israelite refugees from Asia Minor talked of resurrection, the salvation of souls, and other Oriental mysteries, born, it might be, in empty stomachs, but not in any brain.

Men go their way, and think little of it when rebels talk of redemption.

Lenin heard the murmur of these discontented ones, and saw before him the frightful power to be overcome. It had its enemies in the underworld; some of them had crept into scattered conventicles of which each cursed all the others for heretics. But how insignificant was this minority! What did the majority do or think of doing but grow up, procreate their like, and die?

The voice of Theory was firm and prophesied great things; yet Tsarism stood there like granite rock. Lenin had had ten years' experience of the limits of possibility; now under the mansard roof in Schwabing he saw before him all Russia, as from the Sparrow Hills one looks down on the church domes of Moscow.

"One must have something to dream of," wrote Ulianov in the book that became the Primer of the Revolution, *"Where to Begin?"*

Others before him had risen up against the Régime, had, in sign of impotence, thrown bombs; after them had come mere dreamers; their successors had buried themselves in scientific analysis. Lenin took up his position against the Régime as an enemy commander, as an equal, looked out beyond his narrow circumstances, regarded himself as surrounded by the general staff of an army, and not only sketched a plan of action in the field, but at the same time sought for his soldiers.

Most of his friends were not much better than those enthusiasts at whom Lucian had pointed the finger of scorn. But they must suffice. Where, then, to begin? If one were really intent on victory, it would have been ridiculous not to be able to face the much easier task of getting together one's own nucleus troops.

"Men must be trained up who will devote to the Revolution not only their free evenings, but their whole lives; an organization must be developed of such dimensions that within it there can be carried out a precise division of labour for the various kinds of work that we want," wrote Lenin in the very first of his *Iskra* articles.

In *Where to Begin?* he further elaborates his Samurai theory:

"Political thought . . . has progressed far enough . . . to make it clear that without ten leaders of talent —and talents are not born by the hundred—proved, trained to their task, schooled in it through long years, it is impossible in present-day society for any class to carry on any sort of energetic struggle."

Ulianov deals with the opponents who contend that it is easier to rob a movement of ten able men than a hundred dullards:

"You will always be able to get for this great truth the applause of a hundred dullards. . . . I must tell you that it is much more difficult to catch ten able men than a hundred idiots. I shall uphold this principle however much you may rouse the masses against my 'anti-democratic' attitude. By 'able' men, as I have repeatedly emphasized, are to be understood, in connexion with problems of organization, only professional revolutionaries, whether students or workers by origin."

The masses, even in industry, are only armed with enthusiasm on Sundays and holidays; at other times they are taken up with their immediate interests. They live out of hearing of the sounds of the civil war, they cannot see its troops moving, no waving colours urge them on to radiant heights of power and dominance; they cannot be mobilized as the Tsar mobilizes his army. For this very reason, in spite of the prohibition of the carrying of arms, small cadres must be kept in being. These can awaken hopes among the multitude, and at the destined moment lead it through the ravines into the land where freedom's chorus chants. Even the much talked-of class consciousness dries up after Saturday's wages payment; it is unable to develop without the help of the trained professional revolutionaries.

"The basic error," wrote Lenin, "is the idea that political class consciousness can be developed in the workers from within, out of, say, the economic struggle; that is, proceeding entirely (or mainly) from this struggle, resting entirely or mainly on this struggle. . . . Political class consciousness can only be impressed on the workers from outside; that is, outside the economic struggle, outside the sphere of the relations between the workers and the employers."

The doctrine of the iron cohorts of a few leaders of millions represented the first stage of a struggle, the preparation for a military engagement.

Such ideas would have been impossible in Western Europe. Something of the sort may perhaps have been current in the middle of the last century, when Lassalle and his successor, Schweitzer, dreamed of the army of industrial workers as a songful procession to be led by themselves in a black carnival car drawn by white steeds. But five decades had passed since then; the children of the Western factories had more or less grown up, and their mentality conditioned that of their leaders.

Lenin, however, had not half a century before him, he had to face a much more rapid historical process.

It was precisely the elements on the extreme left of the Western European Labour movement who differed from Lenin on these questions of the fundamentals of organization. Thus Rosa Luxemburg wrote:

"The proletarian class struggle is the most fundamental of all active historic movements up to now, it embraces the whole of the lower social grades, and is the first active movement since social classes have existed which has represented the specific interests of the working masses. . . . This, however, disposes of the distinction made between the 'leaders' and the majority that 'flocks after' them, for it inverts the relation between masses and leaders. The only part to be played in the Social Democracy by the so-called 'leaders' is that of the explanation to the masses of their function in history."

Ulianov, too, knew of the unnumbered, the undiscovered masses who must march with enthusiasm through the streets and squares of Russia. He considered, however, that the problems of the organization of their goose-step could be solved only by his company of faithful servants of the movement. At present the only force watching over the multitude was the bayonets of the enemy.

"The task of the commander," writes Count von Schlieffen, "is to inflict on an opponent, even a stronger opponent, of whom he knows neither the location nor the movements nor the plans, destruction or complete defeat." Lenin, whose general headquarters and observation tower was a writing-desk in Schwabing, had a far more complicated mission than that of a commander-in-chief with his army round him. The *generalissimo* knows broadly the field in which he will conquer or suffer defeat. Ulianov's battle fronts extended to regions unknown to military science, into the homes of poor and rich, into the country house and the cottage.

"The field," he writes, "from which alone this knowledge can be drawn, is the field of the relations of all classes to the State and the Government, the field of the inter-relations between . . . all classes. . . . Accordingly . . . it is not always possible to give the answer with which practical advisers usually . . . content themselves: 'Go among the workers.' To imbue the workers with political knowledge, the Social Democrats must go among all classes of the population, must send out their troops in all directions."

He saw his kernel of loyalists and their followers move over this uneven terrain, saw the central mechanism and the process of decentralization, kept in mind the element of voluntary help, that heavy artillery of revolutionary movements. He could not, it is true, give orders to his followers like a general, had at most only a dozen persons whom he could ask to take particular lines of action. Accordingly it was necessary for the organization to be as constricted and as widespread as possible, present everywhere and yet undiscoverable by the enemy, hard as stone and yet elastic.

"At the head of the local movement," wrote a faithful supporter, "stands a committee. It has under it district groups, clubs and factory committees. Some of these, after satisfying the committee, will have come into the Party; the rest will be only affiliated to it."

Lenin criticized existing methods of struggle: "Usually the first attempt at activity is promptly and completely stamped out by the police. This prompt and complete stamping out comes from the fact that these campaigns were not the result of a systematic, carefully thought-out and secretly prepared plan for a long and obstinate struggle, but simply the natural growth of the work of the clubs under their traditional methods . . . but as soon as serious campaigning began (and it began as early as the strike of the summer of 1896), the defects of our fighting organization became more and more evident. . . . We went into battle like peasants leaving the plough with nothing but cudgels in their hands."

With a changed and improved organization, with connexions in all social classes, furnished with organs of hearing that would detect the smallest whisper of discontent, "we should," he considered, "be making our unconscious servants the employees and officials not only of the factories, but of the postal, railway and customs authorities, the administrative offices, the clerical and all other authorities, not even excluding the police and the court officials."

Lenin sums up the whole matter in a postscript to *Where to Begin?*

". . . to comply with all regulations and to obey all the laws and customs of the active service forces in which one is enrolled, and which one has no right to leave in time of war without the permission of the officers commanding. . . . We must have our own regular postal service, skilled and experienced not only in the process of bulk distribution, but in that of delivery at the doors of dwellings and in the ways of reaching them; reading circles for illegal literature, groups entrusted with the supervision of spies . . . groups of agitators and propagandists, who know how to start a conversation and carry it on for a long time while keeping entirely within the law, so that they can speak out without danger to themselves, can pump their listeners, can sound the position. . . . A group of students, officers, officials . . . should in many cases be entirely unaware of its membership of the Party. . . . For instance, the utmost secrecy and military discipline is needed for a group of colporteurs. A group of propagandists is equally dependent on secrecy, but much less on military discipline. . . . The leadership of the movement must be in the hands of the smallest possible number of groups, as uniform as possible, of well-experienced revolutionaries. The rank and file of the movement must be the largest possible number of groups, as various in every way as possible, from the different sections of the proletariat and of other classes."

These forms of revolutionary organization were in consonance neither with the last pages of Karl Marx's *Kapital* nor with the outcome of the Hegelian dialectic; Lenin lays down rather in aspiration than dogmatically this ideal plan of a movement equally subversive and well

ordered. His desires and conclusions were in contradiction with the customary practice of the small groups.
They wounded vanities, ignored habits. The many orators of rebellion, who in the intoxication of their rhetoric
and the spasms of their dramatic gestures almost threw
their arms out of joint, were now to become dumb and
disciplined subordinates, no longer speaking about everything under the sun, but doing little talking and much
co-ordinated working.

Most of his friends were afraid of nothing so much as
moving an inch from the letter of the Theory.

Just as the voices of the Maid of Orleans would whisper to her only what she had just herself decided in any
particular situation, so Karl Marx confirmed to Lenin
the things which he himself felt to be necessary. But
Ulianov did not kneel down in solitude or await heavenly
inspiration; he was bound up with the masses, thought for
them, learned always from them as the fundamental reality. He knew that without the aid of millions of men
and women his thoughts would not go beyond the walls
of his lodging. Yet the idea was his own, born in his
brain—the envisaged Party was his vision. In him potentialities, inevitabilities in the life of all Russia had come
as inspirations and had been given concrete shape.

THE QUARREL OVER THE "ISKRA"

The sternest régimes come to their end because they
are not stern enough. Through the elaborate network
constructed by a hierarchy over the whole country, there
slip individuals whose arms and brains become the weapons of an idea which is the beginning of a reality. Where
thoughts and children are born, the Tsar cannot command
with the authority wielded over a barracks. His police,
who cannot read destinies in the eyes of their prisoners,
had already had Vladimir Ilyitch Ulianov four times in

their hands, and now they began to regret that they had let slip the man whose papers, smuggled into Russia, were becoming a troublesome plague, even though they did not seem a particularly dangerous one.

He himself soon left Munich. The secret press was unable to continue, as its owners had been intimidated into giving up the work.

George Plekhanov and Vera Sassulitch were glad of the change. The Theoretician was an orthodox supporter of the classical German philosophy, though on a reformed system; but he felt happier in countries yet further west. Nor did he care to stay any length of time in the same place; he would always prick up his ears at the news of a fresh centre of émigré activity.

Vera Sassulitch was the only one in this little editorial group who was not altogether happy over the accepted Marxist methods, and, indeed, did not treat them too seriously; she loved her terrorist past, and was obsessed with romantic pictures of a revolutionary Apocalypse. She asked for even less than the others of the good things of this world. When she spread enough mustard for five people on her sandwich, her friends would say "Vera's giving herself a treat." She was the type of the Russian woman revolutionary as conceived by a *wohltemperiert* European bank-clerk or civil servant, with his steady salary.

Leo Trotzky has described her quarters. They had little resemblance to the boudoir of the French *marquise* who read prohibited diatribes against Louis XV and generously harboured their author:

"Vera was a peculiar and a peculiarly attractive woman. She wrote extremely slowly and went through very agonies of authorship. 'Vera Ivanovna doesn't write,' Vladimir Ilyitch said once to me, 'she puts together bits of mosaic.' And she did, in fact, put down each of her sentences one by one, moving slowly about the room, shuffling and tapping along in her slippers, and incessantly smoking cigarettes which she rolled herself. She threw the loose tobacco and the half-smoked cigarettes just anywhere, in the corners, on the window-seats, on the tables, and tipped the ashes all over her blouse, her hands, her manuscripts, her glass of tea, and every now and then her interlocutor."

For Vera Sassulitch the Revolution was a universal and all-embracing conception; she worshipped this goddess in ecstasies of emotion. If her friends analysed the forms of revolt, Vera paled. She wanted to praise her idol, not to know it. Any suggestion of method offended her pious adoration, her silent contemplation; she found the endless discussions of her five comrades, their interest in German problems, the controversy between Reformists and Orthodox, bare and stale as a neglected, long unoccupied room. Sassulitch, says Trotzky, used constantly to say of the German Social Democrats:

"It is always the same; they will make an end of Revisionism, return to Marx, secure a majority, and after all go on living with the Kaiser."

"Whom do you mean by 'they' this time, Vera Ivanovna?" Trotzky would interrupt.

"Why, the German Social Democrats."

Axelrod, unlike his friend Vera Ivanovna, was never tired of discovering in the pages of the pamphlets from the Social Democratic Press something prophetic of coming events. He longed for Russian development towards German orderliness. In those weak moments in which one does not hide one's ideas from oneself, he dreamed that Moscow and St. Petersburg had attained a state in which they used just as much soap as Berlin or Munich.

In spite of their differences of character and feeling, and their fundamental differences of theory, George Plekhanov, Vera Sassulitch and Paul Axelrod were united in close friendship. They were people with European reputations, with authority in the camp of international Socialism; and Lenin was a thorn in their side.

This young man, fresh from Russia, no more than thirty-three years old, hurt their feelings. His language, even when he was not disagreeing with them, was as decided as that of a Governor-General, and he had the organization at his back. Axelrod objected to him as too Red. Vera Sassulitch objected to him because he was always analysing, and had the cheek never to take her over-seriously, and Plekhanov objected on all these and yet other grounds.

After these cronies had moved away from Munich with the light luggage that was all their worldly goods, they started again to cover their reams in London. Here all six stayed together for nearly a year, before again transferring the editorial office to Geneva.

The same sort of faces as those that had greeted him in Schwabing now passed up and down outside Lenin's rooms in London. There was no change in his everyday life. The smell of the soup cooking in the little kitchen filled the two rooms. Ulianov had learnt English in Siberia, and supposed that he would now be able to speak it. But at his first attempts he saw at once that the only Englishmen who could understand him were the very few who could speak fluent Russian. He took lessons in English from an Englishman whom he helped in Russian. Lenin industriously frequented the open air meetings in Hyde Park, to accustom his ear to the still unfamiliar sounds, and now and then to catch and gloat over a rebel phrase. The other editors carefully avoided all contact with their surroundings.

The six writers lived in closer association than they had done in Munich. They met more often, had more opportunities of personal exchange of views.

One morning the slanting rays of the sun lit up two parties. Ulianov and Martov were the schismatics. Martov talked too much, however, to matter greatly. The stumbling block was Ulianov.

Not so long ago he had thought of Plekhanov as one

consecrated to the Cause; now he stood thirsting for the divine radiance of the Master and found him clouded and overcast. Master and disciple had to draw up together the programme for the second Party Congress. They were consumed by the same desire, had the same Theory, which opened to them the same perspectives. Plekhanov wanted their prophecies of economic change put in cautious language. He had the scepticism of a scholar, the turgidity of a critic who knows the dangers of being too lucid.

Lenin, on the contrary, thirsted for confident predictions, hated the comfortable sound of the safe phrase, pilloried the expression "more or less." The Teacher took offence, wondered how his follower could take his doctrine more seriously than he did himself. So the youngest disciple stood at variance with the Authorities.

Dislike was born in that moment. Beyond doubt the difference over principles, which, after all, were so closely similar, was reinforced by personal incompatibilities. In human relations the incidental, the irrelevant carries the day. Each of the six members of the editorial staff had his secrets—Lenin had faith in the Revolution. He saw it, could prophesy though he could not prove, and accordingly he was set on the party and the apparatus of revolt that he described in *Where to Begin?* The others felt that Ulianov was the more firmly planted on popular support, and they also noted that he was working for a dictatorship in the editorial department, and through that for sole domination in the organization in the homeland.

Leo Trotzky had come to London about this time from his Siberian prison, a novice of the Revolution. Ulianov had looked after the young refugee, protected him from Plekhanov's high-and-mightiness, from the Master's irony. Nevertheless, Trotzky, turning to Lenin, gave it as his opinion that the forms of organization at which Lenin was aiming amounted to his elevation to autocracy. Ulianov replied:

"What is there wrong in that? As things are there is no other possible way out."

The author of *Where to Begin?* had no intention of hiding behind the pages of a book. The dream at the writing-desk urged him on. He longed for a party which would carry the policy of his book into practice. His watchwords must become shibboleths. He sloughed off the husk of submission.

To will so much, Ulianov must have foreseen the impetus of forces not yet materialized, association with a power not yet dreamed of by the world, the steadfast purpose of an all-conquering social element. Alexander, the son of Philip of Macedon, declared himself to be a son of Olympus; Cromwell had private understandings with Heaven, in virtue of which Puritans sang psalms, avoided sins and beheaded kings; Wallenstein sought propitious stars; Napoleon had one of his own. Lenin, who had set out to overturn an empire, spent long hours, as Nadeshda Konstantinovna relates, in Highgate Cemetery—whither poor people are driven in third-class hearses—and sat by the tombstone of Karl Marx. The teacher of his days and nights, who lies buried there, had given him a deity and a Providence, History. Ulianov believed in his own strength only because he believed that he was that god's prophet.

THE RULING AND REBEL MINORITIES

In Russia around 1903 there were many advocates of the most varied ideals; many a new doctrine opened wondering eyes on life. The call of new aspirations overbore all else. People clothed themselves in the convention of the new spirit, and readily allowed themselves to be led away from the thought of their personal interests.

In this year there sprang up a crop of new aspirations

and old. The peasant demanded land, the proletarian the eight-hour day, students at college the right to be a law unto themselves, the lords of the factories the national benefits of high protection and constitutional conservatism, literary men not only their existing freedom to write without ideas, but even freedom from censorship; the Minister of the Interior demanded a Labour Party, to be run by the police; Lenin a centralized organization, his Socialist enemies a loose association of men of like ideas; grand dukes, who were also speculators in Siberian timber, demanded war against Japan, and the Empress Alexandra Feodorovna an heir to the throne.

Perhaps the desire of the Tsaritsa was the most difficult of all to satisfy. The Psalms, of which the precepts are eagerly observed in Russia, she read nightly in ecstasies of bliss before retiring to rest, with the silent long-suffering of the martyrs. Daily she sang David's evening prayer: "Stand in awe and sin not: commune with your own heart upon your bed, and be still."

But the unhappy woman could no longer rest content with these simple words to the Almighty; the weeping Tsaritsa was set on ascertaining what was the pleasure of the Lord. "This, however," as is written in the book of the miracle worker Iamblichus, whose doctrine is an ornament of theology—"This, however, is not easily to be ascertained by man, unless he be instructed by a high genius and illuminated by a godly light."

For two years the French veterinary surgeon Philippe of Lyons seemed to be detecting heaven-sent secrets. He took much gold from the imperial privy purse, and assured Alexandra Feodorovna that soft singers of her fame had announced to him that she would become a mother, indeed that the infant was already coming. Count Witte, who had for many years been Minister of Finance, writes:

"The last months of pregnancy had arrived . . . all Russia heard the news. The Tsaritsa's audiences ceased. . . . In St. Petersburg there was hourly expectation of the cannon salvos from the fortress of Peter and Paul, which were to announce by their number a son or a daughter. The Tsaritsa . . . took to bed. Professor Ott, the physician in ordinary, came with his assistants to stay at Peterhof . . . he waited in vain. . . . Then Professor Ott began to try to persuade the Tsar and Tsaritsa to permit him to examine her. . . . Ott declared that the Tsaritsa was not pregnant at all."

In spite of the miscarriage of the miracle, the prophetic veterinary continued to enjoy in the house of the Romanovs the needful authority; for Her Majesty's mischance was but another spiritual trial.

The horse-doctor's accomplices met together in the summer residence of the Grand Duke Peter Nikolayevitch by the seashore at Peterhof, near the imperial pleasure palace. Here, in the spotless radiance of the spirit, many of the faithful held commune with immortal beings. They received from Philippe's hands the pure, unsubstantial host, and heard voices from the grave. John of Kronstadt, the priest, widely known in Muscovy; Father Seraphim, until recently a dashing artillery officer; Nicholas II, Alexandra Feodorovna, Prince Putianin, the Chief Marshal of the Court, Grand Duchess Anastasia, Grand Duchess Militza, Grand Duke Nicholas Nikolayevitch formed an intimate circle of soulful friends.

They were heavily oppressed with anxiety for the arrival of a Tsarevitch and for the spiritual well-being of the countless subjects of the realm. There was much praying; many a famous figure of past generations, dead for decades, appeared to them with face white as a sheet; important decisions were arrived at.

Father Seraphim, of Moscow, considered that great injustice had been done to his famous predecessor, Seraphim of Sarov, who had died five decades before. Countless miracles he had smilingly worked, often in sleep, on this sinful earth, and yet the Synod refused to canonize him. The late Seraphim was weeping over this in Heaven, and the living Seraphim gathered the miraculous, heavy tears in the hollow of his trembling hand. The fount of Sarov also brought warmth from Paradise which could regale even an Empress. If only the sufferer who, in human parlance, had died could get into the Calendar, his gratitude would know no bounds. Their Majesties' hearts rejoiced. They had hope of winning for themselves great fame, of participating in the universal Kingdom of Christ: they would raise the miracle worker of Sarov to the estate of sainthood.

The supreme authority in the Church looked askant on the purpose of the imperial couple. It declared that the all-highest Synod could no more confer the eternal splendour of this title without close investigation than a court can acquit a defendant without due evidence of his innocence.

"The Empress," writes Count Witte, "deigned to remark as to that: 'The Emperor can do all things.'"

Seraphim was canonized.

In June the Tsar, the Tsaritsa, the court and three hundred thousand of the faithful went on pilgrimage to the mortal remains of the Saint at Sarov, in the *gubernia* of Tambov. At the grave Nicholas and twelve abbots bore the silver coffin. Bethlehem floated in the skies over the innumerable company of believers. All that was earthly, ordinary, everyday faded from view, and in their ecstasy the crowd looked for seven days into eternal gardens. A whole people heard the sounds of Paradise; saw how the Lamb is borne by lions, how the elephant disturbs no blade of grass, how the serpent caresses the ape.

At night the Empress bathed in the holy fount.

And the unattainable was vouchsafed. Alexandra Feodorovna actually did bear a son.

The chief Procurator of the Holy Synod, Prince A. D.

Obolensky, relates that the Emperor said to him, with deep emotion: "As to the sanctity and the miracles of Saint Seraphim, I am so utterly convinced that no one will ever be able to shake my conviction. I have unanswerable proof of it."

The Government declared that the pilgrimage to Sarov was the most important spiritual happening in Russia in the twentieth century. The Tsar spoke to his people in a manifesto, and said that he had had reports of evil disposition and discontent. He had, however, promised his dying father "to preserve inviolate the century-old foundations of the Russian State."

But more than four decades had passed since the abolition of serfdom. The spirit of the countryman had undergone a change. Industry had extended to the limit permitted by the remains of feudalism in the steppe. In places it had a modern North American character which created a new outlook and awakened new aspirations in mountain and valley. Already 453 big concerns employed in all 1,097,000 proletarians, or 43 per cent. of all the Russian factory workers.

The lords of the country's industrial wealth united in a great association to demand the regularization of the State, fearing that absolutism would give birth to revolution. They formed the nucleus of a coming Democratic party. The big landowners also voiced their complaints; they dreamed of self-government, and considered that Tsarism paid excessive attention to industrial interests. They joined hands, nevertheless, with the manufacturers, met them at banquets at which a Constitution was loudly demanded; so long as agrarian reform was kept out of the programme they used even more radical language than their brethren of industry. The Liberals and their student sons regarded themselves as shepherds of a great people; they invited workers to their political functions, and the world decked itself in the shining silver of a new dawn.

They called their association the Liberation League, and issued a paper first in Stuttgart and then in Paris, with Peter Struve as its editor.

The intellectuals, at every opportunity of meeting together that offered, at teachers', doctors', pharmacists', agricultural congresses, demanded the benefits of the Belgian or the British Constitution. At the all-Russian cattle show at Kharkov the Liberation League was welcomed, and the belief was put on record that nothing but arbitrary administration "prevents the breeding of a pure race of Russian horned cattle." The doctors' congress in St. Petersburg declared that it was impossible successfully to combat infant mortality, drunkenness, venereal disease, and tuberculosis without entire freedom of speech, of the Press and assembly.

The wealthy Maltzev gave millions of roubles for the advocacy of these widely desired civic rights.

The workers, for their part, were endeavouring to escape from the lethal embrace of the enemy. In Baku and Nikolayev, in Kiev and Kertch, in Ekaterinoslav, Tiflis and Kharkov there were strikes. The strike movement extended to the very borders of Russia. In Odessa barricades were set up. From the benches the justices awarded sentences aggregating hundreds of years of imprisonment. In half a decade Socialism grew into a mass movement.

The circle of esoteric amity at Peterhof suffered under this multitudinous malice of insubordinate subjects. Neither the grand dukes and grand duchesses living there, nor their Majesties and the priests, could find solace amid the silvery gloom of their nocturnal meetings for all this plebeian greed. They regarded the voices of the discontented as fumes from hell, without a spark of godliness. Father John of Kronstadt reminded the Tsar of his duty, taught that the Constitution and the Bible were one, and recited to the rulers and the pale and trembling duchesses the seventh Psalm of David:

"If he turn not, he will whet his sword: he hath bent his bow, and made it ready.

"He hath also prepared for him the instruments of death; he ordaineth his arrows against the persecutors."

Plehve, the Minister of the Interior, also belonged to this circle. At the canonization of Seraphim he had knelt before the remains of the departed, his face distorted by deep emotion. Their Majesties observed with gracious approval that bent, sorrowing head. In the villa at Peterhof Plehve often told how Russia could be saved; Nicholas's spiritual adviser, a "pope" named Vostorgov, emphatically seconded the Minister's admonitions. Plehve querulously demanded of the small but earnest assembled company why the people who lived in poverty were left to the vagaries of propagandists, why they were not gathered and organized against insolent landowners, arrogant manufacturers and Judah. The discontented proletarians, they were told by high police officials, were led by discontented intellectuals. "What would be easier than for us to lead them ourselves?" The owners of the *latifundia* and of the factory machines would then be fried in their own fat; and their speech-making would be confined to the narrow circle of their well-fed friends. In unimportant economic matters it would even be politic to make concessions. A company of saints, the Black Hundred, should direct the rage of the poor against the Jews and the specious intellectuals. Captain-General Trepov, a great friend of the Tsar's, also hugged the idea of these schemes. Count Witte describes General Trepov's line of thought:

"They are agitators; shoot 'em down. They mouth big phrases; give 'em cold steel. The workpeople want to make a revolution; just second a few police for revolutionary service and you have them at your mercy."

According to the official theory, all Jews had to bear the responsibility for the small company who, two thousand years ago, in Pilate's courtyard, agitated furiously against Christ and organized a small pogrom of their own. An argument occurred to a few Hebrews in Crimea. They proved to the authorities that their fore-fathers had been living on the Black Sea coast long before the Crucifixion, peacefully buying there and gently selling again.

The massacring of proletarianized Jews, Poles and Armenians, of students, propagandists and Socialist workers, was from now onwards to accompany Tsarism to its end, staining its path and spreading fresh terrors on top of old sufferings in Muscovy.

The fourteen years' pogrom, unbroken save for short interruptions, began in Kishinev. The procession in any day's work varied little from the general monotony. "You can please yourself," said a high police official, "how you go to work on a massacre, whether of ten or ten thousand people." The masses were left to their own devices.

The barefooted tramp who came out of the country, knew nobody, wandered from town to town, was un-chained. Ikons were carried at the head of the demon-strators, bells were rung and the long procession was set in motion. The armed poor went to the homes of the unarmed poor. They plundered the ghettos, and the nar-row lanes, which knew only suffering, in which even spring found no room, in which dirt was the children's only plaything, became alive with the death-rattle. Curses rang out: a lovely chalumeau tone in the ears of the true believers. Dangerous Jews, not yet in their second year, were thrown out of the windows. Little shoemakers' or tailors' or cheesemongers' shops were smashed up. Manifestos were broadcast, signed by the "Workers' and True Christians' Party."

The Volhynian monk Iliodor circulated an open letter filled with passionate advocacy of passionate deeds: "In the name of the Father, the Son and the Holy Ghost, the great Anchorite of Lavra has ordained in Kiev that the population thereof shall be acquainted that St. Vladimir, who first baptized the people of Russia, has risen from his grave . . . wept with the Anchorite over the fatherland. . . . Gather ye all in the churches and consider . . . in what way the fatherland . . . can be defended. . . . Whosoever receives this letter must make at least three copies thereof and dispatch them to other villages and small towns. He who fails to comply with this injunction within six days will be visited by frightful disease."

Nicholas II did not, like Charles IX during St. Bartholomew's Night, himself shoot down the enemy from his balcony. But the party of the Black Hundred was his avenging arm, provided the cohorts of the imperial villa at Peterhof. The Emperor said paternally to a delegation of the pogromists: "Thank in my name all the Russians who have joined the organization." Stolypin, then Minister of the Interior, reported to the Tsar that sixty per cent. of this league were criminals. The Emperor replied in writing: "The League is the most loyal of all parties, and the most valuable to the Government. It would be well to have patience with it and allow it time for improvement." Prince Uruzov, Governor of Bessarabia, expressed the view that "a word of command from the mouth of the Tsar, or any unmistakable action in this direction, would have done much for the maintenance of order." When Count Witte drew His Majesty's attention to the pogroms, he replied: "But it is the Jews' own fault." On another occasion Tsar Nicholas said: "Yes, it is mistaken; but what can one do? these people are revolutionaries." General Katzbeck reported on a revolt. He was interrupted reproachfully by the Tsar: "Anyhow, too few were killed. Yes, you killed too few." When the general made to leave the room Nicholas called him back and repeated: "You should have fired on them, in spite of everything, General; you should have fired." A soldier who killed a girl under arrest because she looked out of a window against the regulations, received from Nicholas II a present of ten roubles.

On the Emperor's return from a pilgrimage to the relics of St. Seraphim, Plehve said to General Kuropatkin: "You do not understand the situation in the country. To arrest the revolutionary movement we need a little victory abroad." The adventure against Japan was discussed at a night sitting in Peterhof. It was not, however, only a moral initiative for the salvation of straying souls, but also a business initiative. Great timber concessions in Korea promised a golden harvest.

Over against the traditional might of Russian autocracy, of which the supreme elements gathered at the imperial country seat in Peterhof, where the beakers with consecrated wine were poured out over the Empire as far as Vladivostok, there was another minority, far away from the Villa. The imperial and Socialist minorities moved in rapid tempo—they could feel coming change. The autocrats fought for mastery over their opponents, in the name of Order. The opposition demanded room to live, in the name of Freedom. In the camp of revolt Lenin aimed at one day imposing his will on the vanquished autocracy, in the name of another Order. He defined himself and the party of organized obedience:

"Hand firmly grasping hand, we are proceeding, a tiny band of men and women, along a rocky and difficult path. We are surrounded on all sides by many enemies; we are compelled almost always to march under their fire. We have bound ourselves by a freely adopted resolve to fight against the enemy and not to stray into the swamps by the side of the road."

To beat Tsarism, his cohort was to be led in the same way as the serried ranks of the autocracy.

A Tsar of the Reds against a Tsar of the Whites.

The aristocracy of the Revolution had other roots than that of the Romanovs, its flower another radiance. But the soil on which it lived was not less complicated or composed of fewer layers than that out of which Tsarism sprang.

The underworld of the great cities, the rich, Bohemia, the sects, the national minorities, had to be brought into association with the party of extreme intransigence, with Lenin. At once the Liberals were loud in assertion of their standard.

Around these questions the various shades of Socialist opinion grouped themselves at the Congress of 1903, which opened in Brussels and closed in London.

Through the *Iskra* Ulianov had exerted strong influence over the organizations in Russia, trying to build up for the various types—those influenced by suffering, by poverty, by idealism amid circumstances of peaceful subordination, by hatred—a common temple of dogma joined with opportunism.

Terrorism was raising its head again; the party of the Social Revolutionaries had just been founded to resume the policy of assassination. Many of the rebels of Russia wanted to carry the forts of Tsarism by storm.

Lenin reminded them of the necessity of systematic investment of the forts.

He was intent on making terms with all who trembled in awe at the voice of their shepherd and Autocrat but still dreamed of the possibilities of a different world; on saying to these wanderers, scattered like leaves in the wind: "Come and help us."

Not that the sword was to be laid aside or forgotten. A small company of theoreticians, himself at their head, must be in charge of it. These elders of the Revolution would lead their Party to victory, gaining allies through compromises; for only they were strong enough to preserve their revolutionary faith as vestals their girdle of chastity.

The Congress sitting in London was reminiscent of the Convention of 1793. Everyone wanted to speak at once. Every second sentence was interrupted by hissing

RASPUTIN

DEMONSTRATION OF THE BLACK HUNDRED

FATHER GAPON AT A WORKERS' MEETING

or applause. In daytime the hall was ill-lit. By night the lamplight gave the whispering groups the appearance of conspirators. The delegates from Russia brought with them their determination and their intransigence. Shouts of abuse interrupted the flow of speeches. The steps leading to the platform were narrow. Had anyone stumbled, he might have shouted, like a member of the Convention: "This is a scaffold ladder." And Lenin might have answered, like Carrier: "Practise away!"

The chief struggle raged around the opening paragraph of the statutes of the organization. Martov's draft read: "By members of the Russian Social Democratic Labour Party are to be understood all those who accept its programme and actively work for the realization of its aims, under the control and direction of the Party."

Lenin's proposal was: "By member of the Party is to be understood any person who accepts its programme and supports the Party both by material means and by personal co-operation in one of the Party organizations."

Martov wanted to rest content with the supporters' general agreement with the Party. Lenin was concerned for the personal co-ordinated activity and obedience of the supporter. He said to his opponents:

"In itself there is nothing in this difference of opinion, although it discloses subtle differences of principle, which should produce so much disagreement (or, to speak plainly and without circumlocution, such a split). But any difference of opinion is capable of becoming serious if it is persisted in, if it is given prominence, if every root and every branch of this difference of opinion is deliberately and carefully traced out."

When Ulianov caught sight of a resolution he would eye it narrowly, as though he were examining it with a magnifying glass. As a politician he could have no objection to compromises; but they must not interfere with the actual perception of realities, spreading the mantle of Christian charity over uncleared issues. Where he saw opinions and differences of opinion formulated in paragraphs, he watched over every comma and full stop as a sick man over the flowers brought by his betrothed. He affectionately patted well formulated definitions of tactics as a mother strokes the head of her sick child. Lenin concentrated on resolutions the whole of his attention, with the grave sense of self-preservation. He saw behind them realities and their conflicts. Perhaps Ulianov was the most expert formulator of theses of all time.

Martov's formula opened the way for possible armed alliance with the Liberals. Lenin was only prepared to make use of them. Above all, he did not want them in his own Party, and accordingly he set up an obstacle, a wall, in front of the secret membership register; discipline, obedience, was to be the test by privation—a spiritual asceticism, a Puritanism of submission.

"Discipline and organization," he said, "which are such a stumbling-block for the bourgeois intellectuals, are particularly easy for the proletariat to accept, thanks to its factory schooling . . . the Party organization has for the intellectuals the appearance of an enormous factory; the subordination of a section to the whole and of the minority to the majority seems to them to be an enslavement. . . . People who spend their days in loose-fitting dressing-gowns and slippers amid the homely comfort of the clubs, may find the formal statutes narrow and limited, burdensome and humiliating, bureaucratic and an enslavement, and a restriction on the free play of opposing principles. Aristocratic anarchism fails to realize that formal statutes are necessary for the very purpose of enabling the close intimacy of the clubs to be replaced by a widespread party network."

Lenin, at this congress, proclaimed himself a Jacobin.

It was impossible for him to send, as Maximilien Robespierre had done, his opponents and his friends of yesterday to the reformatory of the Revolution, the scaffold. But he felt the same hatred for them; nor could he give his friends provinces to rule, but he was able to provide them with simple formulæ, to offer them the satisfaction which comes from theoretic certainty.

With Lenin, truths put shortly were the fruit of long wrestling. To his supporters they seemed amazingly simple, and the simpler a comrade was, the more he revelled in the simplicity of what he heard.

"The Jacobin," said Lenin, "who is closely in touch with the organized proletariat . . . is the real revolutionary Social Democrat. The Girondist, who thinks in terms of professors and students, is frightened of the dictatorship of the proletariat, and babbles about the absolute value of the Democratic claims, is an opportunist."

George Plekhanov grasped this simple truth with all its implications. He spoke in favour of Ulianov's proposal, pointed out that "discipline has no terrors for the workers," but that "it frightens many intellectuals who are soaked in bourgeois individualism from joining the Party; Lenin's draft may serve as a bulwark against their penetration into the organization, and if only for that reason all opponents of opportunism must vote for it." After the orgies of dazzling revolutionary phrase-making, Lenin had impressed his former teacher by the symmetry, the logic, the daring, the aggressiveness of his speech.

Plekhanov said to his friends: "Of such stuff Robespierres are made."

Not only the whole Congress, however, but the Teacher himself still failed to realize the actual consequences of Ulianov's proposals. Plekhanov especially was entirely against a split, attempted mediation, tried to find excuses for the recalcitrants. "When you listen to Lenin," he said, "you feel that he is right. When you listen to Martov you feel that what he says is not far from the truth. You feel yourself drawn over first to one side and then to the other."

This debate ended in the victory of Lenin's opponents. The struggle now began over fresh formulæ. The defeated Lenin secured his revenge. He proposed that in addition to the Central Committee in Russia a second headquarters should be set up abroad, should carry on the *Iskra* and should be the supreme authority. Here Ulianov won the day in the already divided Congress. He was determined to be the controller of the newspaper and to get his way, in spite of all congress resolutions, through patient detailed work. Above all, Vera Sassulitch and Paul Axelrod must be got rid of from the editorial board; he and Plekhanov must take over the *Iskra*.

This proposal was adopted by 25 votes of the "majority party," the *Bolsheviki,* against 23 votes of the "minority party," the *Mensheviki*.

In the fourteen years that followed, up to the eve of the seizure of power, the supporters of Bolshevism and Menshevism often remained together in a single party. They had their separate groups, headquarters and press organs, but often changed their standpoint or would pass from one camp into the other.

Lenin remained the living centre of Bolshevism.

It was a long-drawn-out battle in which words went furiously in search of paper and of the opposing group. Frequently the flow of eloquence would be interrupted by action, to take then a new direction or return to its original course. Paragraphs of resolutions took form of themselves, like ink on blotting-paper. Groups of émigrés wavered, attacked, replied. Lenin read every sentence in this scrimmage, to discover opponents or friends.

The Minority Party set up its own offices in Russia, and boycotted the Leninist Central Committee.

In the *Iskra* Lenin and Plekhanov ruled alone. All the other leaders declared that they were unable to join the board, as Ulianov had slandered at the Congress friends who had given long service, and had stopped at nothing to drive them from the editorial board. Plekhanov declared that this was a strike of the generals.

He saw six issues of the *Iskra* through with his disciple. By then the man of Theory had become oppressed with a sense of isolation, and wanted to see his old friends round him again.

Lenin rejected this proposal, and resigned from the editorial board.

Axelrod wrote against him, accusing him of introducing a state of siege into the Party, and Trotzky wrote a pamphlet attacking his dictatorial attitude.

"The hegemony of the Social Democracy in the struggle for liberation," wrote Trotzky, "was accompanied, on this principle of the state of siege, by the lordship of Lenin over the Social Democracy . . . and when he announced at the Congress the decision of the Central Committee, Comrade Lenin showed—his fist (we are not speaking figuratively), as the political symbol of the Central Committee. We forget whether this Centralist gesture was noted in the minutes. It would be a great pity if this was not done. This fist fitly crowns the edifice."

Vera Sassulitch, Potressov and Martov returned to the editorial board under Plekhanov. The *Iskra* became Menshevist. Ulianov now transferred the battle to the Central Committee of the Party. Freed from working under restraint in an editor's chair, he tried to make up through organization for his lack of a paper, and to summon a fresh Congress. He was even able to found a paper of his own. But his struggles were pushed into the background by a much greater one. For in the Far East, in virtue of the might of his armies, the Tsar had begun the slaughter of peoples.

THE TSAR'S SUNDAY AND LENIN'S DREAMS

On January 22, 1905, the people and the Tsar parted ways. It was a painful leave-taking; for Death received two hundred souls. There are times when the spectacle of death brings a revulsion in the minds of the mourners. In St. Petersburg Death spoke at the side of mass graves, told the vanquished that they needed the sword, sent from his world a liberating gleam to light the cold morning of the day after the tragedy.

The alliance of the police with the workers, the proletarian unions run by the secret service, could do nothing to still the cry of the poor. The club-rooms of these unions were decorated with cheap portraits of Nicholas II; at the end of the meetings the national anthem was sung, but with something of a subversive ring. The spirit, in spite of the monarchist ceremonial, was in tune with the general feeling and was political.

In the *Iskra* a correspondent wrote from Kiev:
"Many workers are striking without putting forward any demands. The tram-drivers, for instance, were asked what they wanted; they answered 'Nothing!' The grounds of discontent were stated with every possible variation. 'Why are they on strike here?' I asked a droshky driver on the day the strike began. 'Why, can they possibly hold out any longer and not rebel?' he answered. 'In the factories, grinding oppression is the order of the day, and shameless things are done everywhere.'"

But if a Socialist propagandist spoke amid the tension and exasperation of these sickly winter days, if he spoke out and abused the Tsar, he was answered with "What are you talking about? It is not the Monarchy that is troubling us."

The leader of the police unions of workers in St. Petersburg was the "pope" Gapon. He had the same faith as those whom he led. In spite of his position of rebel by official appointment, his convictions as well as his words were influenced by the feelings of his hearers. At the head of the fatal procession to the Winter Palace, Father Gapon talked with Social Democrats. They had no suspicion that the priest's Bible was a gift from the Ministry of the Interior. Gapon himself forgot it at times. His police mentality had been affected by sympathy with the discontented, and he was less concerned for his employers than for the pale faces that his words transfigured.

The Ministry issued an order for Gapon's arrest. In the Cabinet no one knew any longer which were the instigators of order under the Régime and which of revolt. Everyone regarded himself as a crafty little devil, working evil that good might come, controlling coming events through the most elaborate lying.

On January 22, 1905, workers were to make a pilgrimage from every industrial quarter of St. Petersburg to the Winter Palace, and in their name Gapon was to kneel before the Little Father, point to the shivering, freezing mass, and ask of the Tsar a healing drop of justice as salve for their wounds. The priest had impressed on his Social Democratic colleagues that this was a procession of poor people who were loyally faithful to the Tsar, and had made them promise that they would not distract them by revolutionary tunes, seditious words, or even by the banners of prohibited movements. If, in spite of this, they found their path blocked on this Sunday walk, the rear of the procession must press up on the foremost, to open the gate to the Throne by force. "Naturally," said Gapon, "some will suffer, but part of the troops will pass over to our side, and then, strong in our numbers, we shall achieve—Revolution! The Social Revolutionaries have promised us bombs, and the Democrats money."

From every narrow lane the pilgrims poured forth. The

dwellers in the Nevsky Prospect asked one another in astonishment where the multitude were coming from. Suburbs, factories, gin-shops, tenement buildings discharged their humanity; every street poured out into the next.

Ordinarily when anyone emerged from this world of the poor upon the boulevards and avenues, he came with the diffidence of a man in rags who by some chance finds himself admitted to a drawing-room. Now, however, the barefoot mob in the broad streets that led to the Winter Palace felt themselves at home. Suddenly they had made up their minds that they could no longer endure the poverty they were used to; they made great play, as always when the masses put forward demands, with their vision of the rights of man. They marched on in confidence; was not their true and orthodox priest taking them to their true and orthodox Emperor? They were no rebels, but true believers themselves.

Since dawn they had been on the march. The saints' banners looked like dismal sails on a dark sea, a moving Armada of dead men. After a few hours the demonstrators saw the domes of the Palace in which the "Mighty Being" sat enthroned. In front of the walls, from which flakes of snow were slipping down, there stood grey masses of soldiers, shivering together in the frost.

Suddenly murmurs of doubt became discernible among the pilgrims. "Well, what then?" thought the multitude. "The soldiers are part of the imperial power; they will receive us and take us to the All-powerful."

An officer rubbed his hands, made sure that all his coat-buttons were done up, and shouted hoarsely, "Get back!" The crowd remained still, murmuring unintelligibly.

The signal was given. The sound of volleys of musketry broke into the silence of the streets. Raging pain seemed to seize and choke everyone; all started to run, cursing; men fell to the ground, faces streamed with blood, thousands reeled as if drunk. The cavalry plunged into the crowd, the Cossacks' horses seemed to be spurred on by the frost. The crowd melted away; weak and exhausted men attempted to charge, because they were weak and exhausted.

In the side-streets the cry arose: "We want arms! Arms! Get arms!"

In five hours, on January 22, 1905, the Tsar had passed away for a whole people. A new faith proclaimed deliverance. Men concluded a new alliance, no longer with the Throne, but with a mysterious, lustful virago, who gives herself to all, intoxicates all, promises all things, and calls herself Revolution.

Meanwhile, what were the experts in revolt doing, the leaders and wise men of revolution, the men who for a decade past had been waiting for this or some similar event?

Ulianov's group wanted to come to an understanding with the enemies within their Party, the Mensheviks.

He himself, however, barricaded himself in his Geneva newspaper, *Vpered* (*Forward*), gathered a few loyal pens around him, those of Bogdanov, Lunacharsky, Olminsky and Vorovsky, and immediately after the tragedy of January 22 *proclaimed the value of a disciplined striking force.*

For Lenin the Revolution was not only an armed polemic against the ruling power, but also a theoretical final settlement with friends of yesterday, with comrades of the years of exile, with members of the Party in Russia who after the 1903 Congress had envisaged other methods and almost other aims. Such settlements, he considered, would leave the position clear when the day came for action.

The organization in St. Petersburg, which was under his influence, issued on the day after the Emperor's vengeance a manifesto loaded with imprecations.

"Citizens!" it ran, "yesterday you saw the brutality of the absolutist Government! You saw the blood that flowed in the streets! . . . Who directed the guns against the breasts of the workers? The Tsar, the grand dukes, the Ministers, the generals, and the rabble of the Court. They are the murderers! Death to them! To arms! Comrades, occupy the arsenals, the munition stores and the magazines! Destroy the police stations and gendarmerie offices. . . . We are out to overturn the Tsar's Government and to set up our own. Long live the Revolution! Long live the Constituent Assembly of People's Representatives!"

The tiny sheet which bore this impressive proclamation contained in Lenin's view the essence of the Revolution. He heard echoing through it the authentic voice of the masses, source of surging impulses that can refashion the landscape of familiar existence.

Rebellion whispered in the ears of the people, who had too long been content to be guided by inherited custom, by police regulations, by foremen, "popes" and sergeant-majors. She made the dumb cry aloud, stifled fear, unloosed energies; the industrial suburbs now thundered their demands in public squares hitherto inviolate under the orderly régime of unquestioned autocracy.

On such days as this the people awaken to collective life, consecrate events, act under the guidance of an instinct which theoreticians (who must provide complete explanations for all things) sometimes term historic will. When the masses will come together no one knows. Why exactly they appear to-day, and whether they will still be there to-morrow, is as unknown to the uncounted multitudes themselves as to the individuals who lead them. So does the instinctive self-determination of the masses reveal itself in all its incalculability of expression and energy.

Ulianov, however, was not content to leave it at that. He looked for the permanent elements of revolt in order to be able to assess the situation, tried to collect and store up the enthusiasm momentarily evoked, as dreamers of coming technical advance hope to store up inexhaustible forces from ocean waves that otherwise expend themselves unused. He visualized a resolute plan of action by the trained vanguard whose task was now mapped out in advance, expressed the view that "revolt must in future associate itself with an elemental mass movement," quoted with enthusiasm a voice from the camp of the Mensheviks which declared that "it is possible to create an organization which will represent a unifying ferment and in the hour of Revolution will win the loyalty of myriads."

In the first days of a rebellion its individual leadership, though it may enjoy all the honour of the movement, is not tested, is to all appearance a chance leadership and therefore unstable. The revolt has not yet consolidated itself in its leaders. The man whose shouting was the most conspicuous yesterday, whose formulation of generalities was the most in fashion, is lifted above the heads of the mass. Gapon seemed to be this leader on January 22. The mind of the crowd, nevertheless, was by no means so confused as it appeared to be; the people still carried ikons, but only as the last husk of the traditions of a thousand years. Amid the pallor of grief and suffering, the voice of political aspiration already rang out.

The "pope's" petition to the Tsar was entitled "Most Humble Address of the Workers of St. Petersburg." It prayed for imperial benevolence, declared that the men of the workshops were ready to kneel before the bright purple bows of the throne of the Romanovs. But this was merely the style of the petition. Its matter demanded neither more nor less than that the Tsar should formally renounce the prerogatives of personal rule. The petition was, in fact, fantastic. Beggars exhibited their rags, and that done, demanded with bent heads that the Autocrat should abjure his Autocracy. They wanted a "general amnesty," "freedom and inviolacy of the person," "responsibility of Ministers," "equality of all persons before the law," "separation of Church and State."

No one in Russia could have asked for more, and for asking much less many had before then been hanged.

No principle sees the light quite clearly when it comes into the life of the crowd. In the procession of January 22, 1905, "the Saints of the Holy Book" marched "alongside those of Revolutionary Socialism."

Ulianov now applied himself to writing polemics against the Menshevik leaders who, like shy strangers at the opening of this Dance of the Red Veil, had been glad not to be leading the movement on its first day, and had accordingly welcomed Gapon. In Lenin's view the upheaval was the more certain to achieve results since according to the Calendar of the Theory, it ought to have begun long before. For a long time it had seemed to be nearing, as he waited anxiously through nights of exile for signs from the homeland.

"The very obsoleteness of our political superstructure," he declares, "in face of the complete revolution which has been effected in social relations, makes the collapse of the superstructure inevitable: a sudden and complete collapse is quite possible."

But the tocsins which were now at last pealing brought to him also a warning of danger. From the homes of prosperous citizens there were quietly emerging professors, lawyers and journalists who were prepared to unite rebellion in marriage with their relations and clients; they wanted a speedy restoration of the order that brought them wealth. He quotes suspiciously the words of a Liberal journalist in the *Frankfurter Zeitung*. The man had not reckoned with the observant Lenin when he wrote: "The Liberals now have all the trumps in their hands; for they have succeeded in harnessing the workers to their car. Meanwhile, the Government has no one it can count on, since bureaucracy never produces men of eminence."

But had not all the theoreticians of his school been

talking for decades past of the inevitable victory of capitalist rule over Asiatic types of domination? The Mensheviks were accordingly greeting the rebellion of the
proletarians sometimes openly, sometimes in secret, with
the cry of "Long live the bourgeoisie!"

Lenin attacked this conception of historic development,
according to which one condition springs mechanically
out of another like a child's jack-in-the-box.

"Their Philistine souls," he complains, "rightly tell
them that in a period of rapid progressive development it
is more difficult to recognize the right path, and to solve
the complicated new problems as fast as they arise, than
amid the routine of petty everyday tasks; accordingly they
instinctively murmur, 'God forbid!'"

The world broadened out before his eyes. By the quiet
shores of the Lake of Geneva his ideas lifted themselves
above events like clouds above a smooth stretch of water.

But his own perception was too acute for him to be able
to realize that the other disciples of Karl Marx did not
see the same opportunities as he. For him political action
was now at last beginning. This was what the movement
of the masses meant, and precarious possibilities were now
on the wing like doves flying from roof to roof. He saw
sections of the population on the march, and events intertwining. He saw everything in the form of alliances, of
interests uniting or competing.

Ulianov demanded a Republic, giving this characteristic explanation:

"To obviate possible misunderstanding let us expressly
state once more that by 'Republic' we mean not only, and
indeed not primarily, a form of government, but the whole
of the democratic reforms of our minimum programme.
. . . If Russian absolutism does not after all wriggle
unscathed out of its perils, and simply pay for its escape
with an illusory Constitution, if it is not merely shaken
but overturned, then there will obviously be needed the

application on a gigantic scale of the revolutionary energies of all the progressive classes, to consolidate these gains."

Among the millions who, in their hatred of the system that held them down, were ready to consign it to the flames, he counted first and foremost the peasants. It was with them and not with the bourgeoisie that an alliance needed to be concluded. Only they could scale the heights. To this end he called for the dictatorship of the proletarians, the lower middle class, and the rural peasantry. This, however, was not in his view the be-all and end-all of Socialism, and he attacked Trotzky when the latter spoke of "permanent Revolution" and the dictatorship of the proletariat alone.

For Lenin, power was the essential thing. In order to be able to command he was determined to conquer power. This programme was the corner-stone of his thought. Without the ever-present possibility of seizing supreme power, Socialism would have been for him a matter of slight importance. For two decades he had been in pursuit of power, keeping his eyes fixed on its radiant form, listening to its call.

The others had, in their articles, for decades been displaying their intellectual superiority to the Tsar and the Ministers; they wanted to continue to do this, and not to run the risk of marring the ethereal bloom of their thought by the assumption of responsibility. Lenin, faced and posed by the problem, was determined to seize the purple throne and shatter it by force. He had declared to his friends that his first principle was contained in Napoleon's dictum: "First get something done, then look round you."

This outcast, unlike all his fellows, was prepared to rule; did not shrink back from his own conclusions—far from it: he worked them out in actual experience.

Often, however, he too looked beyond the bounds of the attainable and hoped for miracles.

The urge to action cut through the lines of the horizon, where the skies, like a gigantic veil, concealed the farther prospect. In spite of an examination of conditions which showed him the stupendous tasks of a Socialistic society, he wrote *as early as March 13, 1905,* of a *coming world revolution,* which would open up undreamed-of opportunities for Russia:

"At the beginning of the Revolution the true Social Democrat will not simply utter warnings about its 'painful end'; far from it—he will point to the possibility of a better issue. He will dream—he is bound to, if he is not a hopeless Philistine . . . of our success in lighting the flaming torch of Revolution . . . of our success . . . in realizing . . . with unprecedented completeness the whole of the democratic reforms. We shall succeed in reaching the stage at which the Russian Revolution is not a movement of a few months but a movement lasting years . . . and when that has been achieved, then, then the living fire of Revolution will set Europe in flames . . . then the momentum of the revolutionary movement in Europe will in its turn react on Russia. . . . But we shall have more to say about this later . . . speaking not from this accursed exile, from Geneva, but at thousand-headed workers' meetings in the streets of Moscow and Petersburg."

These forecasts did not lead Ulianov into the void. The solitary meditation, the conjuring up of visions of beatitude, made him all the more sensitive to the immediate task. And the immediate task, the next step, was *organization.*

His influence, like that of every opposition party leader, was resisted by some of his own followers. The inertia of his friends was the stone on which he struck his sparks. The forum for his views and ideas was provided by the Party and the Party Congress, and thus without an organization he would have regarded himself as the poorest of beggars.

The two groups, Mensheviks and Bolsheviks, fought over the question whether the leader in Geneva had the right to summon a Congress. Ulianov settled the question by doing it. Martov's friends assembled in Geneva and protested; Ulianov's met in London. The sittings began with mutual anathematizing. Lenin was now the undisputed leader of a following of his own. He defined the immediate task as the preparation and carrying out of armed revolt. His definition of democracy was very short:

"We are for Democratism in so far as it serves our purpose; when it becomes possible we shall be the first to introduce it."

The conspiracy, of the third Party Congress brought victory for the policy of the barricades. To show how to build them he went back with a forged passport and high hopes to St. Petersburg.

THE WORKERS' SOVIET OF
ST. PETERSBURG

At the moment when Ulianov reached the capital, those Russians who could read had been able for some weeks to enjoy an orgy of subversive journalism. Never before (and never again except for a few months in 1917) had the inhabitants of this realm had such opportunities of advocacy and counter-advocacy unhindered.

The little sheets of the émigrés, printed until then at most in editions of ten thousand, suddenly experienced the joy of mass circulation. They had their revenge for all their years of anxious concealment. The organs of the Mensheviks were as numerous as those of the Bolsheviks; in the revolutionary breeze the multitude cared little for the fine distinctions between the leaders. Elemental forces had done battle with the Tsarist heavens in the months just past.

The sublime play of unimagined demands had worked miracles.

In Western Europe the Socialists had for decades been divided at their Congresses as to the potentialities, effects and prospects of the general strike. The German Marxists had declared that the organized workers would lay down their tools if William II interfered in the slightest with universal suffrage. The question had remained undecided whether a general strike connoted Revolution. All that was taken for certain was that the more complete the permanent organization of the proletariat was, the more effectively the strikers would be able to enforce their demands.

But Russia now proceeded to stage a drama unforeseen by Theory.

At the end of January 1905 hundreds of thousands of poverty-stricken little fathers of families, who until then had been ready to kiss every hand that offered a tip, became knights-errant of Revolution. Unorganized workers struck work in every town in the empire. The Idea tautened the tired bodies as a bow its string. The strike took a thousand forms, became the foundation of Revolution.

"Political strikes, economic strikes," wrote Rosa Luxemburg, "strikes as demonstrations and strikes as stern conflicts, general strikes in particular industries and general strikes in particular towns, peaceable wage struggles and street battles, fighting at the barricades, in every conceivable combination co-exist with one another; run into one another, change imperceptibly into one another; it is an incessantly moving, changing sea of phenomena. And the law of motion of this phenomenon is becoming apparent: it lies not in the mass strike in itself, not in its technical characteristics, but in the interplay of political and social forces of the Revolution."

And constantly new multitudes took courage and stood forth. Russia marvelled at her crowded millions. The novices in events became themselves an event. The masses, of whom yesterday no one knew the existence, stood for a moment in dumb indecision on the threshold of the towns, where the rich men's dwellings began; then they marched on.

Russia seemed to be in dissolution; the most sacred conceptions were shattered, while disaffection itself seemed to acquire an odour of sanctity.

These unorganized masses needed a headquarters for leadership and action. There were no trade unions, no co-operatives; the Socialist Parties were divided, they had only a few thousand members. Who would lead the millions? Where was the solution of the enigma to be found? Would not the rioters fire and destroy the towns, or would they, after a moment's daring, once more be mumbling the old prayers of yesterday? The answer came suddenly, born of no programme, pamphlet or manifesto. In twenty-four hours it was a commonplace: the Workers' Soviets.

Neither the Mensheviks nor the Bolsheviks had devised them. In Lenin's absence his Party colleagues rejected the Soviets as insufficiently revolutionary.

It is possible that the Soviets were, after all, the Tsar's own invention. His Government had appointed, before 1905, a Commission, under the chairmanship of Senator Shildovsky, to ascertain the needs of the industrial proletariat from information to be supplied by delegates chosen by workers of St. Petersburg. The Bolsheviks, looking down on this forum from the exalted sphere of their revolutionary ardour, called it the Hocus-pocus Commission.

At the head of the Soviets—not in any organized way, but through its habit of taking the lead—stood the Workers' Soviet of St. Petersburg. It was nicknamed the Proletarian Government. In palace circles, which in their momentary powerlessness allowed themselves the luxury of phrase-making, the question went round: "Will the Soviet arrest the Government or the Government the Soviet?"

Lenin watched its sittings, whether or not he was present in the public gallery. Twice he went to the Assembly Hall of this Parliament which no Constitution had called together. After years of exile, of wandering, of longing, he heard voices of his homeland. But they were no longer the voices of tired or enthusiastic intellectuals, spending their nights in criticism of epochs or universes. Deputies were speaking who did the same daily work as their constituents. The feeling of the streets took shape here in concrete proposals; men who had never before spoken to an assemblage of listeners became orators.

Unnoticed amid the mass of tense listeners, Ulianov noted down what he heard. In the Soviet itself he dared not approach the platform; his friends kept him in safe hiding. In secret committee work the conspirator ruled and directed policy.

In his obscurity and seclusion it was no great trial to him to be shut off from the uproar of these days. His ambition could easily withstand the temptation to be the leader of a week; for Lenin always felt that the organizations which he led were of more importance than himself. He could now control them without running the danger of paying for the transitory glory of a public speech by being next day, thanks to a shot from an enemy, no longer alive. He had, moreover, acquired the habit of imposing on the enthusiasm of his nature a cool tenacity, and reticence with strangers to the cause.

Without a plan, without direction from any head or centre, every considerable industrial town had, between January and December 1905, burst its prison and replaced the Romanov flag by the red flag of rebellion. Many an intimidated Governor had appeared on his balcony and saluted it. Others had proclaimed their loyalty to the ruler by machine-gun fire. The State was dissolved into satrapies; one satrap would obey, another withstand the rebels. The strikes crippled railways and telegraphs. The Government cabled orders to Irkutsk via London and Peking. Count Witte declared that half Russia had gone mad, and that there were hardly any staunch Conservatives left.

"The total number of workers taking part in strikes in the whole of the decade before the Revolution," writes Lenin, "was 430,000. In January 1905 . . . the number of strikers was 440,000. Thus there were more strikers in one single month than in the whole of the preceding decade. . . . The total number of strikers reached 2,800,000, more than half again as many as the total number of factory workers."

Wherever these strikes flamed up there spoke also a Workers' Soviet.

Now, however, after the mountain range of a year of struggle, with its peaks and valleys, everything was pressing to a decisive issue.

The unemployed men and women were struck by no shot from the enemy; another agony was mowing them down: hunger. In battle the fighter dies, his neighbour goes on firing and hopes to survive the hour of danger. Hunger goes to work more democratically, and hits everyone simultaneously; in his train comes starvation. Men's arms sink exhausted; aspirations, plans, hopes, fade away.

The Government was waiting for this moment, the revolutionaries dreaded it.

The rebels thought, however, that an armed rising might defeat hunger, for the victors would then have won the keys of the granaries.

Lenin realized with the rest that the Workers' Soviets and the strikes would bring in their wake many days of bitter suffering. But he could see the promise of a coming dawn. He heard the speeches of the factory delegates and warned these friends not to let themselves be deceived by alluring hopes; for the thing that mattered, the beginning, the armed rising, had yet to come. The leader spoke out mercilessly from his merciless vision. Perhaps

he was afraid lest the rest should once more lose themselves in generalities and overlook the unique potentialities of the moment. The thing that mattered now was
the barricade. He showed now that the whole keyboard
of past demands and slogans needed retuning. "Now,"
wrote the Man in Obscurity, "we must at last openly
recognize and proclaim the inadequate nature of the
political strike, must impress on the masses in every possible quarter the necessity of an armed rising. . . . To
conceal from the masses the necessity of desperate,
sanguinary, internecine warfare as the immediate task in
the action before us would be to deceive ourselves and
the people."

The critical days in St. Petersburg were quickly over.
Tsar and Court were no longer content to sit and bewail
each new turn of events. Their impatience, exacerbated
by the wildest of rumours, was finally stilled by Count
Witte, the Minister of the Interior. He considered that
the time had now come for the arrest of Nosar, the President of the Workers' Soviet. The Count himself has
described the last days of the St. Petersburg Soviet:

"In place of Nosar the Soviet elected a presidium of
three persons. . . . I had intended to arrest Nosar earlier,
but Litvinov Valensky . . . advised me not to; we must
wait, he said, till the workers would themselves welcome
the arrest; that is, till Nosar and the Soviet had thoroughly lost repute; . . . this was . . . very sensible
advice. . . . After Nosar had been arrested I gave
instructions for the arrest of the whole Soviet, which
Durnovo finally carried out on the 3rd/16th of December.
. . . The Soviet was afraid to meet, and hardly had it
done so . . . when the whole of its members, numbering
190 men, were arrested."

Leo Trotzky, the brains of the St. Petersburg Soviet,
one of the 190, the actual first among nominal equals,
gives an account of the arrest in a different tone, set by
his own doctrine:

"The executive committee, which held its sittings on

the second floor, decided to send some of its members
away. . . . Too late! . . . the building was already surrounded. . . . From below came loud shouts of protest
from the delegates. . . . The chairman opened the window and shouted. . . . 'Comrades! do not attempt to
resist! We declare in advance that any shot fired can
only be the work of a *provocateur* or a police official!' A
few minutes later the soldiers came up to the second
floor. . . .

"The chairman (turning to the officer): 'Please shut
the door and let us go on with our work.'

"The soldiers remained in the corridor. The door,
however, was not closed.

"The chairman: 'The meeting can proceed. Who
wants to speak?'

"The representative of the clerical workers: 'Through
its violent action to-day . . . the Government has made
a strike inevitable. . . . The issue depends on the attitude
of the troops; may they rise in the defence of the country!'

"The officer hurriedly shut the door. The speaker
raised his voice. . . .

"The chairman: 'I declare the meeting closed.'

"The St. Petersburg Soviet of Workers' Delegates was
in the hands of the conspirators of Tsarskoye Selo."

And the Russian Revolution was in the hands of the
Secret Alliance of Bolshevist Barricades!

MOSCOW BLEEDS IN LENIN'S NAME

Often the authorities had issued imperial proclamations
ordering the masses to remain quietly at their ordinary
work in home and factory. But still the masses had come
into the streets. Yet more often the rebels had assured the
same masses, in solemn manifestos richly decorated with

notes of exclamation, that the hour of final decision had struck, and had appealed to them to come out into the streets. But they had remained indoors. A few isolated individuals would come out to find the squares empty, and would return quickly home, as inconspicuously as possible, doing their utmost to look like innocent sight-seers.

The man in the street is neither the Tsar's man nor the revolutionaries'.

When the light of eventful days slowly fades, the man emerged from the mass is apt to say to himself: "Only my individual needs are of real importance; everything else is a matter of sentiment."

On the morning after the arrest of their Soviet, the workers in the factories heard of the summons to a general strike. Irresolutely they discussed it in groups. The machines were waiting for them. The factory whistle blew; it was not lavish of promises, but it did offer a little bread. To strike meant hunger. Peace was tempting after so many hard weeks, and most of the workers succumbed to its lure. Even so, eighty thousand struck. But within a week all but three thousand came back to their regular place by the machine.

But now came the turn of the provinces. The glow from the beacon fires of St. Petersburg reached to the Caucasus, to Siberia. Thirty-three towns were in fever; their pulse varied; high temperature alternated with the ague of despair.

Most conspicuous was the call of the Moscow workers' representatives under the influence of Ulianov, morning, noon and night, waking and in their dreams: "Russia, arise."

Lenin had been for weeks in the city of the Kremlin. Its Soviet was Bolshevist. The leader put the issue with his customary energy:

"Either struggle until the final victory, which means a rising; or give up the struggle altogether."

Triumph seemed to him probable. Here, at last, before these century-old domes of the Romanov power, before the cathedral of the Red Square, with its belfry resplendent in many colours, as though to tell of the Tsar's wealth—here the tradition of submissiveness should finally be stamped out beneath the heels of the men in blouses. Now, in the cold morning, victory in the streets should open the way to a dictatorship. The rebels deliberated no longer. The word had been given. Crowned by success, the tiny vanguard would be the nucleus of a Government. He had written, it is true:

"The maximum programme of the peasantry, its final aims, do not extend beyond the borders of capitalism, which would grow yet more luxuriant and firmly rooted if all the estates were divided up."

He himself, however, would have organized the division of the soil as an instrument of power.

The peasants would never forget that the magic hand of a Red Government had conjured reality out of their dream.

The committee of the revolt was composed of his closest friends and most devoted helpers. The opportunity of this December hour was the crown of his existence. Not to seize it would have been to abandon the world in which his thoughts had lived for twenty years, to stand exposed to himself as a romancer.

The Soviet resolved to call a general strike. The soldiers on guard at the factory gates fraternized with the strikers. On the following day not a factory was at work; even the small workshops and the independent artisans were idle. With the works lifeless in the city, not a whisper of doubt perceptible, the Soviet spoke:

"The strike is to be converted into an armed rising."

In some districts there were small collisions. Soldiers fired at houses in which meetings were being held. The men inside replied with bombs.

On the third day a group of Militants went the round

of the rifle dealers, commandeering arms. The railway station was occupied by the rebels. Troops on their way home from Manchuria were relieved of their ammunition. They were glad enough to be rid of their packs, and unconcernedly went on home.

On the fourth day the police disappeared from the squares. Only imperial dragoons and Cossacks still rode through the streets. There were fresh collisions.

The rebel stage-managers thought of an effective tableau, recalling old engravings in living beauty. Two women workers swathed in red flags went out to meet the cavalrymen. The soldiers, impressed by these living flags, if not by their symbolism, did not shoot, but rode off.

General Dubassov, commanding the Moscow district, was not sure of his Moscow troops; after urgent entreaties he obtained reinforcements from St. Petersburg. The railway strikers were not strong enough to prevent this.

Dubassov had four guns placed in the most frequented square. The cold steel of their barrels, he said, would calm the city's fever. It might have been so. But suddenly, like children throwing stones, the guns fired their shells without warning on the astonished passers-by. For no reason, comfortable citizens, non-combatants, only half aware of the rebellion, were mown down.

These shells brought the whole of the population over to the side of the revolutionaries.

"The first barricades in the Tverskaya," writes Maxim Gorky, "were erected amid light-hearted gossip and laughter. The most motley collection of citizens took part in this merry work, from highly respectable gentlemen in expensive furs to cooks and ostlers."

The universal sympathy of large sections of the population provided the rebels with the solid basis for their stand. The actual fighting was carried on by an infinitesimal band of Militants.

"Some seven to eight hundred persons composed the armed Party groups," writes Leo Trotzky. "Some five hundred railwaymen armed with carbines operated in the stations and on the permanent way. Some four hundred volunteer riflemen from among the compositors and shop assistants formed the reserve."

They put up for five days, against an army of twenty thousand soldiers, a determined and deadly resistance. This would have been an impossibility without the support of the inhabitants. Moscow turned itself for the rebel *tirailleurs* into a mountain range in which every ravine offered concealment from the enemy. If Cossacks approached, windows gave the alarm. After skirmishes, the wounded were carried down passages into safety. The millions of the city were the forest behind the trees of which shots could be fired with impunity.

There is no need for an army commander to enjoin "frightfulness" on his soldiers. He can rely on human nature and on wounds that rouse to madness.

Ulianov, however, felt called upon to urge his companions to carry the struggle to the death and beyond it. Victory must be made even more secure by executions. He felt that the rebel spirit would be destroyed if they indulged in the ultimate sentimentality called in literature humanity. The Bolshevist Committee of the Barricades issued "Advice to the Workers in Revolt":

". . . As the first principle, do not work in crowds but in small bands of three or four, not more. . . . The troops will be powerless if all Moscow fills with these small, elusive bands. . . . Do not attempt to occupy fortified places. The soldiers will destroy them with artillery fire. . . . Shoot at the Cossacks from the courts and quadrangles. Distinguish carefully between our deliberate enemies and the unenlightened whom chance has turned against us. Annihilate the former, spare the latter. . . . Do not spare the Cossacks . . . go for the dragoons and patrols and wipe them out. . . . Our next task, comrades, is to turn over the city to the people. Let us begin with the suburbs, and occupy one district after another."

The advice to adopt measures of "frightfulness" is easy to follow. It was acted on with the utmost thoroughness both by the revolutionaries and by Dubassov's troops. Leo Trotzky tells of a Montenegrin in the ranks of the rebels who received fifty cartridges every morning, and complained every evening that he had not had enough. He was the best marksman; every shot told. An officer of Dubassov's troops reports "how difficult it was to prevent the soldiers from firing on defenceless crowds. They begged and implored us, 'Ah, your Excellency, do let us fire at that lot over there!'"

And the officers took no very special pains to restrain their subordinates. A thousand people, including eighty-six children, were wounded by the soldiers' fire in the course of the struggle. The number of Dubassov's troops who were shot is unknown.

The rising in Moscow was the first armed attempt to set up Bolshevist rule. In December 1905, Lenin first left his card at the Kremlin. He was not admitted. But the shadows of its Byzantine towers were never thenceforth to leave him. From now onwards he seemed not merely to have dreamed of Zion but to have seen it; no one in the cohorts of the revolutionaries had drawn near in these sanguinary months more ardently than he to the cradle of Muscovite domination.

Only two years before, under the mansard roof in Munich, the persecuted exile had asked, "What to begin with?" With the book of this reply in his hands, the most daring possibilities seemed more attainable than half-hearted ones.

Even if he were mistaken, Ulianov had for one moment looked power in the face, had given battle to the Tsar's general. He needed that experience to be able to endure the emptiness of twelve years' further waiting.

LENIN FAILS AT FIRST TO RECOGNIZE DEFEAT

It might be said that Socialism, like the Bible, is a garden filled with fragrant quotations. On its borders red roses and white await the nostrils of inquisitive visitors. The main reason why orthodox Marxists call their dogma a science is simply that resolute disciples consider that this description provides the certainty at which they aim.

After the December failure the hearts of the beaten rebels were full of despondency. They began to compare their achievements with the promises of the defeated leaders, tried to apportion blame for the last battle. George Plekhanov asserted that it had been a mistake to resort to force.

And, in truth, what had the Moscow barricade achieved? The holes which shells had dug to bury themselves in were filled in, and people went peacefully on their ways. Millions had struck work, but scarcely two thousand had wielded a rifle!

The Government in St. Petersburg, thoroughly frightened, was determined to blot out the weakness of a few months from its own memory and that of its subjects by sanguinary severity. From the seats of its might it cried, in the words of a German poet: *"Genug kann nie und nimmer mehr genügen."* ("Enough will never, never be enough.") It had a thousand persons put to death without trial; seventy thousand rebels lay in prison, their short springtime over; fourteen thousand lost their lives in countless easily quelled risings.

Since the preceding January, with its Bloody Sunday, the rebels had come out from their dark, fear-ridden, secret meeting-places, and had revelled in the open streets amid phrases until then prohibited. They had greeted unfamiliar faces and shouted, in the words of the

Bolshevik Krylenko: "Down with underground methods! We are tired of their suffocating atmosphere!"

Now, after December, open agitation had become impossible again. The streets had become dismal, the ground was blood-stained, the smallest sign of life called forth further reprisals, and self-chosen prisons only served for short stays.

The Mensheviks were no longer willing to live like snakes in dank crevices; they asked for the removal of the official ban on the movement. All their efforts were directed to acquiring legal recognition again.

Lenin had no thought for them; his thoughts were still of Revolution; he even believed that victory was still probable in the near future. A week after the failure of the rising he wrote:

"The heroic Moscow proletariat showed that it is possible to carry on an active struggle. The new form of action was faced with such gigantic problems as naturally could not be solved at a stroke. . . . Dubassov's guns made revolutionaries of new masses of the people on an unprecedented scale. . . . The movement has not as yet by any means shown its full extent and depth. . . . Disaffection continues to spread among the peasantry . . . one wave succeeds another. . . . We must be prepared . . . to pass over again to illegal action."

The actual experience of combat, the memories of its last desperate moments in many quarters, opened up to him the prospect of still greater crises, coming tempests through which the ultimate peak of Revolution might yet be scaled.

Thinking of all the past gleams of rich promise now extinguished, he tried to forget the dust, still around him, of the street fighting, to attain composure for the work of analysis. In the hour of defeat he would embrace only realities—but where was reality? Here and there shots were still being fired, distant towns were holding out, roving bands of peasants were looting. Were all these

signs of a renewal of the conflict or the last flicker of
dying stars?

To regain his sense of values he thought of Karl Marx
after the defeat of the German Revolution of 1848.
It might be that through a comparison with this he would
discover Reality, despite the remote seclusion. in which
that goddess spins, joins and severs; this reality of an
illimitable empire in which millions of molecules form a
world of events.

This leader of a small band had no laboratory to work
in, no statistical bureau; he could not even venture to
show his face in too frequented places. How could all
the information find its way to his poor little hiding-place
that was laid punctually and in perfect order on the
immaculate writing-desks in his official opponents' big,
quiet, well-lit offices? Yet Ulianov was determined to
get a bird's-eye view of the situation. Friends were waiting for guidance, allies for consolation. He could not
abandon himself to philosophical reflection, must not be
obsessed by the thought of the transitoriness of things;
he must be ready with definite answers. At this stage
Ulianov had to wrestle with the ghosts of his personal
predilections, which were hard to shake off. The flickering gleam of the predestinate goal must not light the way
for a transitory moment only to leave the path in deeper
darkness. Karl Marx must supply the answer.

"Marx," he wrote now, "does not make play with the
idea of Revolution as a mere phrase, does not abandon
political actuality for empty abstractions. . . . Marx
resolves the knotty problem without regard for depression or apathy in particular sections of society. . . . Only
after he had demonstrated the inevitability of the 'exhaustion' of the purveyors of 'actual Revolution' did he modify
his views. . . . We must keep in mind this attitude of
Marx's in the present difficult situation. . . . The inevitability of a fresh rising is vouched for by a whole series
of hard facts. . . . The crushing of a Revolution is the

greatest of civil wars . . . After that our task is to train for a rising . . . and in this task the activities of the Party must be ruled by the principle that war must be carried on by warlike methods. Whoever is against a rising must find us his merciless opponents."

Lenin succumbed to the desire of his heart. He was filled with rage and hatred above all against friends who criticized his darling, the Moscow barricade. They, he said, were judging the conflict by the precept of Russian generals: "If they give, take; if they hit out, run; if you lose, it means you ought not to have fought."

But, after all, there was no denying the fact of defeat. In Moscow General Dubassov was in control, not the Bolshevik Central Committee. There must therefore have been something defective in the rising. Its actual outbreak was, in Ulianov's view, the crown of human existence; the source of error could only have lain in its conduct. He believed that he had discovered what was wrong. *The Party had been found wanting!* Lenin went in search of confirmation of this. He sought out the combatants, talked with them for hours, questioned them calmly, exhaustively, listened silently, absorbed, knew what importance to attach to the legends with which, after the battle, every man surrounded his own part in it, roamed stealthily through the streets in which his Party had fought, pored over maps, reconstructed past plans, tried to determine each sectional movement, would have been glad to know the course of every shot, and came to the conclusion that:

"Organization had failed to keep pace with the growth and enthusiasm of the movement. . . . The orders to build barricades reached the various districts much too late. . . . We, the leaders of the Social Democratic proletariat, were last December like the army commander who posted his troops so absurdly that the bulk of the army took no part in the battle. . . . We ought not to have fought? . . . On the contrary: we ought to have fought more resolutely, more energetically, more actively."

For him, the matter was now beyond argument. But from others there came a medley of conflicting views. The Mensheviks admitted that the Revolution was defeated, had given place to the old daily routine, but they dared not say outright that it ought never to have been attempted. Ulianov made the most of this position. In a circular to the comrades he wrote: "The choice is clear . . . to play at insurrection is unworthy of the Party."

Hundreds of factory workers were condemned in their absence to death. They had not the few roubles needed for a hiding-place, but they had arms, formed partisan bands, and robbed, first, government savings-banks, then merchants and peaceful passers-by. Towns and villages degenerated into Macedonian conditions. Mutual terrorism, punitive expeditions from above, bombs from below, lit devastating fires. Now that looting in the name of a principle was recognized, the desperate Socialist bands were surreptitiously joined by individuals who until then had done the same thing without principle. Heroes of the Black Hundred were equally ready to sharpen their knives in the service of Revolution; barefooted tramps saw a tempting and profitable martyrdom. The Erfurt programme of the German Social Democrats was translated into Russian in the sense of church looting, bank robbery and burglary in general.

The Mensheviks, dreamers and seekers after legal recognition, contrasted these activities of their supporters with the meetings, followed by a collection, which were the fashion in the Western European Parties; they decided in favour of the latter, and recommended that all leaders of armed bands should be expelled from their ranks.

Ulianov defended the bands, wrote in favour of them, investigated their activities, concluded that banditry was an unfortunate development—but that as it was impossible effectively to prohibit this distressing phenomenon it should be made use of in the service of the Revolution. The party should organize the groups in fives, and then impose some formal order on their anarchic methods of expropriation.

"Sad to say, there is a strange tendency in our ranks, really worthy of the Cadets, to poke stupid fun at the fighting bands and their 'Brownings' . . . we are too fond of poking fun at revolutionary military activity."

In Ulianov's view the movement ought not to consider itself restricted to any one form of struggle. It was essentially an underground movement of revolt, and he rejoiced in its very existence; he declined to criticize its every manifestation from the standpoint of conventional morality. "This form of struggle," he says, in regard to the armed bands, "first definitely developed and spread . . . in 1906, that is, after the rising of December. . . . It is not the partisans' activities that are disorganizing the movement, but the weakness of the Party, which is unable to control and lead them."

Whoever carried on armed resistance to the Régime was, in Ulianov's eyes, clad in the shining armour of eternal justice. All that was repulsive in the conventional view in such action, all the human weaknesses it brought to the surface, left his judgment unaffected. His view was that in the process of the immense struggle even the worst qualities of human nature, unleashed in the intoxication of bloodshed, would be an acid disintegrant of the strongholds of Tsarism.

If any stratagem is permissible in war, if the darkness of night, the still sleeping dawn are shelter to be exploited by the rebel, why not also the meannesses, the treacheries, the brutalities, the ignominies of humanity in general and of the outcast in particular?

Not a thread should unite the oppressed with the palaces of the oppressors; no single conception should be shared with them. Sympathy with the powerful? A crime! Reasonableness? Abominable sentiment! Those on top draw much of their strength from the subservient chorus of the sentiments which you poor souls drink in with your mother's milk. These are inherited chains, the links of which pass from soul to soul, holding them in their iron grip. The Emperor and his creatures have one quality in common with the simple subject, and one only —they are mortal. Make use of that; forge every curse into a dagger!

Ulianov did not write thus, for no one trusts his whole soul to paper. But this ingrained attitude had its effect, moved others, attracted those around him as the planets exert attraction in space.

Hatred was the flame that warmed him in days of cold despair, when friends stumbled and fell, when hopes and aspirations perished. Hate kept the rebel attached to the earth, inspired the Furies of Duty, became a spring of fresh water in the desert of defeat.

This hatred supported and strengthened him, made out of one individual—a persecuted beggar—the living, pulsating rock of intellectual resistance against a whole system.

Part of the power that shapes all things creates by the force of reaction such controlling emotions. Ulianov had felt from his youth upwards the vibrations of the myriad pains which are bound up with the existence of one hundred and forty millions. He was able to comprehend those infinite sorrows, all the tragedy of Russia, as though his brain were a lake in a valley, receiving from each mountain-side hut a thin streamlet of tears.

In face of such sorrows, mercilessness seemed to him the first of all duties.

Around this man there now gathered, after the defeat and in spite of it, the loyalty of a following that already counted a hundred and fifty thousand souls.

Once more Lenin had hurriedly to flee, to search for a

new hiding-place.   He chose a spot not far from St. Petersburg by rail—Kuokalla, in Finland.   Finland, though under the sceptre of the Tsar, enjoyed a certain measure of independence.

To this town, thirty miles from the capital, his staff followed him.   Illegality was proclaimed the supreme law.   From here he listened, watched, convinced and commanded.   Near by a class was set up for instructing picked men in the art of street fighting.   Short courses were held for training others to act as the general staffs of armed bands.   He wrote:

"The Japanese War introduced the use of hand grenades; a munition factory has put an automatic rifle on the market. . . . We can and must make use of the advance of military technique, teach the militant workers to make bombs wholesale, help them and our own fighting squads to accumulate stocks of explosives, detonators and automatic rifles. . . ."

"It has been said," he wrote in a defence of the armed bands, "that partisan warfare brings . . . the proletariat down to the level of a degraded, drunken, ragged mob. That is so, but it follows from this . . . that the Party . . . must never regard partisan warfare as the only or by any means the most important means of combat; that this means . . . must be metamorphosed by the enlightening and organizing influence of Socialism."

But at this moment it was this very form of warfare that, in his view, was playing the principal part.   The more the masses kept silence, the more he wanted guerilla bands.   Ulianov wanted to make this the main issue in the voting for the Congress.   "Grouping according to political programmes is not enough.   A grouping according to attitude to armed rebellion is also necessary."

Just at this time, when the conflict was at its sharpest between Lenin and those of the revolutionaries who were determined to see no more of the ominous gleam of days of bloodshed, the current of opinion among the general membership began to flow in the direction of a reunion of Bolsheviks and Mensheviks. In many towns joint committees of the two organizations were formed, for the mass of the members had for years been fighting alongside one another.

Lenin, firmly determined to take no notice of mere majority resolutions, to be guided in his tactics only by events and not by congresses, went off to the Party Congress at Stockholm, the Congress that sought to reunite "Radicals" and "Reformists."

This plenary meeting was morally the tribunal before which a broken rebellion was to hale its leader, Ulianov. The members disputed hotly, called one another traitors; and yet they were all revolutionaries, loved the same goddess, and beneath their mutual attacks lay the ambition of either side to be her truest servants.

The most widely known leaders hurled furious imprecations at Lenin. Martov, *rapporteur* for the Mensheviks, said: "The Bolsheviks represent our cause as progressing from stage to stage. . . . First, the general strike, then . . . the December rising. . . . Well, I ask the Bolshevik comrades whether our retreat was in accordance with their strategic plans, and whether they calculated in advance on our failure and compulsory return to illegal activity."

This Congress, like the following one held in London, showed up the incompatibilities of the two tactics by the light of a revolution that had lost its way.

Lenin returned to Finland, and listened on the shores of the Baltic to the music of old national anthems.

WITTE, STOLYPIN AND LENIN

The rolling stock on the Siberian railway took to Vladivistok in a few months hundreds of thousands of Russians. The peasant was not only paying for the war, he was also being allowed a little first-hand knowledge of it. In the villages he was told of little yellow men who knew nothing of the Saviour, were called Japanese, and were out to rob the true believer of his cow, his hay, his plough and the wife he beat.

From the upper air-holes of the cattle-trucks the countryman could see the hamlets calmly sleeping in their defencelessness, and the clouds that built bright mountains above steppe and primeval forest. The peasant had time to dream of the wonderland of his aspirations. He could no longer count the days that passed; they closed up behind him like the telegraph poles, in a monotonous, interminable succession. For hours he would gaze dumbly at the passing landscape. His homesickness refused to leave him. Only in the aristocratic end of this army on wheels, in the series of coaches that bore General Kuropatkin and his staff, were there thoughts of fame.

Until this the peasant had never been on a journey. His first was taking him to unknown shores. There he would lie and rot, in the grass or the forest, under the snow. His place in his village graveyard would wait for him in vain.

At other times the countryman was forbidden to leave his locality without a pass. If he could not show the stamp of the authorities he became at once the enemy of the whole realm.

"No one," ran a typical ukase of 1900, "may leave his village at night under any pretence, or go away from it in daytime for more than twenty-four hours. . . . Persons found guilty of any unauthorized journey will be punished . . . even if it should be established that the journey was unconnected with any suspicious or illegitimate purpose." In other respects, too, the laws current in the towns had no validity for the peasant. Relatively to him, a citizen of St. Petersburg or Moscow lived in freedom. All the peasant's delinquencies came before a special local court. If he had stolen one of His Lordship's cows, he would be sent to prison for a couple of years or so, or if only one of his neighbours' a couple of weeks. The presiding magistrate had autocratic power. The court could order any peasant under sixty years of age to be flogged within an inch of his life.

Scattered over the empire were countless village communities. None bothered itself about the others. Each was responsible for collecting its own taxes, thus easing for the Régime the first condition of existence. The village community, the Mir, was supposed in theory to be communistic; its inhabitants were supposed to be producing in common and consuming in equal shares. In practice there grew up in its midst little worlds of rich and poor. For the prosperous man the Mir had become a nuisance, for the poor man an extra source of oppression. The patriarchal traditions in the village were at variance with the "free labour" of the capitalist system. Two economic systems, that of industry and that of feudalism, were intermingled. Countless forms of servitude came into existence, just as each separate wave gleams with a different colour when the evening sun approaches the line of the horizon. A nation of picturesque beggars sat along the roadside in the villages, howling as if tortured by inflamed wounds. "In 1860," writes Karl Kautsky, quoting from a report, "the rural population amounted to fifty million souls; at the end of 1900 it amounted approximately to eighty-six millions. . . . In proportion as this figure has increased the area of the average holding has fallen. . . . According to the statistics . . . the average holding per unit of male population in 1860 was . . . 4.8 dessiatines. . . . In 1880 the average holding per male had sunk to 3.5, in 1900 to 2.6 dessiatines."

"The peasants' land," writes Lenin, "was surrounded on all sides by that of the big landowner, so that the Herr Junker was assured of an exceptionally reliable . . . source of income: the fines for unauthorized pasturing.

A BOLSHEVIST PARTISAN GROUP

BARRICADES IN MOSCOW IN 1905

LEO TROTZKY

COUNT WITTE

'There is nowhere for the chicken to go' was a bitter joke current among the *mujiks* which illustrates better than any long quotation could a peculiarity of peasant land-owning that does not emerge from the statistics.

"The essence of the matter is that we have at one pole of Russian landownership 10.5 million farms (housing about 50 million souls) aggregating 75 million dessia-tines, while at the opposite pole there are 30,000 families (about 150,000 souls) with 70 million dessiatines of land."

A system resulted which led the peasant into working for the junker.

In order to compel the landless man or the possessor of an insignificant acreage to go into service with the dessiatine-millionaire, all the former's civic rights were taken from him. He had to be made personally dependent on the junker. The corvée persisted as the last vestige of serfdom, and alongside it "free" labour, wage labour. Many servants of the soil went, with their own cattle and implements, to the lord's estate. If they had borrowed money from the landowner they usually worked off their indebtedness by labour; but in most cases they received their wages in kind. The peasant, however, urgently wanted ready money to pay his taxes, and would give the usurer, for the average wages of a day's work, many weeks of his existence, in fact anything he demanded. He possessed nothing but his two arms and a cow or horse, as lean as himself. Cattle are not so tough as human beings. They diminished in number, while the peasants increased. In 1870 there were 9,329 head of cattle to every thousand farms; in 1900 only 6,474.

"The District Agricultural Committee," writes Alex-ander Kornilov, "calculated the aggregate income of a peasant family (average 6.3 souls), after deducting costs of maintenance of stock, rent and insurance, for the year 1902 to be 114 roubles 35 kopeks; of this, direct and indirect taxation took 58 roubles 14 kopeks; the family had the remainder of 56 roubles 21 kopeks ($28.94) to live on."

Yet from these farms had to come the funds for the military effort in the Far East. Unlike Western European States, in which the financial basis of imperialist policy is provided by capitalist industry, in Russia agriculture was, and still is, the source of economic power, without which military expansion is unthinkable. In Russia capital was mainly in the hands of foreign concession-holders, who developed properties in Russia only on the basis "of the whole profit coming to them, not merely the interest on their capital, so that only the wages of the workers remained in Russia."

According to official statistics the Japanese War had cost 2,500 million roubles and over two hundred thousand lives.

Men are born to die. But the money, which had not the advantage of being bi-sexual, did not replenish itself so reliably or so easily as the Russians would.

The Emperor wept, perhaps not so much over the graves of his people as at the emptiness of his Treasury. He used to go crow shooting, and noted gravely in his diary the number of birds that fell victims to his marksmanship. When the news of the great defeat arrived, His Majesty wrote: "Had a long stroll, killed one crow, and went for a row on the Gatchina."

Lenin was just as fond of shooting as Nicholas. But he postponed his sport till later, and entered in his diary on the same day as the Tsar: "Not the Russian people, but Russian Tsarism has suffered this disgraceful defeat. Through this military defeat the Russian people has gained. The capitulation of Port Arthur is the prelude to the capitulation of Tsarism."

The blue satin tents of the imperial camp had no gold stars left. The sky darkened. Clefts showed in the walls of the hierarchy; they were no longer able to withstand the winds; from without could be heard, louder and louder, the voice of oracles that none understood. Fear, desire, greed, necessity shrieked in the palace for Money, Money! Nothing else could serve. The deficit glowed like burning coals; its fumes were heavier, more revolutionary, more oppressive than the many candle-lights of revolt which lit up in town and country the profiles of unknown, uncanny figures.

The Democrats rushed off abroad and denounced the satraps of their home country as unworthy of credit. The revolutionaries sent out manifestos imploring their comrades of the international proletariat to prevent their Governments from granting loans. Russian Jews spoke of massacres and reminded their co-religionists of the traditional suffering of the whole race from the anti-Semitism of ancient Egypt, so as to steel the heart of the Rothschilds and Mendelssohns even against good Russian ten per cents.

Lenin hoped that the authorities in St. Petersburg would be unable to cover the deficit. "A financial crash is approaching," he wrote, "the gold standard is giving way. However eager the reactionary bourgeoisie of Europe may be to bolster up arbitrary rule, a deficit of half a milliard roubles is impossible to meet."

Everyone was hoping that the financial ebb would leave Tsarism high and dry.

In the sacred chancel of the Government, where there was already talk of putting up the altar of autocracy for sale, there appeared Witte.

He had continually spoken in tones of warning, had stigmatized the war as an irreparable blunder, and had accordingly fallen out of favour with the Emperor. Years before, Count Witte had introduced a gold currency. At the same time he had expressed the conviction that financial stabilization would be impossible without drastic constitutional and social reform. Cautiously and discreetly he had for ten years intoned this Song of Truth. The financier Witte knew that taxes that had fallen into arrear through the acute agricultural depression could not by any possibility be paid up. When in charge of finance, as long before as 1898, he had tried to put through rural reforms. His department had given warnings of the danger of playing with police-run Socialism. Witte had smoothed the way for capitalism, thrown the gates wide open for foreign capital and at the same time built up a system of protectionist tariffs. In 1903, however, he had been overthrown by Saint Seraphim. At the tomb of the miracle-worker one man had wept more than all the others—Plehve. Plehve's advance to favour meant Witte's dismissal. Count Witte was no adept in Spiritualism; he was more of a Russian Caillaux or Rathenau: the typical enlightened, cosmopolitan man of finance, who can show in black and white what bad business wars are, and how international trusts and cartels open up easier and less noisy ways to the plunder systems most in fashion in modern civilization.

"When I took over the Government after October 17/30," he writes, "I clearly realized that two things were necessary if Russia was to emerge from the revolutionary crisis and the house of Romanov to remain invulnerable: first, a big loan, to provide us amply with funds for several years to come; and secondly, the withdrawal of the army . . . to European Russia. . . .

"Possessed of money and troops . . . I was convinced that we could not fail . . . to bring the life of the 150 million souls of Russia back into normal paths."

In December, when the last fires were burning out the working-class quarter in Moscow, the first hundred million roubles of the loan came into the country.

Lenin and the revolutionary leaders knew only in a general way that Tsarism was seeking fresh golden footholds. The poor devils had no inkling, in their hiding-places of sedition, that a ship was lying alongside in the docks at St. Petersburg, from which a confidential emissary of the Crédit Lyonnais, M. Neitzlin, had landed. He had come with a false passport like any anarchist conspirator. He took up his quarters, this guest from abroad who carried in his portfolio the fate of the Revolution, in the villa of the Grand Duke Vladimir Alexandrovitch. All around him manicured fingers were put to closed lips. He dictated his terms:

"For the required 5 per cent. loan of 2,250 million francs, say 845,750,000 gold roubles, the Government undertakes to restore order in the country and to convoke a Duma. The issue price will be 88. The Russian Government pledges itself to take up no other foreign loan within a period of three years."

At this time the Algeciras Conference was sitting: the Franco-German dispute over Morocco.

"Our representatives at the Conference," writes Witte, "were directed to vote for France."

A Russian peasant prophet might have been able to foresee how ten years later millions of men would be called upon to carry out this agreement as though each one of them had signed it.

After all, the Tsar's empire had got its credit. One hundred and forty million subjects are an asset. So knots are tied. Witte was against war, was a seeker after peace, a dreamer of Pan-Europa. But other forces held sway here.

After only five days M. Neitzlin's ship sailed again for her rich home. She disappeared into the twilight, leaving behind her a golden wake. The fifty thousand villages made no more complaint than at any other time. And no old woman, sitting outside her cottage towards the end of the day, read from her cards the name Lenin.

In this moment, all unconscious of it, Ulianov had lost the first Revolution; but in compensation he had won the opportunities of the World War and the second revolt.

Austrian and German bankers also shared in this loan. Herr Mendelssohn-Bartholdy wrote to Witte from Berlin, touched, almost lyrical in his emotion, telling him in confidence the steps he would take on all the bourses of Europe to ensure the success of the financial operation.

"Thanks to this loan," writes the Count, "the imperial Government came successfully through all the troubles of the years 1906–10. A sufficient reserve of money and the returned troops restored order and the self-confidence of the Government."

Witte could now manœuvre to cut the tautened string of the bow aimed against Tsarism.

The epidemic of strikes was filling the middle classes with indignation. Revolution—all very well. Constitution—still better. But one was no longer sure of one's own life and one's own comfort and ease. One day there would be no gas; next morning there would be empty, yawning stations, not an engine stirring; on another day there would be no postman; and on another the banks would be closed. Every week brought some new vexation. And the more thoroughly beaten was the extreme Left, the more fanatically it shouted its menaces.

"The object of the business men's demands and attacks," writes Trotzky, "was the State Bank. This institution served as a hydraulic press for that 'economic policy' of absolutism of which Witte had been the chief protagonist. . . . When, however, the bank began to restrict its operations many capitalists found themselves in dire straits. . . . 'We don't believe it's necessary at all,' they said to Count Witte at 2 a.m. on the night of October 31 and November 1. . . . Count Witte . . . confronted them with the facts! The discount rate rose rapidly. . . . The credits to the private banks rose yet more quickly: on December 14, 1905, they amounted to 184.2 million roubles, against 39 millions the year before."

After the manifesto on the Constitution the opposition split.

Both Count Witte and Lenin were waiting for this moment in which the various sections would confess to the creed inspired by their interests. The revolutionary, however, differed from the Minister in considering that, while the literary men might go astray, economic class consciousness would not. The Count wrote: "October 17/30 brought dissolution in the camp of the opponents of the autocracy . . . so that many, instead of combating the autocracy, thenceforth looked to it for support against their own opponents."

Lenin thought that at the beginning of the revolt most of its novices would be outside party classification. "The whole of society," was his comforting reflection, "will be embraced in a single 'liberating' movement (liberating in reality for the whole of bourgeois society). Everyone will take on a slight socialistic tinge."

It was this split which first brought the clear prophetic note of revolt into Lenin's utterances.

"Whoever," he declared, "has any actual understanding of the part to be played by the peasantry in the victorious Russian Revolution, is incapable of the suggestion that the impetus toward revolution would be diminished by the falling away of the bourgeoisie. In reality the true impetus of the Revolution will only come into play at that moment, the really revolutionary impetus will only come into actual existence at that moment; hitherto, during the bourgeois-democratic phase of revolt, it will have been latent, and can only become active when the bourgeoisie gives up the struggle and the mass of the peasantry step to the side of the proletariat as active revolutionaries."

The Count and the Bolshevik wanted the same thing in the interests of diametrically opposed aims; they were for the moment both marching, buoyed up by the most contradictory perspectives, under opposing flags, towards the breach which had opened between the victors of the hour during the rising.

Witte was dismissed. He had had, like Cardinal Richelieu, to reconcile two worlds: the many hundred thousand square miles of his country on the one hand, and on the other the few metres that surround the throne.

One frown from the wearer of the purple had sufficed to hurl from power the Minister who had saved the throne in its two moments of gravest danger, at the conclusion of peace with Japan and during the financial crisis. He fell because his policy would have called for a steadiness of purpose for which Nicholas had neither the will nor the mental capacity. The Count had hoped to gain the mastery over the cliques surrounding the Emperor.

Ulianov, a man he had never met, was watching closely the actual progress of social change; Witte was concerned with the possibility of successful manœuvres at Court in the shadow of historic events. In the upshot, since the autocracy had no intention of reforming itself, the fanatic Lenin was more of a realist than Witte. The stubborn rebel was concerned to tap sources of energy, longed for the triumphs of the tactics and strategy that were achieved on French soil at Valmy. He knew something of the power of Godefroy de Bouillon's *"Dieu le veult."*

Witte had owed his position to the financial ebb and the revolutionary flood. The Monarch could not but hate this unmystical man of figures, who never spoke of the Saints and rarely of Providence, but had plenty to say of new paths to be trodden. The Tsar found the Count as unwelcome as any other disturber of comfort in idleness. When the last flickers of rebellion began to die away, Witte's star also fell for ever. *He* could not build up hopes on the prospect of Revolution. He had to reckon with the Court caste, of which the reforming Minister writes in his Memoirs no more flatteringly than Ulianov himself.

Perhaps, judged by legitimist tradition, Witte was not Russian enough. He had tried to rule on Western European lines, with as few gallows as possible; to build up that complicated, indirect, moralizing, intellectual structure of government which depends on forms of capitalism unknown in Russia. He had no belief in the necessity of continuing to pursue the aim of a ruler—subjection—by the old methods of the Tartars.

When he died, during the World War, the Emperor gave a banquet, at which he told the French Ambassador of his satisfaction at the death of the man he hated.

In succession to Witte there came a charming old gentleman, M. Goremykin. He was surprised to find himself in power, would rather have continued peacefully entertaining his circle of friends with Conservative aphorisms, and gave it to be understood that the Tsar had fished him out of an old clothes chest.

The Constitution was now promulgated by decree, through the usual channels.

Lenin used all his arts of invective against those who were for entering the Duma. That policy would disturb the peasants in their work of burning down the junkers' property. What his Menshevik opponents were asking was neither one thing nor the other. The leaves were to rustle without moving. They wanted to take part in the elections, and yet not to send their delegates into the Government's Duma but "to cover the whole country with a network of organs of revolutionary self-government."

Ulianov declared that that could only be the epilogue, not the prelude of revolt.

And the blazing torch of rebellion which he had expected from the withdrawal of the bourgeoisie lit up the countryside. The village communities mostly took the lead in the risings. The economic conflicts in the Mir were stilled. It became the organ of local insurrection.

The landowners' farms were besieged, the junker palaces burned down, "so that the owners shall be unable to return." The properties were alienated and distributed by the Mir. Silently the peasant hordes drew near; not lifting up their voices in complaint, speaking very little, thinking in silence of past endurance. In a night there sprang up in their souls a fury of resolution; quickly their passion blazed up. Every new flare told of the darkness of the past. Their hatred knew no bounds. If the landowner offered resistance, that was the end of him. If he spoke to the slaves, if the proud lord of yesterday now begged of them, his cows were not all taken, he was left with one, "to satisfy our conscience," as the rioters put it. Even some fodder was left behind for the animal, "so that there shall be no scandal."

Blow upon blow, fire after fire. Unceasingly the bands marched on to proclaim, as they said, "Justice." The railway stations were crowded with fleeing landowners, with bag and baggage, miserably making for the towns. Until now many of them had been liberally minded, had spoken ill of the Tsar, had made fun of the police, criticized the laws. Oh, how they longed now for the strong hand! How it passed their comprehension that they should ever have been dissatisfied!

After the rising the "Free Economic Union" compiled statistics.

In the actual interior of Russia, in the spring and summer of 1905, 62 districts, that is 14 per cent. of all the *guberny,* and "strikes," as the peasants called their looting, burning and hanging expeditions. At the beginning of November 160 districts were "lit up." In a short period more than two thousand properties were destroyed, or, as the insurgents put it, shared out. "Unfortunately," said Lenin in a lecture, "the work was not thoroughly enough done! Unfortunately the peasants only destroyed one-fifteenth of the total number of rich farmers' properties, only one-fifteenth of what they should have destroyed in order to remove from the face of the earth the shame of feudal landownership in Russia."

This vengeance for suffering satisfied the lust for destruction, but failed to attain the goal of aspiration. The landowners dried their tears on receiving ample compensation from the Government at the cost of the peasants, and all had been mere futility. Rebellion could not overcome geography and make the distances between the village communities smaller.

Ordinarily when the peasant got drunk, and wanted further enjoyment in the next village of the fantasies born of his cheap alcohol, he dropped on the winter roadside, frozen to death; too many miles separated him from the tavern of his desire. Children had to trot away for two or three miles to learn their A B C, and "popes" had to go as far to sell the Word of God to the dying.

This isolation of the villages was the Government's salvation. The peasants drove out a few policemen, danced in front of roofs crashing in flames, and that was the end of their Revolution. While they were quietly sharing out new lands and property, surveying and allotting them with due solemnity, "as justice and the new age demand," a small detachment of imperial soldiery were restoring order in the next district. Handfuls of troops everywhere recovered for the old landowners their family properties.

Neither Lenin's party nor the Mensheviks were able to lead the agrarian movement; they could only await its results.

Meanwhile the peasants, through their electoral delegates, were sending their representatives to the Duma. The Government supposed that the pious farm servant would vote for the Tsar and against the Anarchists and Socialists, against the townsman. There were long discussions in the Mir; the conclusion arrived at was that Christ was never a big landowner, and men were sent to the first and second Dumas who had promised plenty of land. With a stubbornness which they imagined would help them, they continued, in spite of all punitive expeditions, to send revolutionary peasants to St. Petersburg. These Deputies had a single theme in the first and second Parliaments—"Land, we want land."

Lenin had not anticipated that. His thoughts were of hand-grenades rather than ballot-papers; he called the

Duma a great police and Court intrigue; he saw the State machinery for restricting the independence of the voting. He felt, also, the impotence of his party in the villages, but expected that, with the further development of the Revolution, past propagandist blunders and omissions could be remedied. The radical results of the elections showed him the irresistible pressure for land. Himself under the spell of the illusions of illegality, he issued warnings against the illusion of legality, represented law-fulness as a ruse on the part of the autocrats, and rightly gave the Duma but a short time to live.

The results of the elections, which had surprised Ulianov, also surprised and horrified the Tsar's political wiseacres and strategists. At the very moment when, in the towns, many hands were throwing down the banner of the strike, and fists formerly clenched were tremblingly opening for a bit of bread, representatives of the people were shouting with impunity words that at any other time would have brought to any subject that uttered them the hospitality of Siberia. In St. Petersburg there sat the Duma, a Convention without a Revolution, without the energy, power and effectiveness of the Convention; the assembly aspired after for a hundred years. Dreams of the millions were finding a voice in Parliament, as though an idea that was injurious to interests could dispense with a guillotine!

From the bloodstained rock of power there shone forth in the *gubernia* of Saratov the name of a governor: Stoly-pin. During the agrarian revolt none had used the sword on the people so wholesomely as he. Tales of him went from mouth to mouth, and the Tsar sent for him, amid sighs of relief from the depth of his soul. If Nicholas II did not understand his new Minister's plans of reform, he understood his tribunals. The upper classes welcomed him, and Count Saltykov declared, in the name of the aristocracy: "Not a foot's breadth of our land shall we give up, not a grain of wheat from our fields, not a blade of grass from our meadows, not a stick of firewood from our forests."

Stolypin shouted in the face of the second Duma, from the Government bench: "The Left are crying to the Cabinet, 'Hands up!' But we shall not allow ourselves to be intimidated."

He promulgated a new electoral law, under which big landowners, industrialists, house-owners, big merchants, were amply provided with votes at the expense of intellectuals, workers and peasants; at the same time he wrote a circular letter to all provincial governors: "The electoral areas should be arranged at your discretion as seems best, and so composed that everywhere a majority is assured to the elements loyal to the Government."

Between the second and third Dumy there lay the most terrible nights of the Régime, the darkest which Russia was to pass through until 1918. The Dictator proclaimed his policy: "First restore order in the country. After that we shall confer constitutional reforms."

"Never under the autocracy," writes Witte, "was there so much arbitrary action as in Stolypin's time, and the more Stolypin plunged into this gloom the gloomier he himself became."

Twenty-five thousand peasants were arrested, savagely beaten, and transported; over a thousand journalists were prosecuted; a thousand periodicals were prohibited. Death sentences were pronounced by the courts-martial on 2,117 men. "The need of the moment," declared a decree of the Ministry of the Interior, "is to extirpate once for all the tendency of the people to take the law into their own hands."

From now onwards the gallows were always known as "Stolypin's necktie." The reply came from below as bombs and revolver shots. The time was past when only a few youths shot at potentates. This work was taken over now by proletarians and peasants. Terrorism be-

came a mass method. There were months in which conspirators and isolated terrorists murdered over three hundred military, police and civil officials.

Suvorin, the famous Russian publicist, who had served
many Ministers as faithfully as he despised them, made
this entry in his diary on May 30, 1907: "Anyone leaving
St. Petersburg now buys a revolver first and his railway
ticket second. . . . But Stolypin said to me: 'It is getting better now, the revolution is abating.' "

Even though half of the young flower of revolt dropped
dead, still Lenin spoke of the good progress and prospects
of the rebellion. Now there was a rapid sequence and
accumulation, in his view, of the social conflicts which
"come into play but slowly in the periods of so-called
peaceful development. . . . The Reaction's game is
. . . to represent the Revolution as 'elemental mania.' "

At the moment he was in controversy with friends, with
Bolsheviks who refused to take part in the elections for
Stolypin's *coup-d'état* Duma. "Why, we boycotted the
first and second Parliament, and now we are to accept
the much narrower franchise?" asked the puzzled Leninists. But the Master would hear nothing of further
abstention from the polls.

He laughed at his comrades of the Left, who wanted
to proclaim risings and strikes in the existing situation.

"When the battle is raging," he wrote, "extending, closing up on all sides, then it is our bounden duty . . . to
shout battle-cries. But a battle-cry by itself does not
make a battle where there is none. . . . It would be just
as blind to mistake Bolshevism for 'Boycottism' as for
'Activism.' "

Did he now, where he had failed to do so in Moscow
days, recognize defeat? Did he see his sun paling? Did
he envy the dead at the barricades, who lay deep below
the soil and were not called on to renounce their dream?

This was the first time, the only time until Brest-
Litovsk, that Lenin spoke of strategic retreat, and he used

the same language which he was to use ten years later, when at the height of power. "One must not be deceived," he wrote in *August 1907,* "by the mere sound of words which in their time have played a great and famous revolutionary part. . . . In such periods as that through which we are now passing, in periods when the Revolution stops to take breath . . . our duty is to prepare the conditions for the new ascent; but in order . . . that it may begin, there must be . . . no shouting of slogans which have significance only under the conditions of ascent."

His practical policy now was to take no notice of the astonished whispering of his colleagues, and to eschew the reputation of an extremist in the Party. He had to forget his declarations of yesterday if he was not to lose precious time hugging an out-of-date bundle of momentous aspirations.

The tactics which Lenin slowly and painfully learned during the set-back of the two years after the Moscow rising were later to be his salvation in the burning high-noon of power.

He wrote under the influence of Stolypin's repressive measures.

He fought down all revolutionary chimeras of the moment, and resolutely accepted the position. This recognition, contrary to all theory, was not the fruit of a moment, but the result of a process which had continued from December 1905 to March 1907. Every hour had had for two years to bring fresh pains, to bring Ulianov to recommend the agenda of the *coup-d'état* Parliament to his friends' attention. "A speech in the Duma," was his advice now, "will not bring Revolution . . . but the Social Democracy has . . . something to gain. . . . In consequence of our defeat . . . the reaction has driven us into continually worse nominally constitutional conditions, and it will continue to drive us yet further."

This painfully restrained farewell of Lenin's, his matter-of-fact, banal assurance, "We shall always and in all places fight for our convictions," was a silent turning of his coat. His hopes had been for other conquests.

In Russia the economic, political and national elements were testing other solutions than those of the Revolution. Stolypin was anxious to find them. He did not delude himself that his forest of gallows had extirpated sedition. Vengeance was for him the beginning of all wisdom, not its end. Stern measures only justified themselves, in the Dictator's view, when they made reforms possible, opened up prospects of improvement. The tyrant thought, as did Ulianov himself later on, that opposition was the cardinal sin against the change for the realization of which his spirit craved. Stolypin wanted to free the countryside from the last vestiges of feudalism, but without hurting the feudal lords; he wanted to play the part of a Bismarck, and impose revolution from above. But the conditions from which he set out were not those of which the first German Chancellor had had the advantage, and he came to grief.

The Dictator explained the principles of his reforms to the third Duma:

"Inviolacy of private property; and, as its corollary, the creation of a small propertied class, the recognition of the right to secede from the Mir, and the solution of the problems connected with the needed improvement in the methods of cultivating the soil."

Above all, the Mir, those countless strongholds of economic stagnation, whose harvest of destitution left industry without a home market, must be destroyed. Every head of a family was given the right to acquire a due proportion of the land in the possession of the village community, to be held in his own right.

Stolypin openly admitted that the Government was only helping the economically stronger peasant, who could already play a greater part in the Mir than his neighbours; the others, the vast majority, must fend for themselves. He rested his hopes on the new openings for the ambition to hold land, and calculated on the mass of the peasantry—which until then had everywhere had a like experience and outlook—dividing, the contented farm-owners siding with the Government and against the landless proletariat in any new risings.

From the sale of private properties, including the royal domains, a State fund was to be created which would make provision for those peasants who had the means to increase the properties that they now freely held; the State would be prepared to give them financial assistance as well.

The interests of the upper class were not prejudiced by the Agricultural Bank.

The bank had been founded nearly thirty years before, had constantly saved the feudal lord from bankruptcy, was gentle as a rich, fatherly sinner towards his profligate heir. It was now to see to it that the price of land did not fall too heavily.

By January 1, 1908, however, the Government's Land Fund had only reached 27 per cent. of the sum required, according to the Government's own figures, to satisfy the land hunger. One hundred thousand big properties still accounted for fifty per cent. of the land in private ownership. The Ministry put the average minimum requirements for various *guberny* at 12.24 dessiatines for each peasant family. It was impossible to give the peasants land without expropriating the big landowners. Even if that were done there would not have been enough for all who were hungering for a plot of their own.

The system by which Stolypin had tried to stave off revolution led straight to it, just as, a decade later, Lenin's decrees by which millions of new owners were recognized only removed them further from his dream of a Socialist State such as the world had never yet known.

The destruction of the Mir drove hundreds of thousands of small sharers in it into the void. The settlement of peasants on holdings on their former lords' property took from the peasants of neighbouring hamlets all opportunity of leasing. These peasants, now at last set at liberty and, thanks to Stolypin's legislation, given freedom of movement, not only could but had to leave their villages. Before them the towers and walls and factories of the town rose up empty and uninviting. Nowhere was there a green oasis to be found; the world had become desert.

In six years two and a half million landless men left the Mir. In the World War the migration attained even huger proportions, till on the new morning of Revolution the old yearning was satisfied.

The impotent protests of this homeless multitude, that lay along the streets like breathing mire, found their only audible, intelligible expression in the parties of the Populist Socialists and the Social Revolutionaries.

These organizations demanded land for all. Ulianov criticized them, grasped the significance of the Stolypin reform, and gave his view: "No doubt a certain number . . . of industrial workers . . . share the standpoint of these peasants. But the question is, is this standpoint right? . . . The peasants naturally look backwards. Their general outlook and views are the ideologies of yesterday. But the real trend of economic development is not in the direction of an increase, but of a diminution in the population engaged in agriculture."

Lenin knew that there could be no possibility of seizing power without the goodwill of the hundred and ten millions of peasants; he made use of this infinity of illusions, reckoned with it, but did not share it; the nationalization of the soil fell far short of what he understood by Communism. In Communism there must be economic planning to the last trousers button, and not the haphazard buying and selling which meant that the poor man got nothing. "So long as the system of production for exchange exists it is ridiculous," declared Ulianov, "to speak of Socialism." Even nationalization he could welcome,

LENIN IN 1914

THE FIVE ARRESTED BOLSHEVIK DEPUTIES

but only as a step forward under capitalism. The land would be free. "Free?" he asks. "For whom? For every citizen? Not in the slightest. . . . The land is free . . . for the farmer . . . who is able and willing to work it on the lines demanded by modern economic conditions in general and those of the world market in particular."

Ulianov saw that the new order was destroying the Mir, and asked who was going to put through the critical reforms, Stolypin or the proletariat of the towns.

From all the facts he deduced the general conclusion that "the essence of the agrarian problem lies not in the removal of hindrances to agricultural advance, but in the question how these hindrances are removed, by what classes and through what methods this removal is effected.

"The Stolypin method, from above, retaining junker landownership, entirely destroying the Mir organization, and allowing its resources to be appropriated by the rich peasants, is one way, and the peasant method, from below, is another; . . . both forms . . . facilitate . . . the transition to a higher stage."

Stolypin's reform, however, was not the graveyard of feudalism. It did not effectively clear the way for industry, nor did it expand the home market; it merely produced a cheap reserve of unemployed labour. It contained the germs of war, inviting the bourgeoisie to cease following the will-o'-the-wisp of civil strife and painting an alluring picture of the profits to be gained in foreign markets. The Minister shouted in the Duma, "You are after great upheavals; we are after a great Russia."

The Dictator succeeded in governing with the aid of the bourgeoisie, which had been frightened at its own revolution. The Octobrists, the group whose programme consisted of the October Constitution, proclaimed but never carried into effect, gave him their support; even the Constitutional Democratic Party, the "Cadets," who as lately as during the war with Japan had been praying for Russia's defeat, agreed in the third and fourth Dumy with the Government's new orientation in foreign affairs. If they criticized it in any respect it was mainly for its lack of energy in championing Slav aims in the Balkans.

The potsherds in Stolypin's hands were diamonds in the eyes of the bourgeois parties; and their former words of revolutionism made way for Chauvinist phrases.

"The alteration in the agrarian policy of Tsarism," says Lenin in a note on the Stolypin system, "is not a mere fanciful scheme of the bureaucracy. . . . It means a very decided change of direction towards agrarian Bonapartism. . . . This Bonapartism is a definite manœuvre on the part of the Monarchy . . . of a Monarchy which is compelled to seek means of righting its balance on the edge of disaster."

Stolypin had no acquaintance with Lenin. Dictators are not like princes, born in the State bed of direct succession; they know neither where they are destined to die nor who is destined to succeed them.

THE FORCES AND THE CONSPIRACY OF THE VANQUISHED

Der Mensch, der etwas Tüchtiges hervorbringt, legt seine ganze Energie hinein; er hat nicht die Nüchternheit, dies oder das zu wollen; er zerstreut sich nicht in so und so viele Zwecke, sondern ist seinem wahrhaftigen grossen Zwecke ganz ergeben. Die Leidenschaft ist die Energie dieses Zwecks und die Bestimmtheit dieses Wollens. Es ist eine Art von Trieb, fast tierisch, dass der Mensch seine Energie so in eine Sache legt.

(The man who produces something of consequence puts into it the whole of his energy; he does not soberly consider this or that alternative; he does not disperse his attention over so and so many aims, but is entirely consumed by his one true and great aim. Passion is the energy of this purpose, and the definiteness of this will. It is a sort of instinct, almost animal, by which man so applies his energy to a single cause.)

Hegel.

THE CONFLICT OVER THE
PARTY FUNDS AND OVER
THE LORD ALMIGHTY

IT was no longer possible for Ulianov to go on living in the neighbourhood of St. Petersburg, on Finnish soil. The police were watching the house of this enemy who had only half fled. Like every suspect in Russia, he not only heard but felt the tramp of their boots. Defeated, he left Russia.

Exile, the outer world, the void, spread out dismally, like a rainy day that gives no promise of ending.

A decade before, flight before the majesty of the Tsar's justice had been nothing to mourn over. Then he had travelled gladly, full of plans that promised activity and liberation. But now, almost in the forties, must he take up again the labours of youth, go back to that existence?

The offices of the organ of the Bolshevik group, *The Proletarian,* were to be moved abroad. Three friends accompanied him to see to this. He travelled in slow stages to the refuge in Geneva; for there was nothing very attractive awaiting him. In Stockholm and Berlin he broke the journey for some weeks. "It is like returning to my coffin," said Ulianov to his wife, who had followed him.

Gone was the glory of the days in which the issues of his own and his friends' organs brought joy or horror to hundreds of thousands of Russians; gone were those three months in which the translation of the Erfurt programme of the German Social Democracy had been printed off until over a million copies had been issued.

Quickly the past became a chapter of legend.

He had scarcely reached the shores of his Swiss lake

when he wrote to Maxim Gorky at Capri, begged for his aid in opening a way for the paper into their country. "We must at all costs," he wrote in a letter at the beginning of January 1908, "get into touch with the secretary of the organization of the employees of shipping firms . . . which have ships sailing to Russia. We must ascertain from and to what ports ships sail, how often. . . . We must at all costs get a regular weekly transport service running."

Every cellar refuge, every secret dwelling, every secluded corner was as though submerged below maleficent floods, and infinitely difficult to discover. Friends, acquaintances, nibblers at the movement, shook their heads, explained with quiet nods to the scattered and beaten revolutionaries that this was not the time, that the conditions and the things going on made it out of the question for them to help; breathed a sigh of relief when the importunate enquirers went away. In the past, before and during the Revolution, bankers had opened their portfolios to give contributions, elegant women had opened scented caskets to hide secret correspondence in them, civil servants had opened their doors to the rebels and given them shelter. Students had felt in luck if they were allowed to hear the whisper of refugees in the dusk.

Now no helping hand was to be seen.

Ulianov asked peevishly: ". . . Isn't there some higher official to be found—some *bona-fide* respectable employee whom we could pay a retaining fee of fifty roubles a month? . . . We are not in touch with any respectable people now—outside the workers (who are unable to do what is needed). That is our great trouble. . . ."

The fact was that the few thousand intellectuals who formed the backbone of the movement had been rooted up from the placid surface of everyday life and its personal links. Now they asked: "Was there nothing more in our dreams than this?"

Lawyers, doctors, writers, journalists, university lecturers, students and civil servants had believed that the revolutionary cause would be an everlasting source of inward contentment.

The revolt had now cut them off from the intimacies of ordinary life. Now that the sun of illusion shone no longer for them in any social group or class, that sun so much needed to warm the eternally shivering creature, man, everything had changed colour, and they were tempted to find attractions where a little while before they would only have found food for scornful laughter.

Some dreamed conventional visions of wedded bliss, pictured themselves at home in the circle of their loved ones, saw their sons round them, and bent their heads in maiden shame when, in their quiet musing, they seemed to hear, instead of the words "Prisoner at the bar" or "Comrade," a gentle "Papa." Others thought this too commonplace a solution, imagined ways of impressing both themselves and the ordinary respectable citizen by transferring the revolution of their dreams to the individual, sexual sphere, and took themselves for Borgias when they were merely self-conscious boasters.

Most of them went back to the flickering lamp of conventional good fellowship. The lawyer remembered his gown, the doctor his practice, the student his degree, the professor his platform, the official his pension rights, and many workless journalists read the "permitted" Press with ironic smiles at the thought of the much more that they themselves could have put into the leading articles.

The zest of the new pursuits was stronger than that of the groups for which Ulianov had made a home. Menshevik and Bolshevik alike felt it.

Yet the falling away of his friends and the exertions of his Socialist enemies did not subdue Lenin's spirit; he only grew yet more dogged, hated men and women who had once been on the Left even more than the Tsar, and fully realized the natural economic causes of the heavy

clouds that had come over the fair skies of the Revolution. But he was unable to comprehend how the men
and women whom he had known as rebels could so easily
be led astray.

The more the slow hours tortured him, the less could he
understand the attraction for his friends of by-paths that
in his view led them away from the Pantheon of Theory.
The stagnancy formed him, its pain developed him further. The solitude of these three years taught him a surly
endurance.

"Lenin," writes Shapovalov, who went to see him at
this time, "strode up and down the room in his shirt-
sleeves, breast forward, ready . . . to defy any blow.
I looked at the muscles of his arms, which stood out under
his shirt; observed his gait, his expression. I listened to
his words, in which the iron will . . . rang out, and I
said to myself: 'How he has changed in these years!
How he has grown!' "

Ulianov was now the target for the attacks of bored
and idle groups. All sorts of rumours were put together
against him in the empty hours of the *Stammtisch,* and
arguments forged into weapons to fight him with. As
Lenin had defended the partisan struggles, he was now
represented as the highwayman's advocate, added to the
Olympians as the God of Thieves!

The émigrés were starving. Hands grasped at the
scantiest livelihood. The twelve groups of the one Party
tried to save the poor remainder of their literary activities and make money out of them. They all sprayed one
another with their corrosive poison, but no gold was pre-
cipitated. It was suspected that Lenin was holding on to
some. Two of his closest friends, the future Soviet Ministers Shemaskho and Litvinov, were arrested in Western
Europe while changing roubles which had been stolen in
Tiflis. Lenin did not deny these lootings, merely said:
"Such affairs are always magnified by the international
police."

Ulianov wrote to Gorky at Capri that he could not accept his invitation: ". . . I do not know whether I can get enough money together for it. That is our present difficulty." Three days later he writes: "Al. Al. must really put his back into the work of collecting money. In Russia they are howling for sheer lack of funds."

Even if these poor, frozen, ragged plebeians of an Asiatic anarchy were, with very few exceptions, deaf to the rustle of practical work, they were not dumb. At the plenary sitting of the Party in Paris a last attempt was made to unite the "fractions." *Fourteen* unyielding speakers represented *seven* contradictory policies. The dying strains of this Congress were sung to a theme then almost extinct: the Party funds. The Russians were unable to come to an agreement. A German committee of "trustees" was appointed, consisting of Karl Kautsky, Clara Zetkin, and Franz Mehring. The Nibelung hoard amounted to 30,000 francs. Lenin was instructed to liquidate his group, to enable the Party to continue to exist. But he had no such intention.

The Muscovite Social Democracy then finally split.

Many Mensheviks congratulated themselves on being no longer bound by compromising formulæ. In the Party jargon they were called Liquidators; they were determined to lead to heaven by new paths. In the years of the Revolution trade unions had been formed which met with Count Witte's approval. But their Moscow membership was now no longer eighty thousand, but seven thousand. The Liquidators thought they could develop these vestiges of legality; they rested their hopes on the blameless innocence of the unions, and proposed to organize statistical lectures, followed by dancing.

These people received the full blast of Lenin's wrath. "In the plenum," he reported to Gorky in a full account, ". . . (three full weeks the tortures lasted; everyone's nerves went *kaputt*. Death and damnation!) these serious . . . considerations . . . were joined by smaller and pettier ones. An atmosphere of 'peace at any price' developed . . . combined with resentment against the Bolshevik headquarters. . . . So came the break.

" . . . It is disgusting to be in the midst of this gossipy talking, this quarrelling and scandal-mongering, this weary wrangling, this bitter disillusionment. . . . But we must not give way to our feelings.

" . . . The quarrelling will die out . . . will . . . remain outside Russia . . . on the other hand the development of the Party . . . will stride through and over all . . . the difficulties of the present conditions.

" . . . This cleaning up is . . . far from being mere 'literature' . . . it is indissolubly bound up with the kernel of the workers' movement, which . . . is learning along the line of negation, is beginning its march by way of the negation of Liquidatorism and Ostovism."

The Ostovists were members of the Bolshevik group who would only consent not to despair of the Revolution if anti-parliamentary tactics were adopted.

In other ways, too, the dreams of his closest friends seemed to him to be passing whims, seraphically illuminating the garbage of defeat for the consolation of the weak flesh, but not of the Idea. Un-Marxist thinking even dared to enter the editorial office of *The Proletarian,* flying across the Leninist writing-paper like gulls over the troubled sea. His colleague, Bogdanov, who sat opposite him, seemed, as he bent over his "copy," to be seeking for a god.

Never did saint shrink back in more horror from the devil than Lenin did now before the spectre of a religion.

This émigré, worried by the police, by poverty, by Party friends, by chatter around him, by his own temperament, possessed nothing but his Theory. Now old comrades were trying to rob him of that. The greater the defeat, the more necessary the compromises, the more the pathway had to be trod crouchingly, slinkingly, the more angelic needed to be the brightness of the pure doctrine.

If the source were fouled in which the sun's rays shone, where could the stains of the day's dull task be washed away, where could one get cleaned of all the compromises, where could one stretch numbed limbs?

"How do you like *The Proletarian* now?" he asks Maxim Gorky. "It is in a state of desolation. I have never so neglected my paper; I spend whole days reading the damned Machists."

Bogdanov's group among the followers of Mach taught that truth can only be ideological form and cannot be objective; they postulated an explanation of matter of their own, holding that feelings are the primary thing, and that physical bodies are formed out of them.

These ideas found their popularizer in Lunacharsky, who afterwards became the Education Minister of the Soviet Government. He stood for an almost atheist god, arising from the ideal of beauty of the new proletarian culture by virtue of the ecstasy inspired by its vast, historic task. Lunacharsky wrote in the most easy-going feuilleton style, repeating in many variations the sentiment "Don't suppose that where you can't see anything night begins."

Maxim Gorky, a man closely akin to Lenin, wrote his wonderful romance of the barefoot man in search of truth, and laid bare in his description of a "confession" his longing for a philosophical approach to God, even though a God who did not intervene in specific human affairs.

The denial, however, of objective truth leads, as Ulianov's commentator Deborin writes, to unduly indulgent judgments, to opportunism in the field of philosophic thought.

If, Lenin sums up, truth is only subjective, only a conclusion from things heard, seen, experienced, even Rome may be right. "For there is no doubt that even Catholicism is an organized form of human experience."

In face of the battle of conflicting quotations, it can be

maintained that Ulianov in his Marxist philosophy did what Marx had never undertaken. Lenin, in the midst of a discussion, would clench his fist, with a fierce warning: "If you think this and abandon that, you come to results that take away the courage and eagerness of battle." He would simply prohibit an idea, prove its error only from the necessities of the movement, not by philosophic reasoning.

"If," writes this high priest of atheism, "there is no objective truth, if truth (including also science) is only an organized form of human experience, then the fundamental principle of priesthood is admitted, the door is opened to it, the ground is cleared for the 'organized forms' of religious experience."

Karl Marx would hardly have resorted in this way to philosophic blackmail on behalf of a practical end determined in advance.

Lenin, however, was philosophizing for the purpose of attaining an immediate settlement of differences in the group; in order to sweep away opportunism from every field of its thought. If he had not regarded tolerance as a mortal sin, he would not have been fishing in these waters; to do so would have meant nothing to him but a sign of decay. *Nothing in thought or aspiration seemed to Lenin more incomprehensible than tolerance.* For him it was indistinguishable from lack of guiding principle. It was the beginning of contemptible surrender. To this man of great purposes even the enemy's purposes were more tolerable than purposelessness. "A periodical without a policy," declared Ulianov, "is a preposterous, senseless, scandalous and noxious thing."

Feelings—according to the theory of his opponent friends the most important element in the birth of matter, the source of all things—could have no *nuances* in the life of this man with a mission. Consequently they lit up other men in his eyes with a uniform clarity like the southern skies over Mediterranean creeks. The landscape of emotion was not filled for him with dream on the one side and reality on the other, nor did it shade off into vagueness in the twilight. Philosophy was no resting-place for him; his flock must be kept away from its academies. Their corridors, indeed, were hiding-places of the most malignant opponents of the Party. They gave a poor devil a crown of words and in exchange robbed him of calories. Here too he saw only the political aspect. ". . . Apathy," writes this philosopher *malgré lui,* "is political repletion. Only the replete are 'apathetic,' 'indifferent' towards a bit of bread and butter; the hungry man will always take sides in bread and butter questions. . . . 'Apathy,' 'indifference' . . . implies . . . that the person concerned . . . is comfortably ensconced in the party of the replete."

Ulianov was no more successful than anyone else in the matter of knowing himself. He was blind to the fact that in his veins, as in those of all the rebels before him, there flowed the so-called blue blood of despotism. Were not Cromwell, Robespierre and Napoleon despoilers of thrones? *In him the element of domination and Cæsarism found expression in his handling of theory.* No one showed more independence in the interpretation of the Master, but only Lenin must enjoy this licence. What he said had to be accepted as orthodoxy.

He learned from Karl Marx that freedom of thought which he prohibited in others.

Marx, a disciple of German philosophy, taught that theory has no value as truth unless it is practical, not in the sense of producing immediate results, such as the backscratching Councillor who is advanced to the Mayoralty of Tolpuddle wants and expects, but of yielding results in the course of a historic period. Lenin learned from his Teacher how to recognize realities and the forces that formed them. Marx freed him from that blind acceptance of dogma which he imposed on others. This "orthodox" Russian Marxist was able to think more freely and clearly than Cromwell, the seeker after God, or Robespierre, who introduced the razor-blade of the guillotine as the all-sufficing instrument of virtue's beauty-parlour. He tested theory by practice and practice by theory. And in this his thinking could not fail to make use of an important element in thought-processes —scepticism.

He realized the relativity of things, saw the isle of the known threatened by the boundless realms of the unknown, but declared that "man's intelligence may be only a feeble rushlight in the darkness of night, but I am not going to let that flickering little flame be blown out by mystics and metaphysicians." Yet Lenin also gives such anti-dogmatic advice as this reminder of the mutability of all things and of truth: "It must not be forgotten that the criterion of practice can never confirm or disprove any human notion."

He now wrote a pamphlet against every sort of mysticism, not in order to extend the boundaries of knowledge, not to bring new thoughts into the world, but in reaction against the metaphysical hopes that grow up and thickly carpet the ways of beaten revolutionaries. He suppressed his own uncertainties; doubts—those doubts that whisper into the ear: "The brighter, the livelier our intelligence, the more it discovers weaknesses in itself and the less it trusts its own powers"—could find no admittance into his polemic; he believed that he could see deeper than his friends into the mysteries of the combination of the elements of opposition.

This book in which profundity alternates with mere abuse, this cauldron of invective and constructive thought, he called *Marxism and Empiro-criticism: Critical Observations on a Reactionary Philosophy*.

To his surprise the work found a publisher, who printed three thousand copies of it, and even sold three hundred. If anyone else had written it no one would remember its pages to-day. Ordinarily no one would publish for him. "How is it?" he asked Maxim Gorky. "Couldn't *you* . . . place my book on the agrarian question? . . . I can never, never find a publisher. It is simply maddening."

Publishers were avoiding him no more resolutely than men of other callings. These were the blackest years of his existence. Convulsively, like a fever patient, he looked from side to side to see himself, this man of unique energies, bound down by the narrow restraint of the circle of émigrés. The days were oppressive as the atmosphere of a room long closed up. No dreams could restore him to himself, only the one remedy of new creative work.

LENIN'S ROAD TO THE RUSSIAN FRONTIER

Stolypin, the Prime Minister, fell victim to a police experiment. The bullet that struck down the Dictator, in the presence of his imperial master, in the imperial box of the theatre at Kiev, had not been bought by the assassin. He had received it from the secret police, the Okhrana. There were men in the pay of the Government who penetrated into the most secret chambers of rebellion, to discuss murders with the terrorists. Stolypin wanted to have men of his own, silent and loyal, in the ranks of his dynamite-using opponents. In this he was like Lenin, who pursued the same tactics, planting in the midst of unreliable friends and declared enemies Bolshevist "nuclei" which, like sea shells, repeated to him the slightest whispers.

An agent of the secret service had, for once, betrayed not the revolutionaries, but the police. He was actually posted to protect the Dictator when he murdered him.

In recent months Stolypin's followers had been associated with the Conservative opposition. The Dictator had been striding the bridge of Coalition which bound the estates of the junkers with the banks of high finance and the factories of the big industrialists. By the end of 1910, after years of economic stagnation, Russia had entered on a short period of prosperity. The industrialists began to lose their love of peace, began to declare that the farm servants of the landowners were bringing in to their masters more than they themselves were getting out of the factory hands. The little footbridge of peace, which had united all the great ones in the land, began to be shadowed by clouds of incipient discontent.

Stolypin's successor, Kokovtzev, had not the murdered man's talents. He had not Stolypin's success in keeping at bay the ill-humour of his supporters with magic visions of patriotic islands of the blest.

The industrial bourgeoisie began to think that the State was no longer in a position to weave garlands of war. In the fourth Duma they declared that the sword of the empire was blunt and no longer flashed in the light. All the principal posts were in the hands of the grand dukes. Corruption made gay the gardens of a few fortunates with falling flakes of gold, thick as the snow that the sky brought down on the peasants' cottages. For the first time the name of Rasputin was mentioned in the Duma. "Thus," declared Miliukov, "the Church is in the hands of the Hierarchy; the Hierarchy is prisoner of the State; the State is prisoner of a vagabond."

This distant note of dissatisfaction in his homeland at once reached Lenin's ears in Paris.

Sickness at heart seemed to flee at once out of his room. He threw open the windows as though they opened on Russia. One line of news had changed everything, had brought the optimism of a summer morning. Its radiance lit up the inkpot and the bookshelves; the writing-desk looked as tempting as an orchard. The most secret doings of St. Petersburg and Moscow were revealed to his fancy. He began once more to caress every possibility till it smiled.

After five years there now appeared the first "legal" Bolshevik paper in Moscow, *Svezda*. Lenin wrote its leading article, from Paris. When the post from Moscow brought a parcel containing his paper, his hand shook. "To-day," he writes to a friend, "came Number One. Congratulate us. Our little paper, a Marxist paper, is coming out now in Moscow! That was good news to-day. . . ."

And at last, after four years of anguish and hopelessness, the old tune of rebellion began to be heard again. As in the morning in barracks the soldier, with unrefreshed eyes, yawns, still half asleep, at his neighbour, so the man in the factory looked at his fellow-worker to see whether one could venture to challenge the quiet acceptance of things without finding oneself in isolation. The workers attempted to form craft organizations, passed round petitions demanding freedom of action for trade unions. Economic conflicts began again; in 1911, 137,000 workers struck work.

In the Siberian gold-mines on the Lena, a police officer had two hundred strikers shot. "Obviously," writes Count Witte, "the whole of the public police administration was directly or indirectly receiving bribes from this very rich gold-mining company." Explanations were demanded in the Duma. The Minister of the Interior looked into the future with the optimism of every man who holds office, and replied: "So it always has been, and so it always will be."

After the battle on the Lena, in which one side fired and the other died, the number of strikers reached one million and two hundred thousand.

"It smells of 1905," wrote a leader-writer in the *Novoye Vremya*.

The new, narrow streak of revolt was greeted by every group in the Socialist movement, each with its own certainty as to the next step. Lenin's friends reaped better fortune than the other Party groups. In the

days when the mass movement was dying down, when no
more than a murmur remained audible, Ulianov had
forbidden his few friends to indulge in a continual riot
of controversy.   The Mensheviks were dissipated into
a hundred cliques, all fighting one another; the Bolsheviks into a bare dozen.

The masses understood little of the whispered controversies of the Socialists.   They caught the sense of the
first words, then their attention wandered.   Unlike
Ulianov, the Mensheviks now, as before and during the
Revolution, were interested only in organizing the masses
and not their own group.   This, however, was prohibited
by the police, who made arrests, or, where they had to
give permission, bound it up with endless bureaucratic
obstacles.   The Mensheviks, none the less, persevered,
and had a few successes.

Lenin tasted of the fruit of their labours.   But his
main effort was in another direction; he paid no attention to gathering the masses together, but to the propa-
gation of their hatred.   Workers were welcome in his
organization, but it seemed of more importance to guide
their passion.

The hand of the State, in sealing up the door of the
trade unions, worked for Lenin's gospel.   The multitude
were not allowed to collect together, and people with
varying loves could not speak to them of class, nation,
industry, society, falling birth-rate or customs treaty,
could not win from their hatreds a patient hearing, could
not analyse their pain for them.

Demonstrations were prohibited, and trade unions
equally so; accordingly, they chose the course that promised more blessedness: Lenin, the barricade, insurrection.

This stubborn fighter built on the Russian tradition
which, in his Party, friend and foe alike overlooked.   He
repeated over and over again the same words against
Socialist tendencies that smacked to him of opportunism,
with a pertinacity that might seem morbid because it is

strange and unusual. One who was initiated into the secrets of the rebel movement warned him of the possible non-revolutionary outcome of Parliamentarism; Lenin replied that "Russia's history is quite enough to safeguard the Russian workers from such a development. Among us the (class) differences are so acute that there is no need to fear the decoying of the workers into the Reformist camp."

The factory *curiæ* for the indirect election of the fourth Duma sent to it six Bolshevik deputies. The Mensheviks succeeded in winning seven parliamentary seats in the border districts of Caucasia. The Leninists, as the closer adherents of Ulianov now called themselves, used in their candidature a specific from the Master's rich store. During the campaign, on his instructions, they laid no stress on their own particularism, but kept his doctrine in the background. Only when they had been elected did they proclaim Bolshevism as their faith.

The years of suffering under the Reaction had had other results than stifling men's utterances. Some of the masses endured through its terrors. There grew up a type of Socialist new in Russia: mechanics, semi-skilled workers, joiners, weavers, who did not live as professional revolutionaries, seeking through flood and fire always the Holy Grail of the Idea, but in the heart of the masses, flesh of their flesh. To these men Lenin addressed his message. He wanted to put fresh life into his small organization through them, encouraged them amid their hesitations, summoned to him a few out of the nameless crowd, worked on them through his characteristic method of modest questioning coupled with cool and precise orders. An academy of rebels formed round him. "Do send a message," he writes to Gorky from Paris, "to the workers from our school. They are fine fellows. One, poor chap, is a writer. . . ."

"In Paris," he mentions, "there came to me (between you and me) a delegate sent specially by the sailors. . . .

They had no organization—it is absolutely awful! If you are in touch with any of the officers, everything must be tried to get something done."

Elated with new hope, Ulianov broke off all the threads that still linked his group with the priesthoods of other Socialist pamphlets. The very fact of new probable moves made it "necessary," he writes, "not to amalgamate, but to secede." The coming Labour movement must tread the pavement of his road, and it must therefore be laid at once.

The émigré section of the Russian Socialist Party was, indeed, only a small field of work. Amid its groups men and women would stand up, often people possessed by delusions, mania, fixed ideas, and throw inkpots at one another and their neighbours. Ulianov now carried out a *coup d'état* in the small world of his environment, a *coup* which set him free. This un-democrat called his friends together to Prague from their homeland, and constituted himself and his closest comrades a Party. The émigrés howled, cried out that the sun would now shine by night and the moon by day. Ulianov took no notice of the brethren in the land of dreams; with the five and twenty partners assembled in Prague, he dictated the bases of the new Party.

Now, after long years, the domes of a new organization had come into view.

"In Russia," he writes, "there is optimistic revolutionary feeling—actually, definitely revolutionary."

The Prague Congress opened the way for practical work for which Ulianov had been longing now for half a decade. Here, where the illegal workers from home were speaking, the walls of his confinement disappeared. Russian towns came into view. Long sittings considered the vulnerability of the Colossus.

Lenin left Paris for good.

He sought a place to live on the borders of the empire,

stayed, like an expelled pretender to the Throne, from the summer of 1912 to the first signs of the World War in August 1914, in CRACOW. For hours the exile would wander along paths that crossed the soil of his homeland. If the frontier guards did not catch sight of him, he would go past the line which separated Austria from Russia, in order, as he said, "to breathe the air of Russia."

Here and there he would meet a peasant, and listen to what the soil had to say through its serving-man. Like a pilgrim on the white seashore this man, filled with desire, would scan the horizon to see what it concealed. The golden infinity of the plain remained dumb. Would he yet again cross the level fields to see their towns? For twenty long years Lenin had been listening for the secrets of this soil. Did he grasp them, were not the days passing by in disappointment, was not all the effort merely the play of aspiration with indignation? And if one day he returned, what would that hour reveal?

Ulianov did not lose himself in this melancholy of infinity. He had come for other reasons to the Tsar's gates. Conceptions and aims did not fade away like the peasants' cottages that he could see dissolving into specks on the endless blue. And once the world had shown this year-long seeker its only possible truth, *nothingness,* he would quickly return home, where conspiracy awaited him.

For there were constantly friends here from Russia. St. Petersburg newspapers arrived here only three days old. He led the Duma group. Deputies read speeches that he had drafted. The craft associations sent delegates. Leninists were at work in various organizations. "Once more," he writes in March 1913, "our hour is striking. Now we are exulting over the victories . . . in the election of the leaders of the new Metal Workers' Union."

In Lenin's cottage, in the village of Poronin, at the foot of the Tatra range, work was going on busily in the autumn of 1913. His propagandists from the homeland were presenting their reports. The Duma group had come. Representatives of local organizations were telling their tale, in primitive, local colouring. He saw how his ship, albeit still without him aboard, was sailing eastwards. Here there was no émigré atmosphere. He was virtually in Russia. Nor had Ulianov any need to write in papers that appeared in Paris or Geneva. He had an organ now in St. Petersburg itself—*Pravda*.

Every day brought its printed message. *Pravda* (*Truth*) was the great victory after the Prague Congress. It became the popular paper of the industrial suburbs of St. Petersburg, and reached in its first year a circulation of thirty thousand. In order to increase its size he had collections organized. He insisted on detailed reports of the moneys received, to enable him to examine their sources, and declared that this was the best evidence of feeling; he wanted to make the acquaintance of the subscriber of every kopek, made note of the groups which contributed most regularly, kept accounts. Was this the same Lenin who had defended the looting by the partisan bands in order to finance his movement?

Through *Pravda* he was able as never before to lead the workers of St. Petersburg. Every moment the paper was being prohibited, coming out again, dummy editors were going into and coming out of prison. A secret organization brought the papers, still damp with printer's ink, to the workshops and the workers' families. In every issue Lenin published letters of the discontented; had them written if none had come in. Every strike slogan found enthusiastic support, and in the working-class suburbs the first barricade was erected.

On July 23, 1914, the French Ambassador at the Court of the Romanovs entered in his diary: "The frequent demonstrations in the industrial quarters of St. Petersburg were repeated to-day. The prefect of police declared to me this evening that the movement has been suppressed and that the resumption of work to-morrow morning is assured."

The mountains of others labours rose up; the scarcely built barricade disappeared before a greater carnage. No one any longer counted the dead.

President Poincaré and his Minister Viviani came to visit the Tsar.

Sazonov, Foreign Minister, recalled that his guest Viviani had only recently resigned from the international party whose Russian members had time and leisure in the fortress of Peter and Paul to compare their ideas with realities. He was keen to show that the Government of Tsar Nicholas had no fear of the standard of rebellion, wanted also to show pleasant little attentions, and so said smilingly to Paléologue, the Ambassador for the Allied Republic: "The Cossacks of the Guards have been chosen as escort for the President . . . splendid, frightful chaps." He continued: "Their uniforms are red. I don't think this colour is entirely hateful to M. Viviani."

The rebellion in the streets of St. Petersburg died away. Lenin's slogans disappeared.

The first Sunday of August 1914 came.

As though in pilgrimage to immortal groves, to a gracious, bountiful god, enormous masses thronged before the Winter Palace. The Tsar no longer, as on a past January day, had them shot down. For those who now came on pilgrimage to him would witness certain death for the laurels of victory, and would have their share of it.

The Emperor appeared on the balcony. Tens of thousands kneeled; patriotic songs burst forth.

In all Europe, on this day, men looked up, as though bewitched, in gratitude at the leaders of the carnage.

THE PRISONERS' ELDER

The attitude of every man, as he learned from the bawl-
ing placards, the headlines in his newspaper, or his excited
neighbour that war had broken out, decided the fate of
continents.   Every hand was clenched in menace against
unknown men and things that the rulers declared to be
eternal enemies; or else it remained motionless as a leaf
when no breath of wind stirs.

Ulianov learned of the event in his Galician smuggler's
den. Quite recently he had written to Gorky: "Was is un-
likely, and for the present we are remaining here. . . ."
At the same time he had prophesied, like all disciples of Karl Marx, that the day of settlement had
to come, and was only in the dark, like the general
staffs themselves, as to the moment when the slaughter
would begin.   "A war between Austria and Russia,"
Lenin had written a few days later, "would be a very useful thing for Revolution" all over eastern Europe. This
also was one of the declarations which for decades the
Socialists had been in the habit of making, as a mildly
effective warning that peace had better be maintained.

In spite of all, he was seized now with horror.

For a space of minutes Lenin, with a small minority
of others in Europe, was dumbfounded.   Then came
moments in which miracles were awaited. Some amazing
event would perhaps come, and cast existing laws on the
dust-heap! Then, when he had recognized the inevitable,
the exile was swimming, like the rest of creation, in the
vast sea of horror, and so was no longer appalled by the
all-conquering night.

As always at the beginning of his struggles with an
immeasurably superior power, Lenin tore himself from
the narrow field of his everyday life.

This fanatic for organization did not mourn over the
destruction of his Party, as after the defeated revolution

of 1905. The ruling power needed only to lift its little finger and the fine web of patient, underground work was torn to pieces. Lenin's congregation could not boast of eleven thousand office-holders, like that of the Germans. But the work of his Party demanded more from each individual member. Out of this readiness for sacrifice, out of the handicap of this political necessity, he constructed, like all the other revolutionary Muscovites, a radiant, exaggerated revolutionary morality. The Russians would have been just as pleased if they had been able to enjoy parliamentary institutions and a free Press.

To Ulianov his country appeared like a police guard-room that was now unchallengeably in control. *The army was not in his eyes the nation under arms, but the strengthened and mobilized police, an extended Okhrana.*

The home authorities had won an easy victory over his Party. But this did not drive him to despair, principally because he realized the connexion between this and the wider events of the time. Lenin realized the turn taken in the life of the world, and possibilities of which no one else dreamed seemed to him to be becoming a certainty.

In the brilliantly spangled heavens of the war Ulianov detected a star of which he was able to calculate the path. He saw the individual men and women of his country, looked through and beyond the bloodstained background across which coming events were already throwing a faint shadow. The World War, with its general staffs, its endless fronts, its stern efforts put forth by opposing communities, had given birth in that Galician village, in Ulianov's brain, to its opposite pole.

It was as though a fly armed itself against the globe to destroy it.

Lenin lived in an idea that took more and more definite shape. He was operating with causes which had not yet come to the surface as army commanders operate from their staff quarters with actual soldiers; he was giving battle armed with accumulated conceptions.

All the theses on which he was now concentrating, Ulianov communicated a few weeks later to ten very astonished friends.

In these August days Lenin remembered his comrades at international congresses. He could still hear the ring of their battle metaphors, the talk of breaches forced, of bastions scaled, all the agitator's heroics of declamation. At the Stuttgart Congress of the Socialists of all countries in 1907, the leader of the Bolsheviks had pressed with Rosa Luxemburg for a formula to commit Socialists to revolution in the event of war. "Lenin told us," writes Zinoviev, "how he had discussed the wording of the resolution with August Bebel. Bebel had agreed in theory with the basic idea, but had demanded great caution in expressing it, to avoid prematurely frightening the geese."

Ulianov wanted to ascertain the effect of the outbreak of war on the comrades of the Red Flag, to ascertain their attitude and their intentions. He believed he could count on them in a general way as friends, as the resolutions at the Congress went some way toward his own attitude. Throughout his life he attached great importance to such documents.

"It is said," writes Lenin, "that resolutions are of all branches of literature the most appallingly tedious. I am myself altogether a fanatic for resolutions."

At bottom this outcast differed from the rebels of the West in that he did not play fast and loose with ideas, but took Socialism more seriously than anyone else.

The exile had not the time to learn details as to the attitude of the Marxist parties.

In these August weeks every good patriot, if he did not discover an enemy airman, must at least deliver some spies up to justice. Some Austrian concerned for the fate of his country was struck by the exercise taken by a stranger along the railway embankment. He denounced the stranger to the authorities, who shared his suspicion, and Ulianov was arrested in the village of Novy Targ, in the neighbourhood of Cracow.

In the village prison he was helped by his old secret, the art of listening to other people, of learning from everyone, of putting off the tight jacket of his own ego. He could become absorbed in his curiosity over the wanderings and dreams of a peasant, even while he was simulating it for his own purposes.

In these first feverish nights of the war Lenin told long tales to the Galician peasants in his cell. And, three years before he entered into the succession of the Romanovs, he was elected—more democratically than later by Russia—by the inmates of the village prison to be the prisoners' elder.

Accompanied by a warder, he could go out to buy tobacco for the prisoners. Most of the peasants had been put in gaol for debt. Painfully, for he had not much knowledge of the Polish language, their chosen representative instructed them as to opportunities of appeal, ordered legal books from Cracow, was able to take up again his neglected career of advocate, until it was interrupted by the friendly intervention of the Austrian Social Democrats.

The Socialists of the Dual Monarchy gave the Vienna Government full particulars about Lenin, assured the Ministers concerned that Ulianov was the Tsar's enemy and accordingly a potential ally, and effected his freedom through arguments as to the accuracy of which the prisoner did not trouble himself.

Lenin took train through enemy country to Switzerland.

FOR THE DEFEAT OF HIS OWN GOVERNMENT

When Ulianov reached Swiss soil he was shut off from his own country by the long line of trenches. There was no longer any connexion possible with political branch establishments in St. Petersburg or Moscow. Nevertheless, he felt further removed from Western Socialism than from the conventicles of the friends who had secretly remained at home in Russia.

He had never much trusted the plaintive tones of the Second International, had believed he could see many vicious elements and many weaklings in its ranks. Shortly before 1914 its leaders had been trying to bring about a reconciliation between Mensheviks and Bolsheviks. Vandervelde had come to St. Petersburg on this mission. August Bebel, too, had for years been trying to bring unity among the Russian Socialists. Lenin had seen in this initiative only an intrigue of opportunism, and had rejected all outside intervention.

Now, however, Helvetia's guest lit up all the fires of rage against the International. For him European Socialism was a yet more insatiable Hell than the war. "The International," he said, "is nothing but a union for the international support of national Chauvinism."

The downfall of Socialism was so great in his eyes that he could see recovery only in the complete rejection of its existing forms.

He now transferred the bitter intransigence of twenty years of Russian group controversies to that with the International. Lenin had no further cares for the organization in Russia, and he thus found a new field of work here.

This man felt that now it would be for complicated Continental inter-reactions to pluck the Tsar's garland to pieces, and that supporters in St. Petersburg and Moscow had become of secondary importance; accordingly he must have an international instrument if he was to be able to do anything, even on the tiniest scale.

In Russia the church-bells of his dogmatic theses, by which he sought to drown all other voices of rebellion, were, at any rate, echoed by the actual history of the towns and villages.

There was, it is true, even in the country of the

Romanovs a class of the population which—if no one knew into what precise drawer it should theoretically be put—could be·called "petty bourgeois." "With us, however," writes Rabinovitch, "there had been no development of the middle class proper, which in western Europe forms a link between social classes and plays an important part in the economic and political life of the State. . . . It is easy to understand that in a country with so insignificant a middle class the social contrasts are inevitably very acute, and economic crises are bound to take very extreme forms."

Lenin's anathema against rebels at home who were not satisfied with his theory was *partly* in harmony with these circumstances. But his condemnation and lamentation over European Socialism, in whose ranks particular attention was paid to the middle class, was the cry of the wounded piety of his temperament, and had, as sentiment always does have, more of an emotional than a logical basis.

In the forum of the Second International—which never really extended beyond the borders of western Europe, although, according to statistics which imparted a glow of satisfaction when read, its membership numbered twenty-five millions—he remained a stranger. Here Ulianov was what he never became in Russian affairs, even if he stayed many years abroad—an émigré. Yet his earnest, restrained and yet deeply emotional call for internationality represented a national need of Russians fighting against oppression at home—a need expressed sometimes despairingly, sometimes in whispers, sometimes at enormous and eloquent length. Thus the *first* Bolshevist manifesto against the war, as early as September 1914, read as follows:

"If anything is calculated under certain circumstances to delay the collapse of Tsarism, it is precisely the present war, which has placed the money-bags of the British, French and Russian bourgeoisie at the service of the reactionary aims of Tsarism. . . . If anything can render yet harder the revolutionary struggle of the Russian working class against Tsarism, it is notably the attitude of the leaders of the German and Austrian Social Democrats, whom the Chauvinist Press in Russia is never tired of holding up to us as patterns."

For Lenin the liberation of his country was dependent on the German, French and British Socialists turning the sword in chastisement on their own imperialists.

Exile did not bring Lenin into the general uprooted condition. It did not upset the balance of his intellectual powers; on the contrary, it provided ideas which two years later found realization in mass action. He was not tied to any office, any dignity, any mandate, was untouched by the mood of the hour, the attitude of the world about him, the passing words of neighbours; he was free from all the countless influences that bear on human activities in the ordinary political and apolitical arenas of existence.

And, in truth, when the Ministers appeared amid the pomp and circumstance of Parliament and turned the full glare of their own rectitude on the sins of enemy colleagues, no miracle happened. The elected of the people heard the blare of enemy fanfares, shouted for messages of victory, raised their hands in solemn oath or in approval, spoke to the people that had elected them: "Not one life is needlessly sacrificed."

In the chorus of the parliamentary warriors the Socialists sang the national hymns with the rest.

Until then the rebels had belonged to one wide supernational community; Ulianov with them. But in those August days they discovered other laws. They held that Socialism itself demanded that they should no longer listen to its marching songs, but hasten to the wan wastes of the battle-front to measure themselves against the enemies of their nation. Not that they were content to abandon Theory. Had they done that, no one would any longer have been able to distinguish them from the bourgeois. Consequently the rebels managed to see in process in the world around them not the victory of imperialism, but of Socialism. The internationalists of France declared that this was a new edition of the campaigns of the French Revolution, held that the mere marching in ragged service trousers made them *sans-culottes*. The Germans saw in the profitable rationalization of trade and industry for the purposes of the war not war-time capitalism, but war-time Socialism, held that Germany was now the self-sufficing commercial unit of Fichte, given added vitality by a Hegelian extension of the attributes of the State. On the introduction of the grain monopoly a man of the extreme Left characterized this measure as "the greatest practical triumph which Socialism" had "hitherto won over capitalism." Nor did the Russians silently fold their arms; they said the same sort of thing. Plekhanov, who every day for some decades past had dusted his Marx, wrote: "The brigands are at the gate of my country, ready for robbery and murder." To the German Socialists, whose thoughts were even as his, save for a different national colour, he cried, "Oh, shame! oh, shame! oh, shame!" Vera Sassulitch, once a terrorist, wept in raptures over moonlight on the Kremlin, spoke of the menaced field and meadow and forest of her homeland.

Other Socialists lectured on slightly different lines. The war had got to be carried on; there was no reason for concern at the sound of the death-rattle of the proletarian in the other trenches; this unpleasant circumstance did not exclude the possibility of friendship later on. Soon there would be renewed fraternal embraces, and then the registered office of the International, which was closed for a short time only, would re-open.

Each held in his hands the same Table of Commandments, but read from it something different.

Lenin, nevertheless, thought with Saint Augustine: "Though they all betoken themselves with the token of

the Cross of Christ, though all say the Amen and sing the
Hallelujah, though all be baptized, enter the churches,
build basilicas—the children of God are in no wise different from the children of the devil, save only through
Charity."

*But charity meant for him civil war against war, the
duty of working for the defeat of one's own country first
and foremost.*

At the point where great historic processes seem to end,
where the roads of change abruptly stop, where on the
plain of conflicting movements men are being mowed
down, Ulianov sought their deliverance through the
principle which was the most drastic of all, through
Revolution. His closest friends urged that the idea was
impracticable; they spoke of sound common sense. He
laughed at them. Sound common sense! A preposterous
tribunal!

Those who raise their standard at the head of an army
inwardly fear the cloud-capped Colossus of the power of
the multitude whom they command. Lenin believed
that he heard this fear of theirs, that he saw the possibility
of the defeat of all of them.

Ulianov wrote in a modest sheet that he was once more
editing in exile, as ten and twenty years before: "A
Revolution during war is civil war. But, in the first
place, conversion of the Government's war into civil war
is made easier by the military failures (the 'defeat') of
the Government; and, in the second place, it is in point
of fact impossible to work for such a conversion without
thereby bringing defeat nearer. . . . Without such action
millions of words of out-and-out revolutionism are worth
less than a cracked centime. . . . The class struggle is
impossible without injury to one's 'own' bourgeoisie and
one's 'own' Government. And injury to one's own Government in war time is high treason."

This supreme traitor to his country, whom the courts of
any belligerent State would have condemned to death,

was filled with a deep feeling of responsibility. This feeling dictated to Lenin—who opened the newspaper every morning in tense concern and read with joy of any defeat of the Russian armies—a national programme, through which to show to the various peoples of his country that there was a Party in Moscow which was against their oppression.

When Russia later fell apart, when her nations took up arms against the central power, he was able to show his past programme, and so prevent their secession. Ulianov had a national defence policy of his own which he championed against the official policy. In an article on "The National Pride of the Great Russians" he wrote:

"It is not fitting that we representatives of the ruling nation in the extreme east of Europe and in a great part of Asia should forget the enormous importance of the question of nationalities. . . . We are filled with a feeling of national pride; for the Great Russian nation has itself produced a revolutionary class, has itself demonstrated its ability to show humanity a great example in the struggle for freedom and Socialism, and not merely great pogroms, great rows of gallows, great torture-chambers, great epidemics of starvation, and a great deal of sycophancy towards 'popes,' Tsars, landowners and capitalists. We are filled with national pride, and for that reason we particularly hate our slavish past (in which landowners and nobles led the peasants to the shambles in order to strangle Hungary, Poland, Persia and China). . . . No one is to blame for being born a slave, but a slave who himself finds justification for slavery . . . (for instance, describes the throttling of Poland, Ukraine, etc., as 'national defence') is a loathsome creature."

Here Lenin was thinking particularly of Plekhanov. He considered that his former Teacher, who was now friend, now opponent, was putting difficulties, through Chauvinist *obiter dicta,* in the way of "the fraternization of all the peoples of Russia." Whole portfolios of such portrait-sketches were passed round from one little nest of émigrés to another. There were few Socialists who were not, in Lenin's eyes, coming out all over in bourgeois pimples.

He was living again in the void of his customary solitude, only more certain than ever that a new harvest would soon reveal that he spoke truly.

"At this time," writes Zinoviev, who usually had a good word to say for the way the Communists stuck to one another, "there were certainly not a dozen men in the whole world who would have believed in him. Even in our own Party there were none."

Accordingly Lenin took refuge with the younger generation.

This most patient of men shrank no more from the small scale of the immediate surroundings on which he now exerted his influence, than from the great task of his life.

A few young people of Socialistic tendency were living near him in the shadow of their discontent, turning up their noses at this world as at a bad cup of coffee. On the benches of this kindergarten there sat at most fifteen to twenty young people. They were waiting for the World Revolution with the same impatience as for their twenty-first birthdays. Most of them belonged to the Swiss youth movement. Others had come, with very doubtful passports, from other countries. Only after the outbreak of war had they celebrated, amid much noise and rejoicing, their spiritual birth; now they were athirst for anything in the way of revolution. Often Lenin talked to them the whole day long. He took them seriously, and so, without meaning it, flattered their youthful vanity.

The exile had no eyes for the lack of numbers or importance in his audience. This man who, later, would not have hesitated, if the civil war had demanded it, to instruct the people, who had been tortured since 1914 by all the rulers of the world, for the benefit of their

LENIN IN A VILLAGE CROWD

BEGINNING OF STRIKE IN ST. PETERSBURG

souls in some new chemical method of extermination of their fellows, had nevertheless a high estimation of the moral significance of the individual. To him no one was unimportant. Everyone, in his view, had many potentialities. Perhaps it was his own total lack of vanity which accounted for this belief. "One must begin somewhere," thought Ulianov: "I cannot choose the men and women whom I am to instruct, and so I begin with the most willing." These young people seemed to him like the first living beings encountered after crossing a desert. In this spirit, twenty years before, he must have talked to his audiences in the Militant Unions, in this same spirit with the Galician peasants in his cell, and, later, with his loyal subjects as Dictator.

It was not at all in the spirit of the old scene in which the Emperor Napoleon asked his grenadier at the bivouac fire for a pinch of snuff. For it was evident how Lenin himself suffered, how the thought of the tortured faces of the soldiers fighting for ends that were not theirs literally choked him; and yet he did not lose heart, but appealed to every man he met—*"You and I must change it all."* Lenin taught by polemic, pointed out at once the smallest distinction, directed his anathemas not against the Tsar and the official Socialism, but against those friends, the nearest to his own way of thinking, who failed to swear in the identical formula of his own choice. He sought members for his own group, even when it consisted only of himself, his wife Krupskaya, and their two shadows.

One of his friends was solemnly assured by Ulianov that he had a good prospect of making up the number of his youthful adherents in Zurich to six!

When these young people summoned an international conference, Lenin led from a neighbouring café his affiliated group of boys, and built up around every word of his thesis mountains of opposition.

After long effort he at last found once more a Russian

audience. There was a little break in the silence. Now and then a sound penetrated from home. But the days of war died slowly, taking many men with them.

He succeeded in getting together a conference of Bolshevik émigrés. In March 1915 about a dozen friends had joined with him in solemnly preparing for the coming collapse. He had written down a plan of action. Quietly he now read to his comrades the contents of a sheet of paper which was in a few months to become the programme of a catastrophic, mad-seeming rush into the limitless unknown: ". . . The Social framework of the next Revolution in Russia can be nothing but the revolutionary-democratic Dictatorship of the proletariat and the peasantry. . . . Our answer to the question what the Party of the proletariat would do if the Revolution brought them to the helm during the present war, is this: We should offer peace to all the belligerents. . . . There is no doubt that a victory in Russia . . . would furnish exceptionally favourable conditions for the spread of revolution both in Asia and in Europe. . . ."

He wrote this on *October 13, 1915*. No news agency telegraphed it. Correspondents from all the world were in search of news, but they did not read these lines. And yet Ulianov was destined to leave the scene of his present obscurity and to broadcast these pious formulæ in every language to every people of the five continents.

ZURICH, ZIMMERWALD AND KIENTHAL

There fought in Zurich, Berne and Geneva one mark for every German soldier, one franc for every French one. The money did not follow a circuitous career as in the home countries, did not first enter the munition factories, and then, turned into shell, vanish into thin air; nor did it bring any casualties, except perhaps some little damage to souls. It may be that the belligerents were keen to convince themselves that they were fighting for justice, and so spent a great deal of money in order to prove to the neutrals that their cause was the fifth Evangel. Their explanations showed that French *civilisation* and German *Kultur* had agreed on an international terminology. Each was anxious to make the same points. If the Entente were fighting for the liberation of the small nations, the Dual Alliance was fighting for the liberation of the very smallest ones—an even more moral proceeding.

Newspapers and printed propaganda generally were pabulum suited to the multitude. Very few individuals were bought, and even these not always with money. For gold, that inoffensive metal on which so much abuse is lavished, seems fated to arouse prejudice. Many people think it permissible to be convinced by the alluring charms of theoretical arguments, but not by the passing of legal tender. Their scruples had of course to be respected. If the wooed was a believer in the Pope, the French wooer assured him that "my country is essentially Catholic"; the German that "in mine the Catholic Centre Party is supreme." If the convincee was a Socialist he heard from one side, "We are the nation of the great Revolution," and from the other, like a rival bidder at an auction, "We have the biggest health insurance organization and the most hygienic hearses."

The diplomatic organs of the belligerents lost their bureaucratic stiffness, became adventurous, romantic, brightly inventive, prodigal. Every street-corner had ears, hands stealthily made entries in note-books, every sound from abroad was picked up and relayed. The neutral countries were the only window overlooking enemy territory. Not a square millimetre of window space remained unoccupied.

The citizens of Helvetia usually understand three languages, cook with a great deal of butter, attain an advanced age, and are proud of their countryman, the anarchist William Tell. Most of them were peacefully minded men. But in order not to leave in the lurch belligerents who, after all, were human beings, they provided them with a certain amount of war material. Lest any of their neighbours should feel injured, they made these supplies to all of them in secret. This method of export did not cheapen the goods.

On the edge of this world there lived the Russian émigrés. The Muscovites did not produce a Swiss housing shortage. They were content with the most meagre accommodation, but, as picturesque foreigners, lent added life to the café tables. The old groups cheerfully cursed one another with all the old vigour. These possessors of rival certainties had no bombs, and hence were unable to murder one another. But the glances which they exchanged in the narrow space of the common coffee-room were much more malignant than those between the soldiers in the trenches, whose thoughts were less of victory than of their next leave.

Lenin lived like the rest, careless of appearances, amid the poverty that had become his normal condition. He had lodgings in the Spiegelgasse in Zurich, in a house built by a merchant in the sixteenth century. It was impossible to open the windows of the narrow, long-looking room in the day-time, as the court was occupied by a sausage factory which loaded the air with pestilential smells. A wooden table, two chairs, two beds and a sewing-machine furnished the room.

The landlady might have called her apartments "Poverty Hotel." The lodgers collected in the kitchen. There, as the cooking of a very small bit of meat went on, political discussion ran riot. An Austrian barnstormer, the wife of a German baker, an out-of-work Italian had the other rooms. One day, at the gas stove, the landlady cried out: "The soldiers ought to turn their weapons against their own Governments!" Hearing this political *vœu* from his hostess, so entirely in harmony with his own philosophy and that of his group, Ulianov made up his mind that he could be happy here. "We might," writes his wife Krupskaya, "have got a much better room for the same money, but we thought very highly of our hosts."

Every morning, before Ulianov went to the library, at a little before nine, he was visited by a Bolshevik who, though a sausage cost only fifteen *Rappen* [1] in the university canteen, had lost his reason through starvation. His other friends, though they did not lose their reason, were scarcely more pampered. When they were going to the reading-rooms they had first to do a great deal of polishing up, for often the attendants refused to admit them because of their raggedness. Ulianov still had a decent coat and a pair of sound shoes, and was therefore able to finish his book *Imperialism as the Latest Stage of Capitalism*.

The bitter cup of war, from which everyone now had to drink, was not, in his view, formed by the diabolical mania of the rulers, but was cast in the crucible of unalterable laws.

He calculated that the wealth of the four richest countries in securities aggregated 479,000 million gold francs. Britain, the United States, France and Germany together owned "over 80 per cent. of the international financial capital. Almost the whole of the rest of the world plays, in one form or another, the part of debtor or payer of tribute to these international bankers of States, these four 'pillars' of international High Finance. . . ."

Proceeding from this fact, Ulianov set out to show that the special character of this war was due to the existing phase of imperialism.

Everything, in his view, resolved itself into the struggle for opportunities for the export of capital, "which," he declares, "first began to assume gigantic dimensions at the

[1] Three cents.

beginning of the twentieth century. . . . How solid a
basis for the imperialist oppression and exploitation of
most of the nations and countries of the world through
the . . . parasitism of a handful of the wealthiest
States! . . ."

He attacked the Socialists who held that the barque of
war was drifting along in darkness without purpose or
necessity; that at the dawn of a day of reason it would
come to rest for ever in the port of the longed-for peace.
"No," he writes, "the capitalists have . . . every reason
to wage war; they must, in fact, wage war if they want to
keep capitalism going."

The Great Powers live at the expense of Colonies. The
civilized world prospers on the life-blood of Asia and
Africa, and the work of the millions of human beings that
are the population of oppressed nations. Every rock and
every footpath of backward countries becomes a field for
chase and conquest. The rulers of the West have discovered how to win over large sections of the population of their own countries by bribery; with their colossal
resources they have been able to train up an aristocracy
of labour and to drink with it from well-filled beakers
the toast, "Perish the thought of Revolution!"

"The privileged section of the proletariat of the imperialist Great Powers," he writes, "lives partly at the expense of the hundred-million masses of the uncivilized
peoples." This, in Ulianov's view, was why many proletarians found a good word to say for war, why the rulers
were able to find defenders in their bourgeois Labour
Parties.

Lenin, however, would not have been able even to
induce those Socialists who in his belief were avoiding
the groves of the pro-war bourgeoisie to come together
for the discussions that he wanted of present or coming
days. The tabernacle of his faith was scarcely visible;
clouds of wrath blotted it out. In spite of all his stress
on internationality, his language sounded too Muscovite.

In this situation there appeared on the scene a man who, without intending it, was to build for Lenin the supernational platform from which the solitary watcher was able to send out Bolshevist signals.

Lenin no longer had the power to unite, sought for the tiniest groups, was blind to the trend of European tendencies in Socialism. Had he been different, he would perhaps never have attained his goal.

The pacifist seeker in the Socialist camp was Robert Grimm, a Swiss. He was not, like Ulianov, aiming at transforming the world, but he felt that the psychological moment had arrived for a common front for all the Internationalists who did not rest their hope of world salvation on the strategy of their countries' general staffs.

At the beginning of September 1915 there assembled in Berne, welcomed with the necessary unobtrusiveness, the long and eagerly awaited representatives of the Socialist minorities. As in the Swiss capital the agents of all the Legations were distinguished by an insatiable interest in other people's affairs, the members of the Congress went on to the village, hidden away in the mountains, of ZIMMERWALD.

In the small saloon of a little inn there sat down thirty men and women, all that remained of an historic promise that once, in pride of phrase, had covered up with words the slums of the great towns, where gaunt rows of tenements take all of life and leave nothing but the perfection of wretchedness. Now the little room was filled with memories of scenes of the past, of great international congress demonstrations, of symbolic fraternization. There had been times when supporters of the movement had been deeply moved at songs of happy promise; now they were dying to other tunes.

Man has just as little control of destiny-moulding events as of his own grovelling existence. Reason serves him only for the making of technical necessaries, for giving shape to matter, for the production of rails, skyscrapers,

Ersatz.[1] When he has done that, and desires to be master
of the material he has shaped, of economic causes and
processes—they mock at him. It seems as if reason makes
men its playthings. Organizations that have become historic grip the imagination of the smallest brain; the
startled herd streams out of forgotten villages, from every
workshop, every office. Millions are easily moved, easily
as the wind blows the dust.

This condition is called by Marxists "revolt of the
forces of production." Their doctrine teaches that a day
will come when these forces will no longer control humanity, but humanity will control these forces.

Up to now few had been able to withstand this taking-
charge of the forces of production. The elect who met in
Zimmerwald formed the human element in the coming
changes. Their meeting-room is a necessary part of a
complete picture of the war; it was its complementary
colour. The thirty could do no more than sign a manifesto, declare to the nations that this war was not the
Zimmerwaldians' war. "Rag after rag," ran their appeal,
"is falling from the veils that concealed the meaning of
this world disaster."

Zimmerwald was only the starting-point of a process,
no power as yet. But it was to become one. Ideas of
peace now had a shepherd's fire in the Alps. The appeal
rang out, too, in a stillness; for months nothing of its
sort had any longer been in the papers. For many it was
a *Wiedersehen* for which they had almost ceased to hope.

Amid this Socialist minority Lenin was the nucleus of
a yet tinier fraction.

He felt in Zimmerwald neither relief nor disappointment, found himself in the old prison of his customary
isolation. Even the peace manifesto of which he was a
signatory contained in his eyes plenty of false doctrine.

The majority were unwilling to break with the old
International; wanted only to hoist again its neglected

[1] Cheap substitutes for anything.

sails, to praise its tradition. Ulianov was for cutting
loose entirely from the parties of national defence; for
burying even those organizations which showed faint signs
of revolutionary life, and for founding the new, the *Third
International*.

Such formulæ as Trotzky's ". . . true national self-
defence consists in the struggle for peace . . ." seemed
to him mere sermonizing.

". . . Conscientious objection, anti-war strike, and so
on," he writes, "are just stupidities, pitiful and poor-
spirited dreams of unarmed struggle against the armed
bourgeoisie, of the ending of capitalism without a desperate civil war or a series of wars. . . . Away with the
parsonical, sentimental, absurd dreaming about 'peace
at any price.'"

"But to assume," writes this irreducible oppositionist
in his theses, "that the imperialist war will end in a
democratic peace . . . is to mislead the masses by concealing from them the essential truth that a democratic
peace is impossible without a series of revolutions."

The war-weariness of the soldiers, who longed for any
semblance of rest—a quiet garden, a white table-cloth,
the arms of their girls—was in Lenin's eyes a danger.
That would have meant that the dance of the unleashed
furies had been in vain. This longing of men must be
made use of, but the dreams of their desire must be led
into the vats of Revolution. This war must be overwhelmed, taken by assault, but that same attack must also
mark the beginning of world-insurrection.

At the beginning of the war, in the Galician village, he
had for a moment been appalled; then it came to him that
this would be the ultimate funeral procession of imperialism. If all the men who, after a last convulsion, lay
stiffly on the earth had died for the Kingdom of Socialism,
and not as conscript defenders of the export of capital,
Lenin would have sung their praises in death with more
real enthusiasm than all the army chaplains put together.

He loved the sword that the prophet of one faith takes over from the servant of another. Zwingli's statue in Zurich, with weapon in one hand and the Book of the Word in the other, was the monument he would have liked for himself.

Revolution and Pacifism were incompatible with one another.

If he saw anything inspiring in the history of the bourgeoisie, it was only in its insurrectionary courage of days long past; in the destruction of the might of Spain by Dutch merchants, in the bloody scaffold on which England's king died, in the Terror of French revolutionary bayonets. He loved the battles, turned by legend into epics of heroes, which Judæa, Dacia, Spain, Gaul, Germania, Britain, waged against the much more prudent and yet not eternal Rome.

To him Pacifism seemed, not only the negation of Revolution, but of class consciousness and so of national well-being.

Nations must be prepared to fight. ". . . Socialism," he writes in his theses, "cannot reject in principle wars carried on in the interest of the majority of the population. By annexations we understand merely the taking possession of a country against the will of its inhabitants; in other words, the idea of annexation is intimately bound up with that of the right of self-determination of a nation. . . . Every true Socialist is . . . bound to demand immediately and unconditionally the liberation and independence of colonies and of peoples which are suffering oppression at the hands of their own country."

He attacked Rosa Luxemburg's denial of the possibility of national wars, said to her: ". . . If the Great Powers are thoroughly exhausted by this war, or if the Revolution is victorious in Russia, national wars, even successful ones, are entirely possible . . . they are even inevitable, and both progressive and revolutionary in character."

Ulianov was unable to blind himself to the fact of the

existence of the line of trenches thrown, by the chance of battle, across Europe; he was unable to take comfort in the Commandment, "Thou shalt not kill." He was just as furious as Nicholas II with people who applied these words as a panacea for the universal torture. He ordered his supporters to take their places in the imperialist armies. Dread of the slime of the trenches seemed to him as "immoral" as to any sergeant-major in the lines.

"Be in the fight in order to fight against it, to work for defeat," was his slogan.

The other Zimmerwaldian Socialists, even if they agreed with Ulianov, refrained from saying so in and out of season. The forces against them were too strong for them to advertise the qualities of their own weapons—when they had none.

In the eight months between Zimmerwald and the next conference, at Kienthal, Lenin had been able to do a good deal of unostentatious work. The Kienthal manifesto already showed clear traces of his influence.

Zimmerwald and Kienthal soon met in St. Petersburg, and there definitely split up. And the Left Wing of the two Swiss villages was destined to bombard the Right of the same Congresses from armoured cruisers and to prohabit their activities on Russian soil in the name of new principles which were remarkably like the old ones.

THE BOLSHEVIKS IN THE DUMA AND THE WAR COMMITTEES

In the ranks of those who rejoice in the gaudy trappings of war, the poor—the living dust of the factories and the living clods of the fields—are pleased to be allowed to die on an equal footing with the rich.

Here there rules the democracy of shared experience. In the Greece of the ancients the laws which prohibited slaves from going out to war were felt by these workers as a reproach and disgrace. In this same spirit the Mayor of the Russian town of Orenburg had declared, amid the enthusiastic approval of the proletarians around him, that "if the workers are prevented from defending their country, their . . . might will tear down . . . every obstacle . . . they will fulfil their mission."

Opposition to this mass emotion has not much more than symbolic, propagandist significance. Those who seriously undertake it are doomed to lose caste utterly. They are like doctors who have to work during an epidemic among a superstitious population: the helpers are killed. A disturbance of unanimity by the side of a single grave is distressing; how much more so when millions are marching under orders to their death! The man who then strikes a discordant note is the most contemptible of spoil-sports.

Lenin's five Deputies in the Duma (one had been unmasked as a Government agent and had had to resign from the group) had more regard for their far-away Master's smile of satisfaction than for an approving nod from the Prime Minister. In passionate hatred of Tsarism, they alone among the Parliamentary groups of all the world shouted for peace.

The official Russian news agency telegraphed to the whole world, and to the overjoyed leader in Berne: "In October news reached the Government that a conference of a new secret organization was being planned, to discuss measures aimed . . . at the destruction of the Russian State. On November 4 the police ascertained that the conference in question was sitting in a house in Viborg Avenue, twelve versts from St. Petersburg. A detachment of police entered the premises and found there eleven persons, including, as subsequently transpired, five Deputies in the Duma, MM. Petrovsky, Badayev, Muranov, Samoilov and Shagov. . . ."

When the police raid occurred, the meeting was just engaged in reading a Decalogue which their judges were not alone in finding far from devotional or edifying: smuggled theses of Lenin's on the duty of working for defeat. The arrested Deputies declared to the bench that they did not entirely share the views there expounded. Their counsel, Kerensky, who was subsequently to become Dictator, tried to save his clients' lives; he said: "Never have the defendants dreamed of provoking a Revolution during the war. Never have they desired the defeat of our army. Never have they reached out over the heads of those who are dying for their country, to shake hands with the enemy."

The defendant Petrovsky, however, declared that this programme speech from abroad was in general agreement with the views of comrades in Russia. In other ways, too, the men in the dock failed to display a becoming penitence. The note-book of one Deputy was able to prove much more than either the prosecutor or the brilliant defending counsel. It contained minutes of secret conferences with munition workers and soldiers—proof positive of the existence of machinations to destroy the State.

In his Swiss newspaper, Lenin administered a gentle rebuke to his disciples, declared that the defendants' evasions in the matter of national defence were due solely to fear of the court-martial, and held that the prosecution had shown "that the vanguard of the revolutionary Social Democracy of Russia is still inadequately prepared for legal persecution." This said, he proceeded enthusiastically: ". . . At a time when nearly all the 'Socialist' delegates of Europe have come out as toadies of the Chauvinists . . . there has proved to be in Russia a workers' party whose delegates are not . . . distinguished for their association with bourgeois and cultured *salons,* or by the business acumen of 'European' lawyers and Parliamentarians, but in the fulfilment of the modest, inconspicuous, hard, thankless and dangerous functions of illegal propagandists and organizers . . . the line they have taken will leave its mark on the history of the world. . . ."

The five Deputies lost their seats in the Duma and were exiled for life to Siberia.

The arrest of their Deputies did more for the Bolsheviks than an editorial staff and a mass of pamphlets could possibly have done; the condemnation of the Five did not mark the end of the Party, but was a stroke of good fortune for it.

Ulianov's group had only a small sheet, appearing at irregular intervals, published in far-away Saratov.

The wartime censorship saw every line, left not the smallest loophole. Lenin's supporters, unlike the Mensheviks, were unable to publish a line in statement of their views, however cautiously formulated. But the case in court had, through the announcement of the sentences inflicted, been evidence of their existence, had been a manifesto circulated by the Tsar's Government at the cost of the State. Wherever workers were gathered together to listen to a patriotic Menshevist address, a Bolshevik would get up and refer to the Five. The exiles had no opportunity of reply; accordingly, in the eyes of the proletarian public they were always right. The administration of justice had thus simplified debate in Socialist circles, influenced them, given the extreme Left a very acceptable certificate of their formidableness.

No section found this sentence of exile more awkward than the Liberal bourgeoisie.

It recognized that without the confidence of the factories, without the goodwill of the workers who cast the guns or, standing in long rows in ominous silence, produced ammunition components, the war could not be carried on at all, much less won.

Trade and industry were languishing. The noise of the machinery was growing constantly fainter, more muffled, more laboured. The production of gold, copper, pig iron, cast iron, steel and foundry coke was falling. The

Tsar's bureaucracy, to which the very idea of urgency was foreign, went on still in its Asiatic, patriarchal habits, irregular, unpunctual, idly romantic and careless, was incapable of the effort of organization required by the war, understood nothing of modern technical methods, carried on against the enemy armies a peasants' war— pitchforks and horses against guns and tanks.

To every three thousand rounds fired against them the Russians could only reply with a hundred and fifty. To equip the regiments at the front, a million and a half rifles should have been produced every month; only fifty thousand were being supplied. The railway engines ran as slowly as draught oxen and choked up the stations; freight trains were either overloaded or standing empty. Behind the lines there was no attempt at training the hundreds of thousands of recruits.

The *mujik* was only half a soldier, only a recruit because he was mortal. One third of the strength had no rifles. "These unfortunates," said General Belayev of the regiments at the front, "wait patiently under the rain of shrapnel for the comrades next them to fall, so that they may take over their rifles."

Blinded by the sun and the white no-man's-land, with no means of self-protection, there came to their end in the Carpathians, under the fire of the enemy guns, in six minutes, without themselves firing a single shot, eleven thousand men.

The parties of the propertied classes, the Octobrists, Progressists and Cadets, held a joint meeting in St. Petersburg and resolved to found War Committees. Prince Lvov, in a speech at a joint congress of Zemstvos (County Councils) and municipal associations, summarized their aims thus: ". . . All Russia must become one great military organization, an immense arsenal."

In the capital there was set up a Supreme War Committee, under whose leadership the provincial committees were to function.

The most competent among the army officers supported this initiative, realizing how the administration was crippling the troops in the field. A central Advisory Council was appointed, consisting of four generals, four Deputies in the Duma, and four representatives of the heavy industries with the Minister of War in the chair.

The industrial magnates, keen to win their war, agitated, shouted that the country was going under, hoped to revive Russia; all the resources of society were to be enlisted as after a catastrophe of nature. At the same time, however, the committees formed islands of political activity. It was possible to speak in them without fear of the police. It was a first step to a Constitution, perhaps the kernel of a coming Government, if Tsarism in its incompetence continued to strangle the nation. Here there began a conspiracy with the tacit approval or secret support of the military, a conspiracy for victory at the front.

Ministers, governors, officials high, medium and low, now opened battle against this politico-industrial association for arming the combatant forces. The bureaucracy, incapable of administering the country, showed its capacity for sullen resistance to these sole sources of the country's energy. The Court opened its subterranean canals, poured forth abuse of these centres of national resistance. The consecrated circle of the Romanovs felt that they could hear the footsteps of the evilly disposed; the Tsaritsa quivered in pious horror of the Duma. Her friend Rasputin, who knew how to unclothe in less than a minute every timid petitioner waiting in his antechamber to present her case, believed that he had set eyes on Antichrist.

But the British and French Ambassadors gave their support to the Industrial Committees. The Ambassadors' palaces were fortresses covering the Cadets' position. Sir George Buchanan, the British Ambassador, M. Paléologue, the representative of the Third Republic, became the spokesmen of the bourgeois parties with the Tsar. They urged Nicholas II to give the Duma the opportunity to get to work, bought up the newspapers with the biggest circulation, were advisers and surreptitious Mæcenases of the Liberals.

Could not the forces that the country had once gathered up against Tsarism, the floods of 1905, now be poured out against Germany? was asked by the London and Paris Socialists of their Governments.   Everything else had been tried since 1914, and now this ought to be seen to.

In company with the French Prime Minister, Viviani, there came his Socialist colleague, Albert Thomas, Minister of Munitions, to St. Petersburg.   Thomas belonged to the same international party as Lenin.   The two had often taken the same oaths at international congresses.   Now Ulianov sent his biblical curse to accompany Thomas on his way.

"Albert Thomas," wrote the French Ambassador at the Court of the Romanovs in his diary, "is in cheerful mood, beaming, highly amused at the idea of meeting the Tsar. 'Well, old Thomas,' he cries, 'so you are to come face to face with his Majesty the Tsar, Autocrat of all the Russias!'"

The captains of industry hurried to meet and receive this officially accredited revolutionary.   He must inspect the factories.   The vice-president of the Industrial War Committee said to the Ambassador: "My friends and I are very anxious that M. Albert Thomas should attend one of our sittings.   He would certainly have most valuable things to tell us, which we could then circularize to all our factories."

"At one moment," writes Paléologue, "I saw Albert Thomas in conversation with Stürmer.[1]   I came up to them and listened.

" 'Your factories are not getting enough done,' said

---

[1] The Russian Premier.

Albert Thomas, 'you could produce ten times as much. You should militarize your workers.'

" 'Militarize our workers!' cried Stürmer. 'But we should have the whole of the Duma up in arms against us.' "

France not only sold munitions to Nicholas II, but lent him her tame Socialists. The Third Republic, whose civilian war administration made a point of studying the psychology of the lower orders, knew the necessity of willing work for the front. Western Europe's Internationalists, through their organization, enabled the masses to steel themselves to the idea of a long-continued universal struggle.

Russia, with her backward industrial organization, was not only unable to supply guns, but equally unable to supply incentive and enthusiasm. The organization for influencing the masses worked as badly as the railways. The pale victims heard only the blessing of the Metropolitan and the interested clamour for Constantinople. This was not enough to make attractive the long trenches of the mass slaughter.

A leader of the munitions congresses said in a big public speech:

"Certainly the workers are not less patriotic than we. But they are left without the encouragement, the cheerful conditions, the resolution that make muscle more effective."

Thomas was to help Gutchkov, the industrialist and leader of the munitions campaign, and to put spirit into the Russian workers.

But the proletarians of Tsardom were forbidden any sort of association or grouping, any Party. Nowhere were they organized. The military organization had no opportunity of support through such channels.

Gutchkov remembered, however, the health insurance committees, the only workers' organization in the country, and invited them to send representatives to the War

Committee. The Insurance Council for St. Petersburg replied that it had no competence in these questions. Now, for the first time since 1905, there were to be elections in the works. An appeal to the workers read: "We shall only be able to conquer the enemy, who is aiming at hegemony over the whole world and at imposing on the Russian people the yoke of ignominious dependence, if we are able to set up against him a like union of social forces and of technical equipment."

The slogans of this campaign put life into the nearly extinguished fire of proletarian effort. The eloquence of the industrialists in their concern for their country succeeded in giving direction to the underground, trepidant movement that still stirred in little rooms which, for all their smallness, were accessible to a multitude.

Lenin sent from Zurich the message: "Take part in the election, but do not join the committees; take part in it for the opportunity to pronounce a resounding 'no' against the war."

The Bolsheviks of St. Petersburg were in opposition to the Mensheviks and Social Revolutionaries, who were inclined to work in the committees. They said that these two proletarian parties were trying to square the circle in attempting to connect up the defence of the country, in an imperialist war of coalitions which stretched right across Europe and Asia, with revolutionary struggles in Russia.

Ulianov's groups received majorities in St. Petersburg. Pretexts were found, however, for invalidating the election; at a fresh election the friends of the munitions committee, Lenin's enemies, won the victory. In Moscow the election was boycotted.

The workers, however, in this political gunmaking campaign did not hurrah before the war torches, as Ulianov feared that they would, but used the opportunity to speak their minds, and started a general agitation. The police reported to Stürmer, the Prime Minister, giving a detailed account of the campaign; they declared that the proletarian delegates had no interest at all in national defence, and were using the premises of the War Committees for party purposes; and the police were right.

Gutchkov, who was interested not only in munitions but in gaining influence over every emanation of discontent, in order to be able to represent it in Parliament, frequently begged the Cabinet to set free representatives of district War Committees who had been arrested by the local police authorities. As a rule his requests were acceded to. In February 1917, however, the whole of the members of the central organization of the workers' groups of the War Committees found their way into prison.

THE ATTEMPTED REVOLUTION FROM ABOVE AND THE SUCCESSFUL ONE FROM BELOW

Since the battle of Tannenberg, the Winter Palace and the Summer Palace had been like enchanted castles. Rumours danced round the throne like ghosts on evil nights. Over the gardens of the Romanovs Fear hung like a dark cloud. The little brook that purls over a coral bed amid forests of roses had lost its magic. It seemed as if the many million sighs of hopelessness at the front cared nothing for the sentries at Cæsar's gates. Reproaches, deep anxieties, evil dreams came over Alexandra Feodorovna. She laid her head in Rasputin's lap, as on a block of black marble. ". . . My soul," the Empress wrote to the Staretz,[1] "is only at peace when you, my Teacher, are sitting next me and I can kiss your hands and lay my head on your blessed, blessed shoulder."

Rasputin's heart, however, was not heavy. Silently he

[1] I.e., monk.

THE PETERSBURG SOVIET

JULY DEMONSTRATION

LEADERS OF THE WORKERS' SOVIETS

would leave the bedchamber in the Winter Palace for the dining-chamber of rich financiers. There it was not the ghosts that danced, but the war profiteers.

Every Wednesday the banker Manus—he did a great deal for hostels, supported several associations for reclaiming girls who had fallen—gave a banquet at which a seductive, slim, attentive Georgian girl tasted and handed round beakers of unconsecrated wine. His majesty's aide-de-camp; Rubinstein, the lover of army contracts; the Metropolitan of St. Petersburg; Protopopov, Minister of the Interior, and General Voyeikov feasted off gold platters, spoke of the difficult times, of a separate peace, of the eternal radiance of autocracy, railed against the War Committees, and lamented over the base greed of the lower orders.

Then Rasputin went on to Stürmer, Prime Minister and Dictator.

The news agency run by the Okhrana for the broadcasting of secret information was instructed to report that the Staretz was now a bitter enemy of the Prime Minister.

He met him, none the less, every week in the fortress of Peter and Paul. In this bastille the daughter of the prison governor waited the oncoming of night, that the holy man might release her from the pains of hell. This maid it was who knitted the bond of friendship between Rasputin and Stürmer. The two dignitaries discussed the future of Russia.

Nicholas II, who had taken over the supreme command of the army, signed in the imperial train documents that he scarcely looked at. After he had been some time at the G.H.Q. at Mohilev—consequently seeing nothing of his consort, nor hearing her plaintive voice, nor wincing before her reproachful glances—His Majesty, pressed by his indignant generals, dismissed the Dictator Stürmer.

On this, Alexandra Feodorovna journeyed with her children to Mohilev, wept passionately, and handed over a letter from the Staretz. But the Emperor could no longer revoke his dismissal of the Premier. He yielded, however, to the urgency of his despairing consort to the extent of retaining Protopopov as Minister of the Interior.

"So wretched and so base a Government as the present," said Miliukov in the Duma, "Russia has never before known. The Ministers are fools, with the exception of the Premier, who is a traitor."

The leaders of the industrialists, the Cadets, Octobrists, and Progressists passed sleepless nights. After dinner the talk was of the abandoned land where shepherds shall make their folds no more. There were discussions of the crying need for a gesture, for a quickly acting and quickly ended revolution. The company had no fear of the unrest in the industrial quarters. There, thought these conspirators in their after-dinner optimism, all was quiet. And, indeed, no sound found a way out of the abyss; there the dying took their misery with them into their early grave.

The leader of the Liberal nationalists, Briantchakinov, said to the French Ambassador: ". . . The upheaval . . . would be an immense liberation of all the national energies, a noble awakening. . . . After a few days of inevitable disturbances . . . Russia would rise to a greatness undreamt of."

And the representative of His Britannic Majesty, Sir George Buchanan, tells how a Russian friend, "later a member of the Provisional Government, brought the news that before Easter there would be a revolution."

"The army leaders," writes Miliukov, "were fully prepared to give the approaching *coup d'état* their support. Rumour said that General Alexeyev was resolved actually to have the Tsaritsa arrested when she visited his headquarters. . . . General Grimov, Gutchkov and Terestchenko determined to have recourse to a conspiracy of the Guards to arrest the Tsar."

Even the grand dukes fretted amid the confinement and restraint of the palaces of their imperial lord. They, too, thought of the flowery carnival of a coming revolt, were in high spirits at the idea, rose hopefully on the morning after the banquet.

The three sons of the Grand Duchess Maria Pavlovna —Cyril, Boris and Andrew—proposed, with the aid of four regiments of Guards, to surround Tsarskoye Selo [1] at night and to declare the Tsarevitch Alexis Tsar, with Nicholas Nikolayevitch as regent.

The villa of the beautiful friend of Prince Gabriel Konstantinovitch was the scene of much blessedness, under the triple star of politics, wine and love. Many times over would the health of the renewed fatherland be drunk, while princes assured ecstatically attentive ladies that they were really and truly Jacobins.

The first victory of this imperial entourage was the murder of Rasputin.

Overcome with grief, Alexandra Feodorovna and Nicholas II placed Protopopov, the best friend of the dead martyr, in power. The new Dictator always had the latest news from the other world, where the slain Staretz was hurrying from saint to saint, telling of the virtues of the Romanovs.

On one occasion when Protopopov came into the Empress's chamber, writes the Ambassador of France, he fell on his knee before Alexandra Feodorovna and cried, "Oh, your Majesty, I see behind you Jesus Christ."

This last of the Tsar's Ministers of the Interior was originally a hope of the Liberals. He whispered his friends' secrets to Rasputin, and the Staretz in return introduced him into the innermost circle. Protopopov suffered from disordered nerves. Spirits visited him, made themselves entirely at home. And whatever the shades from beyond told him, he passed on to the imperial couple.

[1] The Summer Palace.

This spiritistic Dictator was aware of the conspiracy in progress in bourgeois and aristocratic *salons,* and, in order to destroy all his enemies at one blow, wanted to provoke also a popular rebellion. The Chief of Staff, General Vassily Gurkov, reported to His Majesty: "It is possible to differ in regard to Protopopov's qualities of character, but not in regard to the degree, to put it mildly, of the irresponsibility with which he applies to State affairs the principles of a gambler."

The Minister declared that he felt strong enough to defend Tsarism and the Orthodox Church against any sort of uncomfortable event.

Below, however, in homes grown used to poverty, no one had any thought of insurrection. The power to be faced seemed too immense. The more it brought them bitter days, the more hated and the more invulnerable seemed its ramparts in the eyes of the multitude. They were unable to look, like grand dukes, bankers and industrialists, through the keyholes into the secret chamber of 'Absolutism.

The prelude to the greatest upheaval of which history tells, was not produced in the dark corners of conspiracy in which Russian rebels had felt at home for decades, but in the richest houses of the realm.

Among the Socialists there had never been so little talk of revolution as now. In the early morning of the very day of its outbreak Kerensky and his friends decided that at the moment revolt was *out of the question.*

On March 6, 1917, St. Petersburg was hard frozen, with seventy-seven degrees of frost.

The heating-pipes had burst. Twelve hundred locomotives had turned into immovable lumps of ice. Fifty-seven thousand trucks which should have been feeding the capital were motionless.

Bakers' shops had no flour, housewives no bread. In the industrial suburbs there was panic. Every rumour

By its last ukase the superseded régime appointed a committee to control the demonstrations in the streets.

But when the leading Democrats in this committee looked out of the windows at the long files of soldiers, the serried rows of workers' wives and children, when they heard the shouting, they shrank back as from the glow of a giant furnace.

And in the very hour in which the committee of the Duma was sitting, disheartened through the manner of its birth, frightened of its nominal omnipotence, the Workers' and Soldiers' Soviet was already speaking. How had it come into existence? When was it elected? "Blessed simplicity!" writes an eye-witness of those hours, "to talk of elections—now! Workers, soldiers and rebels came into the Duma, and the Workers' Soviet was complete, ready made. Naturally the Socialist groups of the Duma had to come in too. The Revolution must have a centre, and Gutchkov and Rodzianko were no good for that sort of job."

At the very outset of the rebellion its steep places came into view, its promise of difficult years. Even during the drunken embrace of common joy in victory, the classes were separating out, and new dividing lines were showing their metallic hardness.

The Cabinet, the Provisional Government, was honoured by the membership of Alexander Ivanovitch Gutchkov, representative of the Moscow trading community, who liked to call himself a "warrior in mufti." More than a decade before, when Dubassov freed Moscow from Lenin, Gutchkov had organized for the general a voluntary militia. Now he hoped, thanks to the Revolution, to reorganize the army. Paul Nikolayevitch Miliukov had long taught political geography to the Tsar's Ministers, had dreamed since Stolypin's time of Byzantium, and of how he would one day look from the low hills over the still sea of Marmora and see it black with Russian grain-carriers and cruisers. Now, as the already enjoyed the knowledge of victory, fell in the squares and main streets of St. Petersburg.

Where the masses that should have fought against one another—garrison and population—met, they joined in cursing the existing order, which in that moment they consigned to the past, and swore loyalty to a new era of happiness.

For every century of Romanov domination, the rising lasted one day.

Before the breath of rebellion the walls collapsed, burying here and there under their ruins an old servant who had failed to flee in time. The doors of the fortresses stood open. From all quarters there crept out cringers to the Revolution: Tsarism spitting out its faithless.

As a dead man is followed to the edge of the tomb, but not into the coffin, so all his relatives, his friends, his supporters abandoned Nicholas II.

In his ceremonial robes the priest Vladimir Popov, formerly leader of the extreme Right, lifted the crucifix and gave heaven's blessing to the rebels. Grand Duke Cyril Vladimirovitch had the Red Flag hoisted on the tower of his palace by a lackey in knickerbockers and silk stockings. In a mangy overcoat an old, bowed man entered the Duma, wished success to the new lords, and declared his desire to surrender. It was the all-powerful of yesterday, the Minister of the Interior, Protopopov.

The proudest remains of the army, the Cossacks of the Imperial Guards, His Majesty's Regiment, the Holy Legion, the railway regiment of the imperial train, the palace guards, marched as to a parade, as on the Emperor's birthday, to enter into alliance with the victors in front of the headquarters of the rebellion.

In the streets were to be seen the garrison regiments. Their old banners had sewn on them, alongside the embroidered pictures of saints, squares of red bunting.

The Duma was amazed at the defection of the entire army.

able. [They included too many young recruits. Only a few months before there had been a mutiny, and it had been necessary to shoot one hundred and sixty soldiers. Protopopov telegraphed to the front: the Mohammedan division of Cossacks was to come without delay.

The Tsar went on the same evening to the G.H.Q.

A Bolshevik secret committee issued an appeal to the women. This was the first volley of the word-artillery of the Revolution. There are times when sentences that get home can conquer real guns. The women read in the appeal their own thoughts: "When will all the horror of the war end . . . when the whole of the people rise up and overthrow the Tsarist Government? . . ."

At dawn on March 9 many factories awaited their workers in vain.

In the Viborg quarter there was looting. The bridges leading to the centre were occupied by troops, and the day ended with a miracle: the Cossacks, reputed the best shots in the service of the Régime, hit the police instead of the crowd.

Like a river bursting its banks this news flooded the mean streets, invaded every room, carried everything with it.

On March 11 the last vestige had gone of fear, of irresolution; the authority of the powers that were seemed as though it had never existed. Tsarism spoke for the last time. Like every revolution, the Russian Revolution began with its prohibition. The garrison commander issued a fierce warning:

"All assembling is forbidden. I call the attention of the population to the fact that I have once more authorized the troops to make use of their weapons. They will obey this command, and will stop at nothing to maintain order."

A few troops, one or two machine-guns, did the last honours to this placard. Five hundred rebels, who was believed. The hungry looked at their neighbours' pale faces, in terror of the day before them.

In the factories the proletarians declared that without bread they would do no work.

On March 8 there was a wild outburst of strikes.

But the strikes brought home no food.

Men and women came out into the streets, demonstrating their hunger, threatening; weak and despairing crowds. The men were quiet and grave; the women lamented, wept, cursed. And suddenly, suddenly these slave women recalled all the dragging years of war; suddenly they abandoned faith in their saints, their heroes, the Little Father, the medals for bravery and the malignant enemy. The women refused to return home; they knew too well what the morrow would be, went from factory to factory, called out the men and made for the centre of the city.

By three in the afternoon all the industrial suburbs were alive. Closely packed together, the men and the women stood in the streets, the frost mantling them.

Bakers' shops were destroyed. That filled no stomachs, only added to hunger. But rage and hatred had now a field in which the imagination could see the gold of vague harvests ripening.

The abandoned people closed their ranks, and all stomachs became one stomach, with many, many hands.

The main streets were well guarded. Protopopov at last had his revolt, could save the situation, gain a striking victory, get one in at the Duma. He summoned the commandant of the garrison. In his presence the maps of St. Petersburg were studied. Gordron, General of gendarmerie, showed on his map the spots at which important streets crossed—with a red star. On that same day machine-guns were to be concealed at those spots in the ground floors of the surrounding houses. The garrison strength was 100,000 men. But they were not reli-

THE LEGEND OF A JOURNEY
AND THE RIDE INTO
HISTORY

THE three years of war must have seemed to Ulianov a wall with no visible end. On its perpendicular surface he wrote theories. The curses with which this Man who was Waiting closed his books, pamphlets and articles were outcries in the nervous tension of these Swiss days. The monotonous regularity of the hours tired like a heavy burden. The last winter in Zurich had crawled along specially slowly. In the wilderness of Europe there was reborn every hour the sigh of August 4. As a nomad herdsman Lenin still kept watch over the Idea in the valley of his hope. But when in the morning the sky slowly paled, the exile must have asked himself whether he would live to see the new social order.

One day, at the beginning of March 1917, there came a knock at his door. Without waiting for a reply, a friend stepped in and announced that Revolution, like a thief in the night, had arrived at St. Petersburg.

Waiting lasts an eternity, and then the longed-for comes unceremoniously in a moment, lifts one out of the daily rut, and feverishly one follows the new track.

Lenin ran out of the room as though the roof were on fire, went off to confirm with his own eyes, to see the news in print. The morning paper had nothing as yet. He hurried to Lake Zurich, repeating over and over again the words he had heard, and there on the shore, under a shelter, were the latest telegrams, pasted on a blackboard. From Russia the wire ran:

". . . An executive committee consisting of twelve

members of the Duma is in possession of power. All the Ministers have been put in prison. . . ."

Lenin suddenly felt stifled in this city. He saw nothing of the passers-by. In the wait for the tram, the return to his door, to his writing-table, he seemed to be going up and down between prison walls, monotonously round and round the cell, round and round.

A manifesto from St. Petersburg sent greetings to the émigrés. "The Provisional Government," it ran, "will gladly recall all who have suffered for the country from their exile or their prison."

Five hundred Russians were exulting, in every canton of Helvetia, saw themselves already high on horseback at home, promised their landladies to send them picture postcards, swore that they would send on the arrears of rent, and packed their all in wooden chests, cardboard boxes or cloths.

The British Government, however, though it declared in the Commons through Bonar Law that the Revolution had come as a real relief, since the masses of Moscow's realm were calling for the energetic prosecution of the war, and the French Government, though, through its Foreign Minister, Briand, it said the same, and said it even better, refused to allow more than one hundred and fifty émigrés to pass through their territory.

Lenin could not go. He felt like a dreamer who wants to cry aloud and cannot make a sound, or one who, as often as he tries to rise, is felled by a gigantic fist. One after another he suggested to his wife the most amazing travel schemes. With the help of a smuggler he proposed to travel to Russia through Germany. This man of contraband, however, disclosed himself after the first meeting as a creature of Ludendorff's.

Parvus, a friend of Trotzky's as far back as 1905, had set out to prove that the Master's theories could also bring good fortune to the individual in business life, and accordingly had speculated during the war, as a true internationalist, in Berlin, Copenhagen, Vienna and Constantinople; now, hoping for political laurels, he advised the Foreign Ministry in Berlin to let Lenin pass through.

This secret association would, however, have risked ending Ulianov's activities as a Socialist in St. Petersburg. If he was to go through Germany it must be either as a smuggler, without Ludendorff's knowledge, or, if with his knowledge, as publicly as possible, with no secret clause and before the whole world.

One night, his wife relates, he said: "I tell you what! I will travel with the passport of a dumb Swede."

"It won't do," answered Krupskaya. "You might talk in your sleep and give yourself away. If you dream at night of the Cadets you will shout out, 'Blackguards, blackguards!' and they will know you are not a Swede."

The émigré groups united in order to get home, sent telegram after telegram to the Provisional Government and the Workers' Soviet, received from Miliukov, the Foreign Minister, replies that said nothing, and from the Soviet promises that said no more.

Their friends among the Swiss Socialists tried now to help the exiles. Perhaps they were glad to do their guests a real service and at the same time lose advisers in matters of orthodoxy who combined pertinacity with unlimited spare time. Robert Grimm negotiated on behalf of the Russians with the German Minister, Herr Romberg. The negotiations seemed likely to take some time. Weeks might pass before the frontiers of the suddenly loved country came into sight.

Realizing this, Lenin, the one cool head among five hundred who had gone wild with excitement, broke free from the welter of poignant dreams and projects, took his place as a leader, held that on the tactics and ideas of the two dozen friends in St. Petersburg the fate of the world hung. Instead of composing pæans of unending joy, he compiled theses, and wrote to the Bolsheviks of St. Petersburg "Letters from Afar."

In exactitude of thought he found protection from the unnerving conditions of the moment, from the contradictory news, from all the pestering of inquisitive neighbours and acquaintances. On the fourth day after the destruction of the old gods the exile sketched the outline of the commencing drama, foretold its next acts. He did not see the suffering of the years to come, which were to condemn men and women in every Russian valley, in every town and village to agonies of hunger; on the contrary, he wrote that "every family" would have "bread, every child milk"; but he saw the time when the last earthly remains, the last trace, the very name of the old system would disappear.

As in the garret in Munich, in the December days of the first rebellion, as at the beginning of the war, so at the very outset of this new turn of destiny he saw paths undreamed of by any others. Lenin forgot many elements in things. He and his followers were yet to have many an anxious moment; but he believed that he recognized with certainty the path which Russia must follow.

He felt qualified to prophesy, because his earlier prophecies of civil war had ceased to be mere printed words. Ulianov took from his file a copy of his paper, No. 47, of October 13, 1915, and placed it before his friends in St. Petersburg, like a bill that can only be met by obedience. "It is worth while to point out," he writes of the contents of that issue, "that these theses have been confirmed word for word by the Revolution."

A pat on his own back.

To those men of the Provisional Government who now talked of hastening slowly, of clear and sunny skies, who took for granted that order was now restored, he says: "Gutchkov and company were for civil war for their own ends; they are against civil war for the ends of the real majority."

It seemed to him to be obvious that in the first Act of the Revolution the new masters of the moment must be

THE RUSSIAN DELEGATION AT BREST LITOVSK

GERMAN AND RUSSIAN SOLDIERS FRATERNIZING

THE MOSCOW GROUP OF BOLSHEVIK DEPUTIES BEFORE THE SEIZURE OF POWER

THE FIRST RED FLAG AT THE FRONT

moderates. He did not, therefore, demand of his friends the immediate turning out of the Government; he was for soothing and winning over the ordinary man in the street by showing sympathy with his aspirations and understanding of his burdens. His supporters at home must, however, now that the limits of the possible had been extended indefinitely, recognize the direction in which everything was moving. They were to work for peace at the fronts and to free their fellow-men from the monotonous loneliness of their present fate, while extolling an entirely different though no less sanguinary struggle.

The Provisional Government, however, would declare peace talk to be mutinous; they would even be compelled to do so; for the Cabinet was "essentially a mere employee of the multi-millionaire firm of England, France and Co."

Socialists of other schools sang the same song as in 1905, said that the rising was a bourgeois revolution serving the interests of capitalism. Lenin was not concerned as to this. In 1905 he had been for participation in any provisional government; this time he was against participation. The Mensheviks used to be against, but now were in favour of, participation. Lenin never said clearly at any stage of events whether insurrection should aim at the immediate attainment of that ideal realm, that Olympus which the Greeks of ancient times prudently placed in the past, the Middle Ages transferred to heaven, and modern Utopists assign to a period in the future of our earth. But if the street fighting was merely for the greater profit of the bourgeoisie, "the workers," writes this tactician, "must open the people's eyes to the fraud of the bourgeois politicasters." It was a duty "to rely solely on our own strength, our own organization, our own solidarity, our own armed strength."

Armed strength was for him a hammer wherewith to shape everything, the guarantee of the right course. The poor were to take bread, housing room and arms, their suburbs to become storehouses of the movement that was gathering strength for a fresh insurrection. He proposed that in St. Petersburg a body of seven hundred and fifty thousand men should be enrolled, not only to defeat the old régime, but to trample it underfoot and utterly destroy it. Only dust and cinders of it should remain. This great body could "spend every fifteenth day on militia duty (being paid for the time by the employers), and so represent an army of fifty thousand . . . so that it would be unnecessary to set up either a special police or a special army divorced from the people."

The armed proletarians would bring to their side the small middle-class people, the slum-dwellers and the peasants. The crown and centre of the bayonets, the glade in this primeval forest of firsts, was for him the Workers' Government.

Ulianov's supporters were for him a problem in pedagogy which he must solve if he was to be able to act. Until his "Letters from Afar" could reach St. Petersburg, he was continually asking himself what his disciples in Russia would recognize as of importance amid so many sudden emergencies, and trembling at the thought that they might succumb to the allurement of Revolutionary Unity. He writes to a friend in Stockholm, begging him to forward every communication sent to him:

"I hope you have received my 'Letters from Afar,' Nos. 1–4. If they have failed to reach you please telegraph me. . . . Personally I do not hesitate for a moment to declare, even to declare in writing, that I would rather see an immediate breach with anyone at all in our Party than make concessions to the Social-patriotism of Kerensky and his people, or the Social-pacifism and Kautskianism of Tcheidze and Co. . . . We must explain to the workers and soldiers in very popular, very clear language, with no scientific jargon whatever, that not only William II, but the British and Italian kings must be brought down. . . . No approach to other Parties, none to anyone! Not the ghost of any trust in them. . . . The organization of our Party—that is the thing that matters."

Every day's continued absence from his country made it possible for his friends to regard Revolutionary Harmony through other eyes than his.

But the negotiations between Robert Grimm and Romberg dragged on endlessly.

At last Lenin decided to send a Swiss Socialist, Fritz Platten, member of the National Council, to the German Emperor's Minister. Platten belonged to the Bolshevist group. In negotiating he was to keep meticulously to his instructions. The cautious exile could not give anyone *carte blanche* in a discussion in his name with the Emperor's representative. He would have nothing hidden or veiled making a mystery out of his journey. Lenin therefore summoned his few friends in the camp of international Socialism, and had his view confirmed by them that it was the duty of the Bolsheviks "to take advantage of the opportunity offered to them of returning home to Russia." Paul Levi from Germany, Loriot from France, Stockholm's Radical mayor Lindhagen, and eight others of the faithful signed this declaration as a testimony of immaculacy which should explain to the Workers' Soviet of St. Petersburg the visa of the German military authorities.

Fritz Platten had formulated nine points with the German authorities in regard to the passage through Germany. The train taken must enjoy the privilege of extraterritoriality. The passengers undertook to work for the liberation of German and Austrian civil internees in Russia.

Lenin wanted to leave Switzerland on the very day of the conclusion of the agreement.

Thirty émigrés waited on the morning of April 8, 1917, on the platform at Berne, not taking their eyes for a minute off the engine waiting to start with them. Behind them stood friends, seconding loud entreaties with wild gesticulations, imploring each one of Ulianov's companions not to venture on the journey through enemy territory. He himself spoke not a word in answer to them, but quietly got into his compartment. In the carriage Lenin found a comrade who proposed to go with the party. He was suspected, however, of having been on friendly terms with the Okhrana. "The man," writes an eye-witness, "had made a little too sure of his seat. Suddenly we saw Lenin seize him by the collar and in an incomparably matter-of-fact manner pitch him out on the platform." Ulianov was thenceforward inaccessible to anyone. Another group of friends had surrounded Zinoviev, talking incessantly, in the effort to prevent him from going, up to the last moment before the whistle blew.

All the other émigrés, even the protesters at the first journey, subsequently went, in the same way as Lenin, through enemy territory.

Lenin, however, had now made a beginning. His first move in the Revolution, his first act, had been denounced as madness. Not only enemies, but his nearest friends threw up their arms and lamented. All his subsequent action was to be judged by friend and foe in the same way as the bold venture of his departure.

The smoke of the engine that crossed Germany with its unusual guest did not lose itself in the skies or mingle with the clouds; it shaped itself in all Europe and America into stories believed by millions of an alliance between Lenin and Ludendorff.

Almost always in national upheavals, as in every great event, legend has a realm of ideal freedom. It is the product of the unwritten, mouth-to-mouth news-sheet of rumour. Once evolved, the saga not only is propagated through the mouths of the concierges in houses great and small, but is passed on by thousands of fountain-pens, gives hundreds of street-corner orators the opportunity of earning their day's poor wage.

So the English Revolution, according to many of its contemporaries in London, was the work of a Spanish cabal; the French Revolution, as many loungers in Versailles conceived it, was an English plot; and the Third Republic simply the moving of a pawn on Bismarck's political chess-board.

In his compartment in this train whose passengers, with the consent of the German general staff, had just taken their third-class tickets, Lenin made notes, looking at times absent-mindedly at the landscape. The other twenty-nine returning émigrés spoke across one another, heard only their own voices, sang the Marseillaise, the Internationale, bombarded the Master with questions. When the train stopped at a station they would all look out curiously at the faces that passed by, to guess the strangers' attitude from their expression; but not a word must be exchanged.

Ulianov knew most of the rumours which were now flying like frightened birds in all directions. But what power, what danger could have chained him, of all men, any longer to Switzerland? The barring of the passage through the Entente countries had, indeed, been a trick of his political opponents. Russia's revolutionary Minister, Nabokov, interpreted Miliukov's silence as meaning: "Formally there was nothing illegal in the method of return; but it will completely undermine Lenin's authority."

The exile, thus released, expected to be arrested on return, and discussed the speech in defence with his comrades. He knew, too, that Ludendorff had hopes of the results of the arrival of this train in St. Petersburg. But could Lenin help it if the general had plans? Had not Socialism, ever since August 4, 1914, been an object of speculation on the part of all supreme army commands?

Now that in the realm of the Russians the doctrine of Marx, owing to a Cabinet intrigue, had become the faith of the peoples, there was a ready admittance everywhere for the officially anointed of the Left. Ministers had time for them. The doors of all authorities opened wide, and lackeys bowed low as before real privy councillors. Statesmen clapped the rebels heartily on the shoulder, spoke of "great responsibility," referred to the "changed times," to "organic development," to "inevitable progress." In the *salons* the Socialists at receptions had the first hot cup of tea and the best piece of cake. Acquaintance with a revolutionary was accounted a life insurance, and one which cost nothing.

A few days before Lenin's departure, Plekhanov had set off for Russia, with forty nationalist comrades, on board a British ironclad, escorted by torpedo-boats.

Trotzky, on the other hand, on reaching England from America on his way home, was arrested by the British authorities.

Socialists replaced the British and French Ambassadors in St. Petersburg. Labour representatives came from London to the rebel capital, to convince the Soviets of the necessity for continuing the war. "The Tsar," said a representative of the Workers' Soviet to the British Labour delegation, "made us fight for Constantinople, which is not Russian and never was." One of the Englishmen, writes Mr. Philips Price, laughed aloud, as when children tell grown-ups some specially quaint absurdity. "Damn it! if you don't want Constantinople, we'll take it."

Sir George Buchanan mentions a conversation after a dinner that he had given in honour of the Entente Socialists. Albert Thomas asked him: "What would you have said if you had been told five years ago that I and two other Socialists would be sitting one day as guests at your table?"

"The very idea would have horrified me," replied

Buchanan. "But now—*la guerre change tout cela*—we are all 'comrades.' "

On instructions from Berlin, its Minister in Berne had required of Fritz Platten, the intermediary, that Lenin should receive a delegate from the trade unions. He refused this. Romberg pointed out, however, that this was a condition of the passage through Germany. Lenin told his friends that the leaders of the organizations might come if they liked, but he would not receive them; if necessary he would catch hold of them and pitch them out.

The generals wanted to force the rebels to embrace in brotherly love, like the cattle-breeders who compel their livestock to mate.

In Stuttgart the trade unions' man came into the entirely unsealed coach. A cavalry captain was with him. He spoke to Fritz Platten, sent greetings to the travellers in the name of the liberation of the peoples, and asked for an interview. The Swiss Councillor replied that they could not give a reply to the greeting and did not want to enter into conversation. The representative of the trade unions, Herr Janson, departed, and never in his life could he guess the explanation of the malevolent friendliness of these dreamers.

There were no further visits between Stuttgart and Sassnitz. Ulianov held that negotiations with the men in power were unavoidable, but would only be harmless to the revolutionary cause if the rebels met their partners with the hatred of enemies, wished them death and damnation. He believed that this journey would be the end neither of the Idea nor of Russia, but of a dynasty friendly to the Romanovs.

In this political speculation in bluff only the completest deceiver could win the crown of "moral justification." And Ulianov believed that he saw his early victory in the grey dawn of a Petersburg morning.

All the critical moves in his solitary life had up to now been bound up with this city, in which the sun is so spar-

ing of its rays. Here had come success and defeat, had
lived all his great memories and all his beginnings. Here
departure had often had the pain of a frigid notifica-
tion of regret after misfortune. Here he had come from
the provinces, a youth of twenty. Here the railway had
brought him home from Siberian exile. And here there
had met, in the months of 1905, the organizers of conspiracy. He was not thinking now of himself; but many
moments of the past came and went by as quickly as the
villages through which the train ran. Those who, in
whatever they are doing or passing through, see only their
own reflection, are the poorest of men. They cannot
enjoy abstractions, ideas, the wide spaces of other worlds.
Lenin felt the wonderful gratification of a coming paradise of effective work, heard the hoarse shouts of the
victors, saw the first ripple of the waves of a fresh
rebellion.

The nearer his country approached, the more Ulianov
lost the sense of his surroundings; he scarcely heard any
longer what his friends might be saying. A few hours
after the last little German station, he was greeted by
Swedish comrades.

The contradictory news from St. Petersburg clouded
the picture of events. The Stockholm Socialists were
equally without definite news, and accordingly decided
on a jollification and invited the travellers to breakfast.
"We poor people," writes Radek, who was present,
"accustomed in Switzerland to regard a herring as a dinner, looked at this gigantic table with its infinite variety
of eatables . . . emptied every single dish, to the un-
speakable astonishment of the waiters, who . . . were
only used to seeing civilized people."

In Stockholm Radek took Lenin to a big store and
bought him a pair of boots, that Russia's coming man
might not enter his kingdom with shoes that disgraced
him. But their receiver objected altogether to a new
overcoat and extra under-clothing; declared that he

was not going to St. Petersburg to open a tailor's shop.

When they resumed the journey a Muscovite made a speech in the railway station, recommending caution and wariness. Lenin smiled, and fidgeted at the length of this farewell.

Only a day more separated him from the first Finnish station. The lights of Torneo shone in the cold northern winter night. Here the Baltic pushes far into the land; a thick crust of ice covered it now. The thirty went in sledges to the Russian frontier. Even the youngest and the most talkative of them were now silent.

The first soldiers greeted the returning exiles with smiling curiosity. Lenin waited impatiently for the first train and looked for newspapers. After four years he saw his *Pravda* again, and suddenly, in spite of the significant greeting out of the past, he became censor, found his pupils' exercises unsatisfying, told his friends the bad mistakes he had discovered. The talk was interrupted by the whistle of the engine. A file of soldiers entered the train to travel with them. Was it a guard of honour, or were the thirty under arrest?

In the compartment Lenin entered into discussion with the soldiers. He interrogated them keenly, attentively. Every word he heard was of importance. It was the men of this type who mattered. They were all for national defence. He had no desire either to wound or shock them; slowly and with careful steps he explained his view to them. The talk lasted until morning. Lenin felt now that he knew much, that he came to St. Petersburg already well informed.

Early in the morning, at a small station, friends of his Party came from the capital. He no longer put questions encouragingly, as in the past night, but pressed for details, showed dissatisfaction.

"Shall we be arrested?" was his final question. The disciples were silent, declared that they had no definite information, told him nothing of the reception which his organization had been preparing for days past.

The closer they came to the Finnish terminus in the capital, the graver grew the faces of the party. Gradually the talk died out. Even thought was stilled. The great expectation lulled the travellers in a pleasant weariness. The lights of the outskirts of St. Petersburg, in waving rows that grew constantly nearer together, showed the travellers that they were getting close in.

Even before the engine breathed out its black cloud for the last time, the arrivals heard drums beating as if for an attack. Yells and hoarse shouting, cries of triumph, the hymned Internationale, changed the station into a living stream. Ulianov looked for a moment in surprise out of the window. At once he was wedged in the crowd, unable to move.

Soldiers, at their head the Bolshevik Shliapnikov, made a way for him with friendly words and pushing, freed the leader from the pincers, from the embrace of thousands. Searchlight projectors lit up the station like a burning waterfall, bayonets and the golden letters on red flags blazed out like fireworks. The garrison at St. Petersburg had sent detachments from each branch of the army. A brightly uniformed host roared in rhythmic unison the one word LENIN.

And he, who in his whole life had never addressed more than a hundred people together, who for thirty years had been passing from one group of ten supporters to another of perhaps twenty, who had never been received by a shout in the streets, did not make the slightest slip, wasted not a tear of emotion. Great revulsions of destiny always apply their test suddenly, leaving no time for preparation. And he had passed the test, said at once to himself with instinctive deliberation: "I shall say what I should have said to only twenty people, shall not let myself be tripped up."

A small group led him, with the agility of a troupe of

acrobats, to the Tsar's own waiting-room. In the middle of the hall stood Tcheidze, the chairman of the Workers' Soviet. Lenin stood still for a moment and heard words from a moral lecture: ". . . In the name of the Soviets . . . of the whole Revolution . . . we greet you . . . but . . . we consider . . . . that no division, but union of the Democracy is needed. . . . We hope you will join us in pursuit of this aim. . . ."

The centre of the demonstration looked in embarrassment at a bouquet of roses which someone had pressed into his hand. He no longer saw or heard Tcheidze. Lenin's answer was to repeat sentences from his Swiss articles, as though he had for three years written for this moment: "Soldiers, sailors, workers . . . in you I see the vanguard of the world army of the proletariat. Everywhere the imperialist war for plunder is being followed by civil war. Already we can see the dawn of world revolution. . . ."

The crowd had fought its way up the decorated stairs to the imperial waiting-room. Now Lenin saw in the square in front of the station an endless sea of heads, fur caps, shoulder-pieces, shakos, and the gun-barrels of tanks.

From the Fortress of Peter and Paul searchlights lit up the clouds. The guard of honour of Kronstadt sailors drowned with the battle-song of the Revolution the exultant yells of the tens of thousands. Ulianov was lifted up and set on the roof of an armoured car, which moved forward slowly like a blind thing. The tank stopped at every street-corner for Lenin to speak. And on that day St. Petersburg heard shouts which had not until then interrupted in any capital of the world the melody of August 4: "The capitalist robbers . . . beginning of civil war . . . vile, imperialist, purposeless slaughter. . . ." That was the voice from the village prison of Novy Targ; that was the negative pole of the war; that was the spark of an idea which, it may be, only seemed great because the idea that it challenged, worn threadbare in the war, was becoming continually more petty.

The journey through the city lasted an hour. Along the route there stood, closely packed together, like the ridge of a mountain, workers and soldiers whose sweat intermingled and was thirstily drunk up by the soil of history.

THE PRIMA BALLERINA'S PALACE AND THE VISION OF ANARCHY

An hour after his arrival Ulianov reached the palace of the Tsar's favourite, the *prima ballerina* Mathilde Kzeczinska. Here he was received with curiosity and enthusiasm by the civil colour-sergeants and non-commissioned officers of his Party.

Women and men of the serving class are supporters of legitimacy of succession, despise and hate girls of other than royal blood who in the sleeping chamber of the Monarch incorporate love with democracy. In the days of the French Revolution the summer palace of the *courtisanes* was stormed immediately after the Bastille. This moral satisfaction is the longed-for revenge of the small man, who has no opportunity to bring more variety into his meagre diet or into wedlock. When the rising has won victory and the revolutionary tribunal speaks, the first speech of the new public prosecutor is devoted to offended morality. The public prosecutor of the French Revolution, Fouquier-Tinville, when on 16 Frimaire he demanded of the puritan court of free citizens the head of "Jeanne Vaubernier, wife of Citizen du Barry," had with him every heart that beat in the *halles* of Paris. His speech echoed the feelings of the suburbs, conventional respectability and outraged poverty.

All St. Petersburg, however, knew that Mathilde

Kzeczinska not only had many lovers, but represented a gun factory. When Nicholas II began to devote himself entirely to Alexandra Feodorovna and Rasputin, Grand Duke Sergei Mikhailovitch, head of the ordnance department, took the Tsar's place with the *prima ballerina.* The dancer received a big honorarium every year from Creusot's iron-works; she also obtained exemption for propertied young men from military service; held office, in fact, in the Ministry of War as a sympathetic General Officer for the Receipt of Bribes.

Her house was the first fortress stormed by the Bolsheviks, even before they became masters of Smolny and the Kremlin. The Government tried in vain to protect this private estate. Even people to whom property is an element in divinity were glad of this expropriation by the rough revolutionaries. The Bolsheviks were after no rape of the Sabine women living there; they only wanted to accustom the Russians to expropriations, and used the occasion to emphasize that wealth in general has no better justification than the *prima ballerina's* wealth had.

At a constitutional upheaval every citizen, if he gets no bread, at least gets a bumper draught of morality. And here the Leninists had found not only a gushing source of purity, but party offices.

Ulianov was now enthroned in the palace. The mirrors and the broad white cupboards, the bronze figures, the marble *amoretti* trumpeting with their cheeks puffed out, were smashed to pieces by the new owners in their first transports of joy. All the *salons* were turned into assembly rooms, and the many smaller apartments into offices for the party officials. Only the candelabra, the frescoes on the ceilings, the silky carpets, the broad staircases, told of the pleasant aroma of bygone days. In inconspicuous corners, or on a table laden with newspapers and manifestos, there still stood a few mournful Chinese vases, getting in the way of the workers.

In the great ballroom one delegate after another spoke of eternal readiness for action, eternal love for the leader and the Revolution. The staff said nothing; only men from the factories and delegates from the barracks were allowed to speak. And all these men, in whose eyes the fervour of the Revolution was beginning to glow, who were holding the masses together as grass the sand of the dunes, looked up at Lenin as children at a lost father recovered.

The leader rose up.

Lenin read his theses—two hours' continuous speaking. It was a lively, illustrated, exciting pamphlet, with the effect of the printed page which can be had for ten kopeks, but now become flesh, thinking, emphasizing each separate line so variously that in the end all other opinions, purposes, feelings, vanished from the minds of the listeners.

After ten years of exile, Ulianov felt at home at once in this camp, knew it as well as his writing-table in Zurich. He saw that his investigations, his hypotheses, had not deceived him; looked at these pale, thin faces, took into consideration the many individual variations of outlook, divined the immense result that a single will, carrying with it many others, would achieve.

But the staff paled. They had expected other views from the Leader. The Party officers were getting used to positions of authority. In the Workers' Soviet, in the Commissions, in the army, they were on the Left, but only Radical in a general way. This man at the speaker's desk was cutting them off from all the comrades of allied groups. Would not all this cost them the new glory of their epaulettes; would not this new departure condemn them all, after a short spell of oratory, to eternal silence?

Ulianov was satisfied with his first appearance. And from this April 16, 1917, to the hour of the onset of his lingering malady he worked as though every single day of all the years of waiting had come to him from the grave of the past and said: "Take me."

On the next morning he spoke in the Taurida Palace.

In the white Chamber, where seven hundred Deputies used to sit, where they had debated through decades, had passed the war budget; where the Cadets had exhibited their profound historical culture and their political helplessness, while the foreign diplomats in their boxes smiled at the ineffectiveness of these debaters on the floor of the House—there now sat and stood fifteen hundred workers and soldiers. In fur coats, with caps on, with rifles and revolvers, they listened to the speaker. For three hundred years the Russians of the foundries and factories had not been allowed to speak. Now anyone was free to pour out his life-story.

In a remote room in the palace the leaders of all the Socialist groups were assembled. Every *nuance* had its representative. Political views that had been repeated for a century past, repeated ever since the fall of the Bourbons, were conceived differently by each one of those present. To-day the magic was to work. The fighters over the heritage of the Romanov autocracy proposed, by the end of the sitting, to understand the same things by the words "Socialism," "Marxism," "Democracy" and "Revolution," proposed to deliver to the fifteen hundred waiting people, in uniform tones, a common message.

Ulianov came in.

"I only arrived," he writes, "in St. Petersburg on the night of April 3,[1] and naturally, in coming forward in the meeting on April 4[1] with a statement on the tasks of the revolutionary proletariat, I could only speak in my own name."

He read theses, showed in this fraternization-sitting the contours of a gigantic receptacle which in the coming

[1] Old style.

months had to take in millions of human wills; he developed his tactics, took pains to be rather more cautious in utterance than the day before, but to keep silence on nothing of importance.

". . . Necessity of the transfer of the whole power of the State into the hands of the Soviets of the workers' Delegates, so that the masses may grow out of their mistakes through their own experience. . . . Not a parliamentary republic . . . but a republic, embracing the whole country, of the Soviets of the workers', rural workers', and peasants' Delegates, built up from below upwards. . . . Removal of the police and the Government officials. . . . In our land programme the transfer of the centre of gravity to the Soviets of the rural workers' Delegates. Fraternization at the front. . . . Thousands of congratulations are being exchanged over the Revolution. But not enough thought is being given to what the Soviets of the workers' and soldiers' Delegates are. . . . The Government must be turned out; it is an oligarchy, not a popular government. . . . It cannot bring peace, bread and entire freedom. . . . It cannot be turned out at once; it cannot be turned out by the ordinary methods. For it depends on the other Government, the Government of the Soviets of the workers' Delegates, continuing to support the bourgeoisie. And this other Government is the only possible government. To become a government the class-conscious minority of workers must win over the majority; so long as it has not the control over the masses, there is no other way to power than through the Soviets. The petty bourgeois element in the Soviets—the Social Democrats, the Social Revolutionaries and so on—is hesitating, and hindering this emergence and liberation from our difficulties. . . . That is the actual relation of class forces by which our tasks are governed."

His audience looked at one another in astonishment. "Who is this man who only arrived yesterday from abroad? What does he want? Are his words merely wasted breath; can the lamp of his aspirations ever really be lit?" Now his opponents spoke. Each one got into difficulties; they were choked with indignation, had so many arguments that they did not know which to begin with. One who later was his friend held that Ulianov wanted to set up in the tomb of Europe the throne of Anarchy, the throne which had been vacant since the days of Michael Bakunin. Then his Party comrades spoke. The Bolsheviks wanted to make excuses for the Master. Lenin, said his later Press secretary and editor of the official Communist organ, was as yet insufficiently informed, and consequently was speaking in exaggerated terms. A little sleep after the long journey would certainly restore him.

The victim dispensed with a reply, folded up the manuscript of his address, put it into his case, and hurried to the palace of the *ballerina* to save the organization from mistaken friends.

Next day the Press was jubilant. A man, the papers wrote, who talks such nonsense cannot be dangerous. "A little while ago," wrote the organ of the Cadets, "Lenin seemed, in the distance, a sphinx; in the moonlight his silhouette had an attraction for some people. Now, however, everyone can see him in broad daylight; he is his own enemy." Plekhanov declared that his former disciple had gone raving mad.

"Miliukov," writes the French Ambassador, "said to me early this morning, beaming: 'Lenin came absolutely to grief yesterday before the Soviet. He defended the peace idea with . . . such shamelessness that he . . . had to withdraw amid shouts of abuse. . . . He will not recover from this reverse.' "

The Bolsheviks shamefacedly shrugged their shoulders. The Social Revolutionaries declared that the Government had shown the utmost stupidity in putting difficulties in the way of the return home of the leader of the extremists; there was not in all Petersburg a more harmless man than Ulianov.

Amid this derision Lenin asked the hostile Socialist Parties to protect him against the sensational stories of his being in league with the Hohenzollerns. But the main thing for him was not the defence of his reputation but the conquest of his own organization. The staff of his Party continued to rebel, longed for the position of Opposition under a proper Parliamentary system.

The Bolsheviks reminded Ulianov of his own theory of the first Revolution, of the watchword of the December 1905 days. At that time their leader had declared their prime purpose to be "the revolutionary-democratic dictatorship of the proletariat and the peasantry"; he had written that in the dankness of the autumn of capitalism the first task must be to build up the bourgeois republic with Jacobin fists. They, his opponents, were the Leninists; he, Lenin, was disavowing himself.

Ulianov replied that consistency with the past may mean betrayal of the present. His friends ought to be offered to the "old Bolsheviks' record office" as "pre-revolutionary curios."

This man had as keen a scent for realities as love for Utopia. And, if Lenin was a dogmatist with pen and paper, he was not to be bound, in face of reality, either by his own or by anyone else's books.

"We do not presume," he repeated many times, "to maintain that Marx or the Marxists can tell us the way to Socialism in perfectly concrete terms. That would be absurd. We know the direction of this road; we know which class forces lead to it. But in the concrete, in actual practice, only the experience of the million men and women can show it when they begin the actual work."

He held now that "the revolutionary-democratic dictatorship . . . has already been realized, but in an extraordinarily original way, with a number of exceedingly important modifications. In our actual present experience it has already changed; there has resulted an extraordinarily original, new, unprecedented intertwining of the one element with the other. Alongside one another, existing at one and the same time, we have both the supremacy of the bourgeoisie . . . and the revolutionary-democratic dictatorship."

Russia, he continued, was now the freest country in the world. In spite of this, the bourgeois were carrying on their war, had their Government, because they had lasted a century, so that, though they were no longer defended by arms, they were supported by a voluntarily endured repression. A majority must be secured in the Soviets in order to teach them to command.

For him, however, the majority was not fifty per cent. plus one. That was a majority only in arithmetic. The political majority in a rebellion is the majority in active insurrection.

While he was still abroad, Ulianov had expected a harder, more solid resistance. Now he felt it with his fingers and found it yielding.

The Provisional Government, Kerensky, the majority in the Soviets, were in his eyes not a power that could be compared with the past million-army of the Tsar, with the battle of 1905, with Dubassov's regiments. And was he now to be less daring than then? To him the new lords seemed players on a stage that might collapse beneath them at any moment.

Before, he had written: "No Socialism, only a Republic"; now, he proclaimed Socialism and Dictatorship. Before, the enemy was strong; now, he was weak.

And the first task of all, in his view, to-day as thirty years before, was to gain power.

"I maintain still," writes Lenin, "that a political party . . . would have no right to exist . . . would be degraded to political nullity, if it allowed the opportunity of seizing power to pass by without using it."

Now, however, Ulianov's insight had conjured up a picture of a process already beginning.

He saw how along the front-line trenches the moon was losing her brightness and the sun his warmth. Here the everyday life of Russia's humanity had suddenly snapped. The soldier knew that the Tsar no longer ruled, and believed that his neighbour at home would receive land *at once,* but he *only after the war.* With the many new possibilities of his life, Ivan preferred to go on living rather than to die; while his superior officer's life mattered less than the soup in the pot. So now he murdered his officer, at the sound of whose voice right up to yesterday his blood had run cold. He dispensed with all the formalities of a revolutionary tribunal, and thrust his bayonet into his officer's body. In the ports the sailors ran to the stores for sacks, seized their commanding officers by head and legs, thrust them into these coarse shrouds, and threw the heavy burden, amid roars of laughter, into the water.

Suddenly every peasant and every worker seemed to have inherited the memory of the lives of past generations. It was as if each one felt on his own back the blows of the knouts which had been used on his grandfather, before and after the emancipation of the peasants; as if each one vividly saw and heard all the curses and the sharp practice of the landowners endured in the past, the crookednesses of the bureaucracy, and now these days and nights in the trenches. "It was," writes Serafimovitch, "as though space had been cloven, and something never before heard or seen, but always present in its most secret depths, had come up to the surface. Something that had never before been expressed in words came into view, clear, simple, intelligible. . . . Age-long hatred, age-long oppression, age-long slavery, at last forced their way up through this cleft."

The thought of the redistribution in his village possessed the soldier: he must hurry. He was determined to return to the spot from which he had been taken to be thrown down here like dung—back to Siberia, to the Ukraine, to Kuban, to the Caucasus. And regiment after regiment, infantrymen and cavalrymen, Cossacks and artillery, set off homewards. If the O. C. Railways objected to getting a train off, what was a man's gun for? If the crate on wheels was full, if there was no room left on the engine, on the steps of the coaches, on the roofs, then the commissariat or ambulance trains would be cleared out. If these too had been appropriated by more fortunate chums, the soldier would go afoot to the next station. There was much in the towns that the peasant could take with him; he helped his brothers loot. For the rich man everywhere was the enemy. And everyone was rich who did not wipe his nose with his hand.

Six months were to pass before these swarthy peasant masses were to devastate Russia under the Bolsheviks. But Ulianov saw them now, foresaw how the hungry would come from the low hills, could feel how they breathed anarchy, and set to work to save the country from this pestilence.

He knew that the successors to the Ministers of the Romanovs, before they sat down every morning to sign papers, glanced first in the crystal mirror in their antechamber to note a resemblance to Danton or Mirabeau. He declared that the new lords knew the beauties of Revolution only from the verses of Victor Hugo. For Lenin every day read Kerensky's speeches:

"You are the freest soldiers in the world. Ought you not to show that the system on which the army is built up is the best? . . . Let us dash forward, then, for the peace of the whole world, with faith in the destiny and the greatness of our nation. . . . Every single aim is sacred. . . . But I ask of you only one thing: Wait at least two months longer. . . . I shall not allow myself to be distrusted, and, through me, the whole Russian democracy insulted . . . we want to respect one another without the knout, without the stick, and to carry on our State affairs differently from our former despots."

Ulianov had not a moment's doubt that all these rhetoricians and Napoleons of defeat would be helplessly consumed by the oncoming flames to which they were blind.

And then?

Then, when no engines were running any longer, no mines, no factories at work, when the looters had crept into their old haunts of slavery with a watch, a bit of cloth, a billiard ball or a mirror, some dashing general, a Romanov cavalry officer, with many orders and a long moustache, would come forward as saviour of the country.

If Kerensky happened to be hissed, if he were not speaking merely to the hysterical Society women who a few months before had been wild over Rasputin, he would thunder: "Is it possible? It must be that the free Russian State is, after all, only a State of mutinous slaves. I wish I had died two months ago: I could then have carried the splendid dream with me to the grave."

As early as July 1915, Ulianov had written: "The war is bound to let loose in the masses the most violent passions . . . and no revolutionary tactics are possible without bearing in mind these new violent passions."

Now had come the critical moment. Now, in his dread of the White leader, in his horror at the incapacity of the new rulers, he felt bound as never before to get into power.

"I recall," says Anna Balabanova, in writing of these days, "how at the end of the sitting Lenin was standing by the window, and I asked him what would happen now. He answered, 'Now there will come either Revolution or Counter-revolution!' That amounted to saying that . . . there was no time to lose."

Ulianov felt that he alone could command the masses,

if not at once to end this rush to destruction, at all events
to stem it and divert it. Only his Party, which was bound
by no tie of interest with the tortured and murdered lords
of yesterday, could bellow at the rioters: "Deserter, hero
and murderer! Stop killing! Take your gun and defend
the country that we have determined to call Socialist.
Sailor and drunkard! Keep order on your warship, that
you have christened *Lassalle,* and protect Petersburg.
Peasant and extortioner! Take at once a bit of land, but
sow it and don't plunder your neighbour's bit. Proletarians of the town! Take over the factories, sack the
manager, but work. Work, everyone! You will not find
roast pigeon flying into your hungry mouths even from a
Communist oven."

The will to power meant now, for Ulianov, the longing
for responsibility, in consciousness of strength to control
Anarchy. In the disorganization which threatened to
inundate and sweep away every town and village, the
Bolsheviks' Party was the best organized constabulary,
the one remaining source of authority!

This solitary being, this single individual in a realm
of 140 million souls, had the power to prove to himself
all these essential things only because he felt bound up
(and yet not in any constraint) both with the visible conditions—anguished humanity, unprotected, hungering,
and without light or a guiding voice—and with the invisible, the idea, the theory of world Communism and world
Revolution. Only the strength of this as yet unpro-
claimed faith enabled him effectively to act, allowed him
to be no more deterred by the pains of the suffering than
if they were flies smitten by a plague.

"Whatever may be the case with Lenin's Utopianism,"
writes his opponent Miliukov, "in regard to other countries, his realistic insight into the situation in Russia is
entirely proved by his tactics."

The union of his dreams with his penetrating insight
into reality gave Lenin something more than the mere

formula of Dictatorship of the Proletariat. For half a century past Socialists had again and again returned to this idea, sometimes singly, sometimes in chorus, and, as in everything else, so on this subject there were countless schools of thought. Ulianov, however, believed that he saw the realization of the idea in the instrument devised for it by the course of events, the Soviets of Workers, Peasants and Soldiers.

BETWEEN THE BATTLES

From the *prima ballerina's* palace the propagandists went out into the country, into the by-ways of the towns, the slums and wherever crowds assembled. Enormous mass meetings of men and women were held, rejoicing in the Revolution, facing it like children who have received the gift of a mechanical toy and do not know how to make it work.

The crews of the Baltic Fleet mutinied. While Kerensky was making an eloquent speech at a sailor's committee meeting, an able seaman got up and interrupted the Dictator: "I assume that we have not come together for a propaganda meeting. . . . In my opinion the Honourable Minister should go straight on to the question in hand."

Lenin began to preach patience.

He tried to calm the various garrisons around St. Petersburg, who were all for turning their guns without further delay against the headquarters of the Provisional Government; he strove to make plain that even in moments in which time loses its normal regularity, on days in which an unknown divinity eggs on the works of all the clocks, patience is still the condition of victory.

He wanted to collect yet more life-stories, to win over the majority of the most active, and to send the doubters into the opposite camp. There they could disorganize the ranks, and so strengthen the Bolshevik army in the coming crisis.

His speeches and pamphlets stood out as models of lucidity against the deluge of words which was turning the soil of all Russia into mud.

Ulianov's Party gained the day in meetings, in the discussions of workers, peasants and soldiers, because what the Bolsheviks had to say was the thing the people wanted as anxiously as they wanted the peace that would not come and the bread that daily grew scarcer. Slogans fought like men in a hand-to-hand scuffle; and the more substantial and simpler bore down the others.

John Reed reproduces this from a dialogue between a student and a soldier: "You realize, I presume, that . . . you are making yourselves the tools of murderers and traitors?"

"Now, brother," replied the soldier, "you don't understand. There are two classes, don't you see, the proletariat and the bourgeoisie. We——"

"Oh, I know that silly talk," broke in the student. "You jabber . . . away like parrots . . . what you are fighting for . . . is just plain pro-German anarchy!"

The soldier, hot with embarrassment, replied: "You are an educated man . . . but still it seems to me . . ."

"I suppose that you believe Lenin is a real friend of the proletariat?" interrupted the other. "Do you know that Lenin was sent through Germany in a closed car? . . ."

"Well, I don't know much about that," answered the soldier, "but it seems to me that what he says is what I and my likes want to hear. Now there are two classes, the bourgeoisie and the proletariat——"

"You are a fool! Why, my friend, I spent two years in Schlüsselburg . . . when you were still shooting down revolutionists . . . and I am opposed to the Bolsheviki. . . . How do you account for that?"

The soldier scratched his head.

"I can't account for it at all. To me it seems perfectly simple—but, then, I'm not well educated. There
are two classes, the bourgeoisie and the proletariat . . .
only two classes," went on the soldier doggedly. "And
whoever isn't on one side is on the other."

Peasant and student talked the same language; yet
neither understood the other's words. The *mujik* was
filled with hatred, the educated man with contempt. The
malevolent faces of the ignorant showed, as the intellectuals saw them, nothing but despicable treachery.
Bolshevism, in their definition, was Socialism for the
illiterate. Had not countless young men and women from
the universities looked longingly out at the free air from
their prison windows? Had they not sacrificed for the
masses all the joys of life, the lips of the loved one, success,
clean underclothing, green fields, in order to dream over
the prison soup-tins of a coming realm of justice? More
than thirty thousand men and women of the professional
classes had been condemned to death by the Tsar.

And now, now in this summer of 1917, were they to
reap not gratitude, but a swarthy onset of barbarism?

Rebels of all shades of opinion in the movement, who
had been writing for many years about Socialism and
living on their dreams of a kingdom to come, faced now
with chaos and the impatience of the sans-culotte, lost
all resolution and desire for action.

Lenin, however, who had no more fear now of any
Utopia or any awkward fact than in 1905, when the
extremists had found themselves supporting the robber
bands, wrote: ". . . These good souls were ready to
recognize the Social Revolution, if only history would
convey us to the Revolution in as peaceful, quiet and
orderly a way as a German express train comes into the
station. The jolly guard opens the carriage door and
calls out: 'Social Revolution Station! All change!'"

Was this Mongol, thought the intellectuals, this man
with the strong lower jaw, with the bright and humorous

eyes of a smart tradesman, this man who lectured with the cut and dried finality of a dervish, was he likely to succeed in gathering in the bell-wethers of the illiterate? And this demagogue aspirant to the throne promised no victories like Napoleon or Cromwell. He talked of defeat, capitulation, the dissolution of the empire into an endless variety of national groupings. He wanted to put all the world into workaday smocks; if anyone had two rooms, he wanted to take one away; he would steal every easy chair, every soft cushion; he laughed at the ideal of liberty, and declared that every cook-housemaid must learn to rule. The wildest ideas ever conceived or put on paper by the bitterest enemies of Socialism, their maddest inventions about Communism, this man seemed to be intent on putting into practice.

History is merciless with the vanquished; like a grasping shopkeeper, she cares only for results; it may, indeed, be that when Fate throws the dice the result is always right. But the suffering of all these cultured classes in the nation is not the least of the sacrifices demanded by Revolution. And never had a rising brought such discordant complainings in the ranks of the Bastille-stormers as now, never given birth to such disillusionment in the moment of rejoicing.

The intellectuals thought that the war was only now beginning in earnest; the workers, peasants and soldiers that it was now ending. The *mujik* was demanding land; the educated revolutionaries were demanding, on the strength of their past services, moral credit. Only the Constituent Assembly, they urged, could provide for all things needed, and had, as the first Russian Parliament elected on the basis of universal suffrage and the secret ballot, sovereign power to settle every problem; at present there was nothing but a Provisional Government. A transition stage? But Kerensky had begun his offensive, was addressing troops at the front, kissing the earth before the soldiers, declaiming, weeping, imploring.

"Provisional?" thought the man in the trenches. "They're sending me to the attack, to death, and that's not provisional!"

Only a few of the battalions of death marched; a regiment of Amazons, who interpreted women's rights as the right to throw bombs, rushed against the enemy; officers spat in contempt at the motionless soldiers and went alone to the attack.

Defeat was a foregone certainty. The Foreign Minister, however, went on declaring that the Russian Revolution was bound to win against the enemy somewhere along the front.

Lenin had made loud and menacing protests against the offensive. In his eyes it was a glacier trip by a party of madmen. He was convinced now that the army was definitely demoralized, and that this would make his future task more difficult; he tried, therefore, to show where the responsibility lay for this initiative:

"The offensive is the renewal of the imperialist war. . . . Even after the Revolution of March 12 Russia has remained in the all-powerful hands of the capitalists . . . the same secret treaties, the same policy of alliances. . . ."

He threw the blame on the Mensheviks and Social Revolutionaries, and roundly abused them: "It is these very parties that are responsible for the renewal of the imperialistic war . . . for the further consequences of the economic ruin which must inevitably follow on the offensive. . . . The unhappy experience of the new stage (the stage now entered on) of the war, of the fresh ruin accentuated by the offensive, will inevitably produce the political collapse of the parties of the Social Revolutionaries and Mensheviks. . . ."

Ulianov was saddled with the blame for the defeat.

Kerensky adopted the well-worn theme of the stab in the back.

Lenin, who but a few months before had been regarded as an absurd nonentity, as the clown of the Revolution, suddenly became the Demon-King who can create defeats, lootings, disasters. What his own tiny press could not achieve, the press of his opponents achieved for him. It carried the tale of him into the farthest trenches, the loneliest cottages. Daily his name was read by the citizen returning home from work. And out of the five letters that belonged to a man who was said to want to "share out" everything, who called on the soldiers to desert, the illiterate made the programme of their Revolution.

But Ulianov could not interpret every impulse of the masses. He had not yet the key to their minds any more than the other parties had. He had no barometer for exactly determining the popular pressure. Were the enthusiastic voices of the mass deceptive? Did not clouds interrupt the view and perhaps conceal the unexpected?

There were many proletarians to whom what had already been attained seemed high festival, who read over supper the Government's promises in the newspapers, and found them as comforting as though they were already dipping their bread into rich gravy. Others were full of mistrust; they came in crowds on to the boulevards after their day's work, looked sourly at the well-dressed loungers, turned menacing eyes on the brightly lit windows of the houses and restaurants, waited impatiently for the longed-for signal, and began to say: "The Bolsheviks are like all the rest; they won't make a move; they only want to copy Kerensky and go to sleep in the Tsar's bed."

Ulianov could see the splendour of the coming conquest of power, could feel the exhilaration of the dawn of victory, and so was against attempting a critical move by the light of a chance torch. He warned against it: "A rising would be ill-advised at present." A little later he explained his reason for waiting: "A rising . . . would . . . have been a false move. We should have been unable to hold on to power, either physically or politically; not physically, even though for the moment St. Peters-

burg was at our mercy; for our workers and soldiers
would not . . . have been prepared to die for the possession of St. Petersburg. They still lacked the fury, they
lacked the . . . hatred. Our people had not then been
made careless of danger by the experience of the persecution of the Bolsheviks. . . ."

In the giant factory of conspiracy he could see that the
boilers had yet to be riveted which would be able to con-
sume every despair, to make every will effective.

An army commander can, to a certain extent, test the
spirit and efficiency of his army in bloodless manœuvres.
A leader of insurrection, who must take into count more
incalculables than a general, would be glad also to lead
his subjects in mock battles, to hear the echo awakened by
the battalions of Revolution in the millions around them,
to test the unknown and yet crucial factor—the popular
spirit and feeling; to steady the restless in his own ranks,
to encourage the hesitant.

Ulianov, however, had also to say that "the workers
and the poorest peasants are a hundred times further Left
than we."

In the barracks many companies were declaring that
they intended that the next snows should find them at
home and no longer in the trenches.

At the conference of the Bolsheviks of St. Petersburg
there appeared representatives of the machine-gun regiments, demanding of the assembly in outspoken language
and with impatience that the final struggle for the dictatorship of the Soviets should begin. Volodarsky declared in the name of the assembled Leninists that only
the parties and not the barracks could resolve on insurrection. The Communist soldiers were in duty bound
to oppose action on the part of their comrades.

This deeply longed-for power of the barricades, this
sinless harbinger of salvation, seemed now to the most
radical of the rebel elements to be anarchic.

The most influential of the Bolsheviks hurried to the

factories to urge their followers to take no part in any demonstrations.

One evening in July, however, there came up to the palace of the *prima ballerina* a massed crowd of soldiers and workers. The Bolsheviks at work in the palace read on the banners in the procession the Leninist slogan "All power to the Soviets!" Two of them went out to the waiting crowd, urged them to be prudent, declared that the country was still dreaming of possibilities of a peaceful issue; months must pass yet before the Day. A wild, confused chorus of threatening shouts was the crowd's answer to the Bolsheviks. For the first time the insurrectionists were thundering against them.

On this July evening Lenin had been out of St. Petersburg. He was hurriedly informed by a scared disciple of what had happened.

The demonstration which he had wanted, in order to test his influence, had been begun by the people without him; and his disciples had been taken unawares.

"It was agreed," writes Stalin, "that it was necessary to revise the decision that had been made, to take action, and to secure the leadership of the movement that had begun."

When, on such days as this, the armed supporters of the opposition march out, but the soldiers of the ruling power, bombarded with news true and false, tired and bored, continue to defend the treasury of law and order, then the legendary first shot is fired! It is so that, without the leaders on either side of the barricade ordering it, the main battle may begin.

Lenin knew that, but he also knew that the insurrection must at no cost be left without leadership, knew how impossible it is entirely to rule out chance, had no desire to hurt and discourage the shouters for battle; the mutineers must not be allowed to feel that they had been left in the lurch.

"To rail . . . at lawless unrest and uprisings among

the masses leads to renegadeship, if it is indulged in
by Bolsheviks; it is a normal failing of the petty bourgeois."

It was all-important that every breach made by the
masses in the serried ranks of established order should
have his approving comment. These threats from the
market-place should put fear into the Workers' Soviets,
should remind them that the Soviets are replaceable, that
they were brought into being for the purposes of the
Revolution, and must either act or go to the wall.

Lenin pressed for the formation of factory councils and
their affiliation to a central organization. These councils,
still closer to the heart of the discontented, would keep the
Soviets up to the mark.

All his efforts were directed to perfecting a system of
revolutionary pressure. The fury of the workers would
frighten and spur on the factory councils, the factory
councils the Soviets, the Soviet of St. Petersburg the
Executive Council of the Soviets (which also sat in St.
Petersburg), the Executive Council the Socialist
Ministers and the Socialist Ministers their bourgeois
colleagues.

And Ulianov did, indeed, succeed in guiding the spon-
taneous movement along the lines that he had set. On
July 16 the revolt seemed to have gathered fresh life.
Passionate indignation had brought half a million men
and women into the streets. His slogans alone were to be
seen on their banners. Not one Menshevik catchword
was to be seen. In his own camp his most resolute supporters were unable to understand why there should be
any more waiting; for a whole army was beleaguering
the fortress of the rulers, the Taurida Palace. "The 1st,
2nd, 3rd, 5th, 6th, 7th, 8th, 13th, and 14th companies of
the first machine-gun regiment, the 4th heavy machine-
gun company, the whole of the first infantry regiment,
the whole reserve pioneer battalion," and the sailors of
Kronstadt, were on the march.

The terrified Government fled to the Executive Council of the Soviets.

Below, at the doors of the Soviet of Soviets, was a howling crowd; its cries beat like stones on the windows: "Take over the power! All power to the Soviets!"

Two Socialist Ministers tried to speak, to stem this wild song by gentle words. "Here we are in the Government," they thought—"all the privy councillors greet us, our official motor-car is waiting—what more does this mob want?" They were convinced that they could not solve the problems created by the war without the help of the old hierarchy, and they suspected that these cries from the mob were merely a Bolshevist intrigue. Voices from the crowd threatened the Ministers with lynching: Trotzky rushed up and rescued them.

The Executive Council let the blinds down, turned up the lights and continued its sitting. All the leaders of the Mensheviks spoke, all the successors of the party of the old terrorists, and the Social Revolutionaries. The shorthand-writers' pencils omitted no word spoken.

Revolution, in her bridal garb, was waiting expectantly beyond the drawbridge of the fortress. For decades men had written of her wonderful treasures, her noble gait, the ecstasy of her favours, the glory of her splendour; for she was Power. Now half a million souls were carrying her train. But the Council was afraid to join the bridal procession and was unprepared for the wedding. It rejected the crown, more sincerely than Cæsar. But the Soviet must make a statement, give an answer. After long discussion it gave a very short one: "The demonstration is counter-revolutionary," and made Kerensky dictator.

In this Executive Council the moderate Socialists were predominant. To them—much more spontaneously than later to Lenin—the Hour had offered to entrust the fate of the peoples of Russia. But they were honest, asked no more than their due; perhaps also they knew themselves.

Their leader declared at this sitting, "We cannot rule alone for a single day."

The Hour heard these words, and the Bride came never again.

For the hour from which they shrank, Lenin was striving. He was confident that he could rule longer than a day; he had faith in himself. Three months before, on the day when Lenin had declared in the Workers' Soviet that he was prepared to form a Government, there were roars of inextinguishable laughter. But was not the mocking scepticism of his audience unconsciously directed against themselves?

Kerensky now consulted the generals. At his call, and in obedience to his Soviet credentials, sixty thousand men came from the front to St. Petersburg. The Minister of Justice had pamphlets, setting out to prove that Lenin was an enemy agent, distributed in the barracks. Tseretelli, the Minister of the Interior, at once declared that the statements in the pamphlets were deliberate untruths, and the dispenser of justice had to resign. But the "proof" of treachery was more drastically effective than the troops.

The majority of the garrison of St. Petersburg, which would have marched anywhere at the order of the Soviets, remained in barracks. The mutinous regiments and bands of workers were surrounded by a well-disciplined and superior force. An iron wall moved against the rebels, threatened to crush them in a corner. At once, on the very next morning, Ulianov was prepared to lead the retreat from an encounter which he had not wanted.

"Seldom," writes Trotzky, "had Lenin's strategy to mark so complete a turn-about."

He had moments of anxious apprehension, something of the giddiness that follows a blow.

Would not everything come now to confusion and disaster? Had this unexpected turn in events torn to pieces the plans all ready for the morrow? The immediate task, however, was to soften the effect of the blows received and to find a way out. His most disciplined supporters, men of the Putilov works, marched through the streets to banish fear, to prevent rear-guard fighting, to clear away barricades, to advise isolated groups against resistance, and so to give the enemy troops no opportunity for claiming a victory. Nor must the unsuccessful demonstrators see the black pall of defeat. Enthusiasm must not be allowed to die out in the industrial suburbs.

Ulianov accordingly took pains to drown the clash of the swords in strains of peace, set out to compose a song of hope for the defeated. His manifesto spoke of the day's events, and continued: " . . . We call for the conversion of this movement in the regiments and factories into a *peacefully organized demonstration* of the will of all the soldiers, workers and peasants of St. Petersburg."

Kamenev and Zinoviev negotiated with the Workers' Soviet, assured it that the Bolshevik organizations would oppose by force their forcible dissolution. The negotiations ended in the Soviet undertaking to protect Lenin's strongholds from looting.

Ulianov had no faith in this peace. He calculated the power of the enemy, had no belief in their hesitating, could feel the hatred of his opponents.

"Now they will send us packing; this is just their opportunity," he said to a friend.

Once more outlawry spread its cloak over him.

THE HUNT FOR LENIN

There were a few days of desultory fighting, and then the flame of legend spread and blazed.

The victors in St. Petersburg introduced the picturesque. Their success demanded heroes, and inventive braggarts shouted in the market-place.

All great events that stir men's emotions are accompanied by the most wonderful lying. "Tolerance seems to be the virtue only of the ages without faith." At all other periods revolution lies and persecutes in the name of revolution, counter-revolution in the name of counter-revolution, war in the name of war, and everyone in the name of that truth which he serves.

The Government troops lounging in the streets, the cadets of the military academies, the officers, were acclaimed by enthusiastic citizens. The passers-by clapped, flowers were thrown from balconies, and all the fine ladies dreamed of heroes.

The restaurants were brightly lit; waiters were kicked in the old Russian style, lackeys' ears boxed; Tseretelli, Minister of the Interior, sent a circular telegram to all the Government Commissioners instructing them *energetically to put down* any attempt of the peasants to take the solution of the land problem into their own hands; the Duma turned up again, declared that the Ministry had no authority to reorganize the administration; the patricians gave banquets and talked of the dangers overcome in the days just passed. How quickly the spirit had changed! But two or three months before every coffee-stall man, every civil servant, every Governor had been talking of the "changing times," of "reforms," of "reasonable Socialism," of the "living forces" of democracy.

Pale and trembling with indignation, the respectable citizen now called for the strong man, for the gallows, for exemplary punishment, and spoke of the army of murderers in the suburbs. Sensible people, good Liberals, elderly Democrats, philosophizing aristocrats went out of their senses. Their terrified hearts became a prompter's box whispering to their brains catchwords of violence against all that smacked of sedition—newspapers, Parties, theatres, congresses, assemblies, demonstrations—against all their own hopes and aspirations of the day before.

The fanaticism of property is no less passionate, no

keener for destruction than the fury of poverty. In this matter a good bringing up, the best of nurseries, a thorough classical education make not the slightest difference. If the man in the saloon bar is offended to find that the man next to him disagrees with him about sheep breeding or the eclipse of the moon, how he must be maddened when his peace of mind is threatened, still more his interests!

In this, revolutionaries and counter-revolutionaries are true to tradition. As Cromwell, Calvin, Zwingli and Robespierre in their day, so in a few months from now the victorious Leninists were to declare that their opponents must go to the stake as a matter of course, since the Conservatives were mere vestiges of the past, dead branches on the living tree. It was a duty to destroy them. For while a revolutionary party could not be exterminated by terrorism, a counter-revolutionary one died out after a few *coups de grâce*. The Legitimists, for their part, say that the insurrectionaries must be put to the sword because the voice of the rebel is an insult to every mother of a family, to the memory of the dead and, in short, to to every well-disposed person.

And now in St. Petersburg there spoke up the returning defenders of the old régime.

In the critical moments of the street fighting there had been not the faintest sign of them; now they were all the more plainly there for all men to see.

The offices of the Bolshevik newspapers were looted, their printing machinery destroyed, their propagandists beaten in the streets, their leaflets burnt, their party headquarters sacked.

But the Soviets that had saved the Government now shrank back. They saw how the dignitaries of the old régime, who until now had stood petrified, were demanding all too openly to wield the flaming sword of justice. They heard how Purishkevitch, the pogrom leader, who once had spat at the Socialists in the Duma, had congratulated the Government, had advised it to "push these people, who had nothing in common with workers and soldiers, but were receiving money from the German Kaiser and the house of Hohenzollern, into the abyss."

Some of the Mensheviks and Social Revolutionaries recalled the binding promise of the Executive Council of the Soviets not to allow the strongholds of the Bolsheviks to be reduced to ashes; they hurried to the Ministries, appealed to their comrades in office, and struck a compromise. Ulianov's supporters must be brought to justice —but not for their extreme views, only for their common treason.

Orders were issued for the arrest of Lenin, Trotzky, Kamenev, Lunacharsky, Zinoviev, and many others. Trotzky and Lunacharsky, who were still going about openly, were thrown into prison; revolutionary regiments were disbanded; the death penalty was promulgated.

The public prosecutor of the Central Criminal Court of St. Petersburg published in the Press the grounds on which the authorities had decided to prosecute Lenin and his immediate supporters; Lenin was charged with high treason, for there was evidence that he stood in illegal touch with agents of enemy countries. His activities had resulted in certain military units having refused to march against the enemy. The public prosecutor declared that the investigations had revealed that a widespread German espionage organization was at work, and that certain undeniable facts indicated that Lenin was its leader. The public prosecutor declared expressly that the investigations had nothing to do with this man's political views; with these the court was not concerned.

And every hoarding, every newspaper bill, all the Ministers, the generals, the admirals, the leaders of the Mensheviks and the Social Revolutionaries, all the hotel-keepers, lift-boys, barbers shrieked, "Lenin, Lenin!" Military cadets, police officers, students, secret agents, went in search of him. The Prime Minister declared to journalists: "It is my deepest conviction that our breach of the Lenin front is an event of much greater importance than the advance of the Germans against our south-western front."

To Ulianov this crop of blind hatred, this cry for vengeance, brought no surprise. He went into hiding. In his conspirator's life he had grown thoroughly used to that. For whenever he had returned to his country— short engagements with decades of "resting" between them—he had been unable to come out from the wings, had had to be on his guard lest the man next him in the restaurant, in the railway carriage, in the street, were an agent of the Okhrana; had never ventured to present himself to the authorities with a passport in his own name. These echoing reverberations of enemy voices merely showed him how frightened his opponents were. Danger awoke in him his old talent, which he had many times brought into play in the past, for the ingenuities of underground work; and the nearness of victory made this man of caution yet more cautious.

This man of the scholar's study disguised himself as sailor, soldier, peasant or factory worker, and remained in the suburbs of St. Petersburg or in Finland.

In the first days of the storm Lenin lived in a cottage next to a haystack, spending hours in discussion with the sixteen-year-old son of the proletarian family who were his hosts. The boy was a follower of the anarchists, and tackled Ulianov for his lack of Left-wingism. The fugitive did his best to defend himself, searched out all the reasons that brought the boy to his conclusions, and was disappointed at being unable to convince him that he was mistaken.

In his disguise Lenin listened attentively to sailors, dockers, deserters in hiding, tried to ascertain their views on Bolshevism, was keen to discover how the confused situation affected these men's attitude.

In the glory of the orator's desk, in college halls, in the

committee rooms of party headquarters, in elegant or
disorderly editorial offices, politics are a battlefield of
abstract ideas. Ulianov wanted to see how things strike
the proletarian—to whom everyone had daily for six
months past been appealing—to visualize the pictures
produced in the mind of the masses, when they hear the
words "nation," "class," "revolution," "dictatorship,"
"democracy."

In the one room which his hosts had, and in which
Ulianov was living with them, dinner was put on the
table. The bakers' shops were selling white bread once
more—for the first time since 1914. The bright, browned,
appetizing crust, thought the city authorities, would serve
as an argument against Lenin. Did not the March
Revolution come because bread had been lacking and
hunger had distributed the munitions of its despair?
Now, thought the Home Ministry, the best way to beat
Bolshevism was to empty the grain-stores and supply the
poorer suburbs with flour—for a few weeks at all events.
The people would then say: "Where the White standard
waves there is white bread going."

Ulianov was tensely observing how the Government's
argument, which he himself ate with appetite, worked in
this environment, and listened with interest to the family's
remarks. "My host," he writes, "said: 'Just look at the
splendid bread; 'they' don't dare now to give us bad
stuff!'

"I was surprised at this . . . acute judgment of the
events of July. My thoughts passed to the political significance of what had happened . . . to the question of
the situation which . . . must have produced this zigzag course . . . to the changes needed in our slogans and
party organization. . . . I had not . . . thought of the
bread. Bread had always been to me a matter that needed
no thought, as I obtained it from my writings.

"But a member of the oppressed class had hit the nail
on the head . . . with an amazing clarity of perception,

from which we intellectuals are poles apart. To him the matter was perfectly clear. The whole world fell into two categories: 'we,' the workers, and 'they,' the exploiters. . . ."

Days and nights of wandering passed without Ulianov becoming "their" prey.

As he was nowhere to be found, the sensation-mongers reported that the leader of the Bolsheviks had fled to Germany; others declared that he was in hiding in Kronstadt, in Schlüsselburg, in the Urals or the Caucasus. The French Press stated that Lenin's real name was Goldberg. An Israelite paper, crediting the suggestion that he was a Jew, demanded his expulsion from the community: he was a disgrace not only to his country, but to Zion.

The Minister of Justice hit on a ruse for saving the authorities from further labour and annoyance. He declared that Lenin was in honour bound to come forward. If, as his friends declared, he was innocent of the crime of treason, he could easily disprove the evidence of the gentlemen of the law. Lenin might safely approach the bar of justice; for if he were not guilty he would leave it triumphantly in freedom.

This impressed some of Lenin's friends. They urged him to place himself in the hands of the Provisional Government. Ulianov answered from his hiding-place: ". . . The courts are an organ of the powers that be. . . . But what are these powers? Who are these powers? There is no Government; it is changing daily; it is inactive; the thing that is active is the military dictatorship. To speak in that connexion of a court of justice is ridiculous. This is no question of courts of justice, but an episode in the civil war. . . . No courts of justice but a drive against the internationalists—that is what the powers that be want."

In his quiet hiding-place, sheltered beneath the grey canopy of the working-class suburbs, Lenin finished his book on the destruction of the bourgeois State. Even if his opponents had their desire and he were lynched, his volume, he felt, must remain behind him, that his followers might not forget the Doctrine. His work, *State and Revolution,* is thus in effect a testament or a programme speech.

"Dear Kamenev," he wrote to his friend, *"Entre nous,* if they should get me, will you see to the publication of my *Marxism and the State* (it is in safe keeping in Stockholm), in blue cloth covers? It is a compilation of all the passages in Marx and Engels and also Kautsky against Pannekoek. . . . Also a quantity of notes and comments. It only wants putting into shape. I think it could all be done in a week. I think this is of importance, for Plekhanov and Kautsky are not the only people who have been writing nonsense. Only, one thing: let it be strictly *entre nous."*

He was continually giving his friends practical advice for the moment, retained control still in his hands. Amid the mass of incalculable shiftings of opinion and policy which accompany the dying hours of a régime, he sought the traces of the positive and calculable.

"When a revolutionary party," writes Ulianov, "has not the support of a majority either among the vanguard of the revolutionary class or among the rural population, there can be no question of a rising. A rising must have not only this majority, but: (1) the incoming revolutionary tide over the whole country; (2) the complete moral and political bankruptcy of the old régime—for instance, the 'Coalition Government'; and (3) a deep-seated sense of insecurity among all the irresolute elements."

Lenin's enemies had, after all, some comfort in the failure to discover his hiding-place; for the Bolshevik Party Congress met without Lenin's presence.

His opponents supposed that the extreme Left would now be without a leader. But this strategist, even though he was not present, was able to prescribe the essential lines of the resolutions, and to hear at second hand the confident shouts of victory which rose from the assembly. The Party already had 126 branches aggregating 200,000 members. In a number of towns the Soviets were already Bolshevist. In the principal working-class districts in St. Petersburg his supporters had gained the majority at the municipal elections.

He felt that the more disorganization spread among his opponents, the more the State fell into dissolution, the more firmly based was the rising pyramid of his own hierarchy.

His friends' statistics showed that the conditions of victory were present. Nothing remained but to throw the gauntlet, and the power would be in his hands.

Impatience beat more and more insistently on the door of his hiding-place.

CAN THE BOLSHEVIKS MAINTAIN THEMSELVES IN POWER?"

In bitter disappointment the Democratic leaders had united in declaring that only dictatorship could "save the country."

Kerensky would gladly have ruled as *Imperator*. But he lacked two attributes of the Napoleonic: the *virtus* of the ancients and the eagle quality of success.

If he spoke of final, decisive, draconic measures, all that men heard was a hoarse voice and all they saw, a threatening forefinger. His heroics had behind them neither a great idea nor the argument of bayonets. Yet he symbolized one sort of dictatorship—that of impotence. With a tireless rhetoric never before equalled, this Minister, holding three portfolios and supreme command of the army, tried to frighten the Revolution with the generals and the generals with the Revolution. Next day, at best, there would follow pettifogging little police measures that failed entirely to hurt the opponents of the Government, only irritating and annoying them, and, above all, revealing to them its impotence.

Some of the officers in high command inferred that power was an unclaimed estate, belonging, as under Roman law, to whoever was first to take possession of it. They saw how over ten thousand army officers had been driven away by the men at the front, heard how Russians of rank and culture were aping the peasant in his Soviet by gathering together in all sorts of conferences and councils, provincial and national, to applaud and hiss and get nothing done.

But if the politicians lived only for the splendour of rhetoric, the field-marshals were no wiser: they exaggerated the saving sense of their nags and the usefulness of their cavalry attacks. General Kornilov, like many of his colleagues, negotiated for a long time with Kerensky. In the end he lost patience, and decided himself to march against the centre of the plague, against the mother of anarchy, against St. Petersburg, against the Provisional Government. His offensive was planned as a crushing blow against Bolshevism, his anathemas were aimed against Lenin. ". . . The enemy," declared the mutinous commander in a manifesto, "who, thanks to bribery and treason, is raising his head in our country as though it were his own, is aiming at the destruction not only of the liberty but of the very existence of the Russian people. Men of Russia, awake from your mad delusion!"

Over the heads of the political rank and file, who were bolting from one camp into another amid a fearful hail of words; above the whole machinery of government, which was now but a convoy stuck in the morass; high above the mere paper existence of the institutions of the State, which were robbed now of all reality—there stood working against one another two enemies: Kornilov, in the splendour of his staff, and the outlawed Ulianov.

"For a short time," writes Miliukov, the leader of the Cadets, "the choice was free between Kornilov and Lenin. . . . Driven by a sort of instinct, the masses—for it was with the masses that the decision lay—pronounced for Lenin."

Kerensky's Government set free the sailors and soldiers who had rebelled against it in the July rising and had been imprisoned; it greeted them on their liberation and entrusted to them the defence of the State against the mutinous general. Lenin's supporters mobilized the industrial suburbs against Kornilov.

But before the battle began the power of the cavalry leader melted away like an ice cream on the terrace of a country restaurant. When he made to swallow the first spoonful the delicacy had dissolved, and the disappointed Kornilov found himself in prison.

Ulianov was now concerned lest his own community should succumb to love of Kerensky. The Provincial Government must be preserved, but only like game, that it might in the end come up to his table.

The action of the mutinous general had brought complete disorganization into the army. Now the conscript soldiers were definitely convinced that the officers' shoulder-straps were the mark of the Beast, and Lenin saw his forebodings of anarchy realized.

He was still in hiding in a Finnish village, only to be reached with difficulty by his closest friends. "If you should want to come here," he writes to an acquaintance, "ask Rovio to telephone to Huttunen, the Deputy in the Finnish Diet, and say that someone wants to go to see Rovio's wife's sister."

Occasionally he left his refuge to go to St. Petersburg to the meetings of the Central Committee.

He was torn with impatience. He was continually

urging "Now or never." He felt Kornilov's attempt as a personal insult, was outraged at the thought that another should have dreamed of robbing him of his own darling child, power. It seemed to him as if the morning would never come, the evening never end, and the whole day seemed to consist of unchanging minutes which repeated, as often as the second hand moved, "It is getting too late, getting too late!"

He was living in panic. He implored his friends to act, as a drowning man might cry for help to a steamer majestically ploughing by. Letter after letter, pamphlet after pamphlet he sent to his Party, called his most devoted friends traitors, tried to impose his whole soul on others, to pass on to comrades his determination, his agitation, his conviction.

This usually tedious writer, whose collected Works were as necessary for their own day as its daily bread, but are to-day (for they were written purely for the needs of the hour) like the remains of a meal, this foe of fine writing wrote now, in utmost haste, letters of which the sentences are impregnable barricades. He poured out his whole soul on the paper, composed in a few hasty minutes harmonies with the ring of the Marseillaise. He had suddenly become a poet of terse urgency.

Until the moment of the seizure of power he was sending to every authority of his party such appeals as this to the Petersburg and Moscow Committees of the Bolsheviks:

"Events are dictating our task so clearly that dilatoriness would be absolutely a *crime*.

"The peasant movement is growing . . . sympathy with us is continually increasing—99 per cent. of the soldiers are with us in Moscow; the Finnish troops and the fleet are against the Government. . . .

"The railwaymen and postal servants are in conflict with the Government.

"Under such conditions to 'wait' would be a crime.

"The Bolsheviks have not the right . . . to wait, they must seize the Government . . . otherwise the wave of anarchy may become too strong for us.

"It would be a crime to hesitate; to wait for the Soviet Congress would be childish punctilio . . . treason to the Revolution. . . .

"There is no absolute necessity to 'begin' with St. Petersburg. If Moscow 'begins' without bloodshed, it will certainly have support. . . .

"The word must be: Power to the Soviets, land to the peasants, peace to the peoples, bread to the hungry.

"Victory is assured, and it is ten to one that it will be bloodless.

"To wait would be a crime against the Revolution.

"Greetings,
"N. LENIN."

For months he had been giving quite concrete advice, which continually grew more definite. As early as September he had written to his friend Smilga from Viborg:

"The latest events have . . . confirmed the accuracy of my view that a political problem has become a military one. I am afraid that the Bolsheviks are forgetting this and lulling themselves with the hope that a wave of indignation will sweep Kerensky away. . . . We must get together the most reliable of the soldiers into a secret committee, go thoroughly into everything with them, keep control ourselves of the whole movement, and have exact information of the strength of the troops in and around St. Petersburg, and also of the possibility of transporting Finnish regiments thither. . . .

"We must make use of the services of the sailors and

soldiers who go home to their villages on leave, for purposes of agitation. . . ."

"We must put our brains into the rising," he tells the Central Committee of his Party—"we must . . . not lose a moment in organizing a staff for the insurgent troops, apportioning our forces, detailing the reliable regiments for the principal points, surrounding the Alexander Theatre, occupying the Fortress of Peter and Paul, arresting the general and the Government. . . . We must mobilize the armed workers, call on them for the last, desperate, decisive struggle; must at once seize the telegraphs and telephones, post our staff in the central telephone exchange, and connect up with it by telephone all the works, all the regiments, every point of the armed struggle, and so on."

Still some of his friends refused to listen to any idea of insurrection. The very fact of the general sympathy for the Bolsheviks, declared Zinoviev and Kamenev, made any sudden seizure of power needless, criminal. Why run the extremest risk when the Constituent Assembly which had to be elected would bring success by peaceful. means?

Lenin mobilized against these leaders the mass of the party membership, declared that the moment for the critical move could no longer be postponed. The country would no more wait than a raging fire would. He resorted to the ruse of assuring his comrades that only his Government would really allow the Constituent Assembly to sit, that the others were in dread of the elected of the nation.

At last, at the end of October, the Central Committee of the Party assembled to make its final decision.

Here three policies fought for mastery: Lenin opposed any further delay; Zinoviev and Kamenev were against a rising; and a third policy was advanced by Trotzky.

Leo Davidovitch Trotzky was the chairman of the Petersburg Soviet, which had lately become predomi-

nantly Bolshevik. He wanted to summon the second All-Russian Congress of Soviets early in November. This assembly should declare the Provincial Government deposed. The preparations and the rising, in Trotzky's view, should take place in full publicity. The threat implicit in them would intimidate the opponents and would arouse popular enthusiasm. The garrison of St. Petersburg was prepared to defend the All-Russian Congress from any attempt at violence.

Ulianov was against Trotzky's plan; he feared that the other side might, by rapid action, put an end to the preparations for the congress. He was quite unable to understand why Kerensky had not yet arrested the Revolutionary War Committee of the Petersburg Soviet, which Trotzky had just formed.

It was agreed, however, to begin the rising in the first week of November.

Lenin went home towards the morning more at ease, sat down at his writing-table and answered the question which was still to remain for a long time an anxious one for millions. More calmly and more objectively than all the outside observers, Ulianov, before anyone else, examined the problem. The pamphlet which he wrote on it a week *before* the seizure of power was called:

"Can the Bolsheviks Maintain Themselves in Power?"

He reviewed the results of all the elections which had taken place so far, and concluded:

"Thus the majority of the peasants are against the Coalition. . . . Objectively regarded, the situation in Russia is, no doubt, that the proletariat is not at this moment isolated from the majority of the petty bourgeoisie. . . . The proletariat is not in a position to 'conquer' the 'machinery of State' and to set it in motion. . . . On the other hand, it is in a position . . . to set its own new type of machinery in motion. . . . It will be necessary to proceed with the utmost energy . . . against the highest officials, as against the capitalists. . . . These methods

of control and of *compulsion to work* are more effective than the legislating and the guillotine of the Convention. The guillotine only intimidated, only broke the *active* opposition. *That is not enough for us.* We must compel the officials to continue at work within the framework of the recognized State. . . . 'If any would not work, neither should he eat!' That is the fundamental principle, the first and the most important of all. . . . The Soviets will introduce the work-card for the rich and then for the rest of the population. . . . After the Revolution of 1905 Russia was governed by 150,000 landowners . . . and is it suggested that the 240,000 members of the Bolshevik Party cannot rule Russia in the interest of the poor and against the rich? . . . No great revolution in history escapes the phase of civil war. And only those who are out of touch with the world can suppose that civil war is conceivable without bringing extraordinary complications and difficulties. . . . Our Revolution is invincible if it is not afraid of itself."

From the first days of power to the moment when Nature robbed him of speech, and, as if in mockery, left him with reason, the difficulties were much more enormous than he had pictured to himself in his quiet hiding-place. Considered in the abstract and at peace, his ideas came in orderly succession, made way for one another, danced to the measure of their natural logic. In a few weeks the abstract was to vanish, theories were to be but an evening prayer; the concrete was to pile crag on crag, to open abysses across which no guide could show the way. All these measures, for which Ulianov called when the hope came of an early seizure of the helm, were attempted, but succeeded only here and there, giving the effect of stray palm-trees in a landscape bare as the face of the moon. Every step called for in this pamphlet struck at the interests of thousands; each step was a separate campaign with its victories and defeats.

Not until at least a century has passed will it be possible

to discuss the results of this pamphlet. Not until predilections and prejudices and individual faiths are no longer offended—till none of the hopes raised remains to ask for fulfilment and no witness of those days continues to breathe—will History, that clearing-house of all apologias, be able to give its judgment. When the day comes for that, the verdict may well have its surprises both for Lenin and his disciples and for his victims.

But before Ulianov laid down the lines of his future programme—in spite of all the expectations which were releasing him from the deep spell of thirty years' longing—a day had come, at the beginning of September, when he thought of compromising. It might, Lenin felt, be necessary to take this indirect path to power. A *ruse de guerre* would perhaps hasten matters. He proposed, therefore, to the Mensheviks and the Social Revolutionaries that they should cut themselves free from the bourgeois parties and the representatives of property, and themselves seize power; the Bolsheviks were prepared to give them *loyal support* as a benevolent Opposition.

"The question of the moment is one not of a compulsory, but of a voluntary compromise," wrote Lenin. "Now and now only, perhaps only within a few days or one or two weeks at most, could such a Government be formed and consolidated by entirely peaceful means."

". . . Ilyitch," writes Trotzky, "loved all the stratagems of war, the throwing sand in the enemy's eyes and getting the better of him by ruse. . . ."

The Mensheviks and the Social Revolutionaries, however, were not prepared to stand up against Ulianov unsupported by a Coalition. They continued to negotiate in endlessly prolonged meetings with the Cadets; formed, as it were, over and over again the very same Government, only to bring it down again a few days later; abandoned demands to-day, pressed them again to-morrow.

"After long negotiations," said a report from St. Peters-

burg on October 6, "the Mensheviks gave way, and abandoned the points to which the Cadets had refused to agree, such as the dissolution of the Duma, a compulsory loan from the richer classes, and the immediate transfer of all landed property to the Agrarian Commissions."

Every change of portfolio was at last attempted to save the situation. Every time a Minister went and was replaced by another, such newspapers as the *Retch* wrote: "The present Coalition is the last effort to defend the country from the man-eater Lenin."

Kerensky, however, who still enjoyed the applause of his many secretaries, repeated what the last Tsarist Minister, Protopopov, had said before the March Revolution. He declared that he was fully prepared, and wanted nothing better than a rising of the Bolsheviks. Two days before his flight through a back door of the Government Palace, disguised as a cook, the Dictator met Sir George Buchanan. "Kerensky," wrote Sir George in his diary, "was inclined to be optimistic. In the talk I have just had with him he cried out more than once: 'I only wish they would come; then I will make an end of them!'"

Hurriedly this orator, who was so confident of victory, summoned troops to St. Petersburg. The Council of the regiments marching in to the capital telegraphed to the Soviet: "We are being sent to Petrograd. No idea why; please explain." The Soviet replied begging the soldiers to come, to help the Revolutionary War Committee.

Kerensky had given orders some days before this for detachments of the garrison to be sent to the front. Trotzky had replied, in the name of the Revolutionary War Committee, "No!" The Soviet had demanded control over all the actions of the Officer Commanding the St. Petersburg area. The Provisional Government decided not at once to resort to force, but to negotiate first. The insurrectionary committee wanted nothing better than this delay; it gave the Bolsheviks plenty of

time to study the map of St. Petersburg and distribute
their forces.

Kerensky, however, was anxious to protect the already
weakened authority of the State from further disintegra-
tion, and thought the moment for firmness had come. He
gave orders for the printing-offices of the Bolshevik newspapers and the organ of the Soviet to be sealed up. At
the same time the garrison commander issued a proclamation warning the population not to attempt any fresh
rising.

Some miles from St. Petersburg, on the banks of the
Neva, there rises like a sullen wall of rock the forbidding
façade of the Smolny Institute, originally a *pensionnat*
for young ladies of birth, built at the desire of Catherine II close alongside the Smolny convent, whose five-
domed cathedral majestically dominates the whole neighbourhood.

The halls and rooms of this palace no longer echoed
with the girlish laughter of the young students. Along
its interminable corridors there went to and fro the delegates from factories and barracks. Those people who
came up its stairs for the first time would wander about in
search of one or other of the many committees sitting
here. The old plates were still on the doors. Alongside "Ladies' Class Room" and "Teaching Staff Office"
one might read cards inscribed "Socialist Soldiers'
Association" or "Factory and Workshop Delegates."

In room No. 18 there worked the Bolshevik Parliamentary group, and in Nos. 10 and 17 the Revolutionary
War Committee.

For days past the men in these three rooms had not
left Smolny. Pale, suffering from lack of sleep, reduced
to a bundle of nerves, they were listening to the voices
from all parts of the capital, from barracks and factory.
The last effort before the seizure of power consisted of

countless oratorical duels. Ambassadors from the three rooms appealed to regiments and works employees to make up their minds to an immediate rising. The indicator on the scale of public feeling jerked to and fro, until the workers consulted resolved, amid shouts of hope and joy, on a renewal of open insurrection.

On this 7th of November the men in the three rooms made their final throw.

Their first command had the ingratiating tone of one of Nicholas II's ukases before an engagement; it appealed to the workers' heroism in the style of a thousand-years-old tradition. The Revolutionary War Committee annulled the Government decree of confiscation of the Bolshevik newspapers and the Soviet organ, and entrusted the "famous Volhynian regiment with the honourable duty of protecting freedom of Socialist speech from counter-revolutionary violence."

Then followed command after command.

The offices of the Petrograd News Agency, the banks, the general post office, the railways were occupied without opposition.

About 1 p.m. Leo Davidovitch Trotzky, in the name of the Revolutionary War Committee, declared the Provisional Government at an end. For a moment he stood still at the speaker's desk in the Soviet hall, as though under the spell of the splendour of an unknown sea; then he spoke, sharply accenting every separate word:

"We, the Soviets of the Workers', Soldiers', and Peasants Delegates, are on the point of making an experiment that has not its like in history."

Only a few shots were fired in the city. Whole blocks of houses were occupied on telephoned orders from Smolny. Negotiations went on with members of the Government and with the representatives of the moderate Socialist parties, who knew nothing of the arrests of several Ministers which had already been effected. "While the rising," relates Kerensky, "was actually in full

LENIN, BUCHARIN, ZINOVIEV, AND PAUL LEVI

TROOPS PARADING BEFORE TROTZKY

GENERAL BRUSSILOV AND TROTZKY INSPECTING A REGIMENT

progress, and the Red Armies were at work all over the
city . . . Bolshevik Deputies . . . were trying to dupe
the representatives of the democracy. These artists in
debate passed the whole night in the discussion of various
formulæ. . . . By means of these methods of conducting
negotiations the Bolsheviks gained time. . . ."

"The truth is," writes Trotzky, "that the Bolsheviks
who took part in the negotiations were those who wanted
to put an end to the rising. . . . Viewed objectively, the
efforts of these Deputies were undoubtedly of some service to the insurrectionary movement."

Ulianov had already been staying for some days in a
suburb of St. Petersburg. From such news as he heard
and read he had to infer that the Military Committee
was negotiating with the Government.

Towards midday on November 7 he left his place of
concealment. Cautiously, like a scout on reconnoitring
duty, he approached Smolny. The streets had their everyday appearance. Only a placard, which brought no surprise to the new Prime Minister and Dictator as he
crept along the side-streets, announced the end of the
old régime.

At last, towards evening, Ulianov reached the revolutionary headquarters.

"Lenin said to me," writes Trotzky, " 'Are you fellows
agreeing to a compromise?' And he looked me through
and through. I replied . . . that it was only a manœuvre. . . . 'Well, that's fine,' said Lenin, with hearty
emphasis, full of joy and enthusiasm, rubbing his hands
excitedly and beginning to walk up and down the room.
'That's splendid!' "

He was a prey to nervous excitement; every minute he
asked how things were going. Nothing short of complete
victory seemed to him to be of value. But half an hour
later this conspirator was the calmest man in the whole
directing body: he could feel now how everything was
proceeding steadily through the development of the

masses now in motion into an organism; he pieced together the incoming news, and was able quietly to observe the course of the events of the next few hours. He remained perfectly cool-headed, and brought a corresponding influence to bear on men around him, who were feverishly issuing orders, trusting to their winners' flair to inspire the right thing at the right moment.

In the great hall of the Smolny there met the second Congress of Soviets.

Amid an uproar and confusion of applause and protests, amid wild torrents of words, the Presidium was elected: fourteen Bolsheviks, seven Social Revolutionaries, three Mensheviks and one member of the Gorky group.

The advocates of Socialist gradualism disappeared for good and all from the stage. For six months past they had continually shirked the responsibility of commanding in the name of the impatient fury of the armed masses and had fought shy of the task of reducing their opponents to impotence.

Now they were themselves reduced to impotence. Men untainted by their dilettantism, broad shouldered and resolute, rose from the midst of the assembly and took their place in the Presidium.

Suddenly the walls shook. The dull, regular boom of cannon was heard. The hall went wild, as though its voices wanted to drown the roar of the guns, to tell them in what direction to fire. The Mensheviks raged, shouted curses at the majority: "Bandits! liars! murderers! you have occupied the city behind our backs like highwaymen! You have arrested the Socialist Ministers!"

Martov attempted to speak; like Ulianov, he was for peace. If this rebel of many years trembled now before the thunder of civil war, it was not out of fear, but out of anxiety lest the Revolution should go to its downfall. He proposed negotiations for a united front. "Victory is the only way out," replied the majority.

The minority left the congress.

Lenin was no longer in the hall. He was waiting in a small room in the Smolny; it was already late at night. Trotzky hurried to him. The room had no furniture; a few blankets were brought, and the two victors lay down to rest. Trotzky was called up every ten minutes.

The two tried for some hours to get some sleep. Messengers came again and brought the latest news: Kerensky had fled, the Winter Palace had been stormed!

The night had passed; a blue dawn awoke the sleepers. Lenin, pale with exhaustion, said with a tired smile to his companion:

"The climb from outlawry and vagabondage to power is too steep—one gets dizzy." This remains the one recorded sentence in which he expressed his personal feeling.

Summoning his utmost physical and mental resources, he went down into the hall, where deserters from the front, workers from the factories, literary men who had been living in exile for a quarter of a century, and idlers from the suburbs, hung about waiting for something to happen.

THE STATE GIVES BIRTH TO REVOLUTION AND THE REVOLUTION TO A STATE

St. Petersburg is the city of Russian effort.

Here the dreaming of the steppes, the play of fantasy along the strand of southern seas, the softly murmuring woods, are stilled.

The river banks are cold. Wage-earners, year in and year out, must hold the Neva in captivity.

In the sodden flats and islands, wooden piles must be rammed into the earth before roads can be laid and houses built.

This city was built up on human lives; countless sacrifices went to its making.

Here the landscape loses the enchantment of stillness and is instinct with historic movement. The keen west wind that blows over the city unleashes human forces from the ordinary life of Russia, spurs men on to effort, endows them with the faculty of providing for the economic, political and military organization of the State.

Here Peter the Great reached the open sea, crossing himself, as he approached its keen air, like a Crusader at the gates of Jerusalem. In Riga already he had sacrificed to the ocean, throwing down a glass vessel and saying: "Which of you, my soldiers, would have believed thirty years ago that one day you Russians would be building ships here on the shore of the Baltic, and therewithal, clothed in the German style, be feasting and carousing with me here?"

Peter, like every reformer, saw already the realization of ideals of which but few of his followers had any inkling; he could see his future capital, with its walls and domes, of which no stone was yet laid, and tell of the scientific advance which in his belief gave life to earth as the circulating blood to men's bodies. He concluded the banquet with words of aspiration and prophecy: "I can see how science will leave her home in England, France and Germany, and come for some centuries to live with us."

Peter the Great set out to prescribe the course of events, just as he had laid down that the *mujik* must shave his beard, wash himself and cut his nails, and that the children of the noble families must learn arithmetic and the propositions of Euclid, "in default whereof they were not to be permitted to marry until they had learnt these things."

But, just as Peter forced European ways on his subjects, necessity forced on him the provision of a solid social structure, a State and its apparatus of power. This he had to do or be destroyed by his neighbours.

Absolutism had its first real beginnings under him; he envisaged and created the fundamentals of autocratic rule, built a social substructure which resembled that of St. Petersburg: labour and the bones of dead serfs.

The unrestricted power of the dictator is as necessary for this State as the piles of its capital: the might of the Tsar was no invention of the Evil One. As a bridge over the waters will not only join one bank with another, but cross on its way islands of the most varied elevations, so the central power unites all the phases of civilization which exist within the bounds of this realm. Within the millions of square miles of Muscovy there live, in its northern primeval forests, savages; there live hunters whose food is raw fish; dwellers in its steppes pray to stones; and in the towns men and women work with the latest appliances evolved by scientific advance.

If all this were not to fall asunder it must be held together by a colossal State mechanism. But the very immensity of this structure, the fact that its summit rose high above the ordinary levels of human life, made it a thing apart from the nation, a law unto itself.

The monarch, that pinnacle of the State adorned in glittering splendour, became no longer a servant of the needs of society, but a dreamer living in the realm of mystical invention. The whole weakness of absolutism lay in the danger that the all-powerful ruler might become no more than a being with human needs. Nature had her revenge: the crowned head that commanded all dwellers on this earth suffered from the repletion that this right brought with it. To the last of the Romanovs a message, a tear from the Unknown, seemed a thing of more importance than all the seas of Russia. The logical development of two centuries of power ended with its slipping from the hands of Peter into those of Rasputin.

When Nicholas II, stupefied with incense, sank and disappeared, the intricate structure of power collapsed with him.

On this evening of November 7, 1917, the moon lit up the ruins of Autocracy, which in its faintly quivering rays seemed desolate as the Forum Romanum.

This man who had shaved off his beard so that the police should not recognize him until the hour of triumph, who on the eighth day of the eleventh month of this year became Prime Minister under an assumed name —his pseudonym Lenin—had written his theory of the State expressly for this moment while still an exile, with the same matter-of-fact inevitability with which a crown prince might have his proclamation prepared for the hour of his succession.

"In 1916," writes Riazanov, "I had the opportunity of observing Lenin at work in Zurich. We were working at adjoining tables in the Library, and I noted with admiration the diligence and concentration with which this fiery revolutionary often read for hours the books he needed, how he surrounded himself with mountains of volumes, how tirelessly he undertook 'excavations'—as he called them in his book—what astonishing capacity he had for discovering new apt quotations and for throwing fresh light on old ones."

The fruit of these labours was the work on *State and Revolution*.

On November 8 this industrious reader was keen to come before the Soviet, to recall to it how fruitful each dig with the spade had been, and to show it his plans for the now homeless nation. Ulianov was the only one who at that moment had in his head the complete scheme of a new organization; he was ready with the play five minutes before the first night.

Was it chance? Was it historic continuity? Was this book the revised issue of the testament of Peter the Great?

Lenin, however, had not constructed his theory of the

State out of legends of the Ruriks, out of the archives of the Romanovs, out of the libraries of Byzantine monasteries or treatises on orthodox theology. He took it from German philosophy, from Hegel, Karl Marx, from the reports of sittings of the French Convention and the journals of the Long Parliament.

His theory was thus a Western fruit, but it was to be tested out on Russian soil. The work was garnished with German, French and English quotations; but its conclusions demanded the same blind obedience as the ukase of Peter the Great. His subjects were to be allowed to wear beards, to let their nails grow, even to marry without passing in algebra; but they were to be impressed into the service of the modern principle—that of Socialism—as resolutely as the Tsar had impressed them two centuries before into the beginnings of capitalism.

In the old palace of autocracy the rooms of the hierarchy were in excellent order. Every little door had its placard. The inscriptions—Imperial Mews, Okhrana, Police Guard-room, Holy Synod and Privy Purse Department—were plain for all to read. But all these rooms had long been disused. Through their unwashed windows it was no longer possible to see the blue sky. Parrots hopped from bundle to bundle of documents, repeating the same phrase over and over again; ravens flitted about in search of jewels. The prouder the magnificence of these apartments of majesty, the softer was the tapestry that padded their walls, that no intolerable sounds of the commonalty should disturb their peace.

Ulianov was for putting up great halls in *his* palace; his State was to become a warm shelter for thousands. But could uncounted numbers find room in it? The Master was to be stern in casting out; every porter was to be a policeman, and to admit no one without the mark of the true faith. The staff was to be changed, and the servants of the new form of State, coming from the masses, were to have rather less contempt for the voices from the fields, factories and barracks than their predecessors, even when their brother-workers were not present.

"New States," once wrote the brilliant pamphleteer of monarchy, Rivarol, to his irresolute master Louis XVI, "can only be built up on mud, blood and brutality; they are erected from the bottom upwards."

The first pale dawn of a new social order flowed into the great hall of Smolny amid cries of direst need and of eagerness for new activity. Here there waited young soldiers, workers from the farthest of the outlying factories, men of every race of Russia, shouting in the bewildered intoxication of their accession to power. Most of them could neither read nor write, were nothing but waves of the boundless dark sea of the people, attracted by the Revolution as by a moon and flooding in a tidal wave through this educational institute of Catherine II.

The accredited representatives of the foreign States were already receiving the news of the birth of the new Power. "I have the honour," wrote Trotzky, as M.C. of the insurrection, "to inform you, *M. l'Ambassadeur,* that the Congress of the General Soviets of Russia installed on the 8th instant a new Government of the Republic, formed out of the Soviets of the People's Commissars. Vladimir Ilyitch *Lenin* has been appointed President of the new Government. The conduct of foreign policy has been placed in my hands. . . ."

The new Government entered the assembly hall of the Soviets; Lenin was the first to take his seat in the Presidium.

"A thick-set figure," is the description given of him by an eye-witness, "with a big head, rather bald, set on a stout neck, with small mobile eyes, a big kindly mouth and a powerful chin, now shaven; though the familiar beard, which he was from then on to wear once more, was already making its reappearance. In shabby clothes, with trousers much too long for him. . . ."

When the assembly recognized him, all shouted deliriously, shouted their enthusiasm at the realization of their dreams of success. Their whole faith seemed to them to find expression in Lenin's features.

For a moment he did not know what to do under the storm of applause; awkwardly as an actor on the stage who finds his own hands an embarrassment, he turned the pages of his manuscript.

Lenin let the others speak first. Kamenev reported progress; then a Menshevik thundered denunciations. Only yesterday the moderates had declared that they were leaving the Soviet for ever; but their political activities consisted of resignations and their withdrawal; they came as a warning and left as a warning.

The new head of the Government looked observantly round the hall during the debate; his eyes seemed to wander in search of each individual delegate. There they sat now before him, these enthusiasts for whom he had longed through thirty years.

Chins supported in the hollow of their hands, they listened attentively to the speaker, their faces distorted with rage or radiant with enthusiasm. Would this crowd of followers belong still to him to-morrow? He was determined to remain where he was, determined as he had been in working and longing through decades for this moment of power, as he had worked for this day in Stockholm, Berlin, Cracow, Paris, London, Zurich. Now, now for rapid action—now, in the hour of consummation; now, when only hope was vocal. Difficulties would come, but not until the morrow, when these peasants and workers would be dying for the Republic on every front.

Certainly the hall of the Convention had been a more magnificent one. There had sat the talents of a century, a legion of thinkers had thronged. There had been Carnot, builder of fourteen armies; Lacanal, who sketched the plan of the public elementary school system; Saint-Just, who knew only how to win victories and write poems; Danton, the saviour of Paris; Morveau, who built a hundred hospitals; Tutien, who spread over the country a network of museums; Condorcet, the educationist of genius. In the hall of the Convention scholars had sat as closely packed together as the illiterates here on the floor of the Smolny. "But if we are to wait," the head of the Government had written, "till people are ripe for Socialism, we shall have to wait another five hundred years."

This Smolny was Russia as the Convention had been France.

It was not scholars that mattered, or whether an idea was right or wrong, true or false, but whether at the critical moment it was good or bad, useful or harmful. Who could say whether Lenin, when he saw Socialism there realized, was not floundering in error in company with the men at his feet? But these men were the power without which no community can live.

The last speaker had finished. Lenin stook up to speak, at last emerged from hiding. He who until now had only led from the background, from gloom and seclusion, had had plans too big to leave room for personal ambition, came now along into the centre, heard and seen by all, to give his whole message from this platform.

He stepped to the desk, waited for the applause to end, and spoke, as always, without heroics or peroration. Every speech he made ended simply with the sentence: "That is all I had to say to you."

He gripped the sides of the desk and began:

"What is the significance of this Revolution of the workers and peasants? The significance of this upheaval lies, above all, in the fact that we now have our own organ of power, in which the bourgeoisie have no part whatever. . . . The old machinery of State is being razed to the ground . . . a new administrative machinery is being set up. . . . One of our first tasks is the immediate liquidation of the war . . . we must at once publish all the secret treaties. . . . We secure the confidence of the peasants by a decree expropriating the

landowners. . . . We shall introduce a real control of
production by the workers. . . . In Russia we must
now occupy ourselves with the building up of the proletarian Socialist State."

After this Government statement a Menshevik stood
up to speak, and asked whether the Head of the Republic
was prepared to sign any sort of peace.

Lenin did not accept the traditional unwritten law of
opposition, "When in power, forget everything you have
said before," as sound advice for the statesman. But he
could no longer speak merely as a propagandist and con-
troversialist.

The first few moments of power had changed everything.

He was responsible for the soldiers at the front, for
peace and war. Ulianov was aware of the powerlessness
of the army and the hopes this was arousing among the
Germans. The Premier resorted at once to the diplomacy
which he had used in past battles with coffee-house opponents. The curiosity of his questioner was welcome. Un-
initiated into the etiquette which the Head of the Government should observe, he sprang up at once, without waiting for a sign from the Presidium, and spoke the words
which became the starting-point of Soviet diplomacy:
". . . We are not afraid of a revolutionary war. It
may be that the imperialist Governments will leave our
appeal unanswered. We shall not deliver an ultimatum
which they would easily reject. . . . For some of our
conditions we shall fight to the bitter end, but for others
it will perhaps be impossible to go on fighting. The
point is that we want to end the war."

The delegates caught their breath; the dream had come
true—the war was over! If the general staff of the enemy
could have had a photograph of this room, with its magnificence and the ragged men in it, filled with passionate
longing for peace, they would have demanded the annexation of Russia up to Irkutsk and have imposed on

the rest of her territory—as far as Vladivostok—the acceptance of a treaty of friendship and fair trade.

But one thing which the generals on the other side of the now non-existent front could not have seen, and would not have annexed at any price if they had seen it, was the spirit that inspired that evening's gathering.

Every tramp, aristocrat or beggar is an artist while he sleeps. Few can tell or even feel, once they wake, the colour and line of their dreams; but now, in this moment, the hidden harmonies in the unconscious souls of these four hundred men were merged in the melancholy strains of the revolutionary anthem:

> We've too long been the vulture's prey.

Amid the rhythmic swell of their song the men looked at Lenin, who stood with sunken head, his eyes fixed on his desk. He felt their glances as a soft caress; they were currents of power from a giant realm, which flowed into his brain and gave Ulianov a scale by which to weigh imponderable things, an instinct for the problems of the coming years.

A Frenchman who had seen many things, had invented more, and had lived through similar moments in the French Revolution, used whenever changes disturbed his soul's peace to utter the maxim: "In life one encounters sooner or later everything and its opposite."

The god of historic change could not permit anyone in this palace—unless, perhaps, the few servants who remained—to indulge in such thoughts.

LENIN IN POWER

The first snows were beginning to fall in St. Petersburg.

In the open space in front of the Smolny, groups of delegates discussed the Soviet Congress just ended. They hurried to the railway stations, some entering each of the departing trains, or got into military motor-cars. Their voices disappeared into the white gloom of the evening.

These men were the officers of the new régime. The Government had no troops to give them, no guns, at most a revolver and credentials addressed to all and none; more than this the Soviet of Socialist dictators did not possess. But the revolutionary committees were lavish with the one possession that they had—words.

The delegates set off, laden with manifestos. Each of them carried a heavy burden of exclamation marks. They took with them to their Siberian, Caucasian, Ural villages, to the Asian provinces and to the borders of the Black Sea, the news of events in St. Petersburg, the message of peace and of the destruction of the old system of landed estates. Each village was to act by its own authority and on its own initiative.

What would Russia say in reply? Would memories of the past close men's minds to the new gospel?

All over the country there were repetitions of the scenes which had been witnessed in the factories and barracks of St. Petersburg on the eve of the seizure of power. The rebellion of those days gave birth to a confidence that inspired millions of men.

Universal as the tender gleam of the light of dawn, which opens the corolla of every flower in the meadows, was the effect of the Revolution: it missed no single hamlet or peasant's cottage.

Lenin had not the power to command in every place where men came together. And if his action had been nothing more than the arbitrary exercise of force, the violent subjection of the nation, he would now, to be able to enforce his will on every man in Russia, have needed infinite legions.

Critical changes had been coming unobserved, not only in the whole realm, where old truth and error were fleeing to make room for new, but also in the room in the Smolny Institute, in the centre of the country, where Ulianov was moulding the new structure of power, taking his material, sound and faulty, as he found it.

This bad stylist was now within the gates of power. But power was not yet conquered. The few machine-guns which protected Smolny were the new Government's whole armament.

Would not the declaration of yesterday, the programme announced, remain mere brave words, like snowflakes that gleam in the moonlight and sink to earth, to vanish for ever?

For four thousand years the poor had rebelled amid the same sighs and shouts. Here and there, in the Egypt of the Pharaohs, in the land of Olympus, in the gardens of Sicily, in republican and imperial Rome, in the Southern France of the Albigenses, in a cathedral of mediæval Germany, in the Paris Commune, the discontented had had short hours of victory—moments short as the twinkling of an eye in the great historic process. Such risings would merely cover the palace of the fleeing rulers with a few daubs of colour, which the next rain would wash from the walls, leaving them free of all trace of the ineffective assault. Was it possible that rebellion should this time maintain its hold of the throne?

Yes, declared Ulianov, if it ceased to be a rebellion and took the shape of a new order! In that moment he became a statesman, and all the qualities developed through thirty years of opposition became evidences of governing power.

But how, with the tiny governing staff around him, could he guide the tens of thousands of the Soviets, who must take the place of the old hierarchy and its hundreds of thousands of officials?

It was only four years since, after long searching, he had found a few men with whose help he could found a newspaper. "I hear," wrote Lenin on September 30, 1913, to Gorky, "that you . . . are dissatisfied with *Pravda* . . . but this defect is not so easy to overcome. We have no helpers. It has been with the utmost difficulty and only after twelve months' effort that we have got together a tolerable editorial staff in St. Petersburg."

And now, a few hours after the seizure of power, he said to a friend: "We have great difficulties ahead of us. We are old, hardened revolutionaries; we have not learnt to carry on industry and the State; but we shall learn."

He was the same man who, close under the mansard roof in Munich, had written *Where to Begin?* He had been the only one at that time to evolve a plan for reducing his opponents to impotence, and he was now having the luck of the game. Now, however, he must find ways and means of building up a new edifice. The new task could not wait for a fair breeze to fill the sails of his will; they must take the winds at once.

The fraternity had grown twenty years older since Munich, habits and attitude to life had crystallized, had become second nature. He was surrounded by a company of people who had never worked in a disciplined way, most of whom were only unceasing talkers, constantly saying the same thing, living without any ordering or mutual division of their work; people who, even in their own fields of politics, literature, history and economics, had had no experience of real effort, had been content with the product of their native talent, and had therefore remained mere talkers. In these people's trunks, their pockets, their portfolios there was the same disorderly mess as in their brains. They were beggars, as vain of their poverty as uncultured millionaires of their wealth.

With these anarchists about him Ulianov succeeded in building up his State.

In the long corridors of Smolny on which the rooms of the members of the Government opened, there also met men whose characters had been steeled by the fugitive days of the past; but their number did not exceed a dozen. The best help that Ulianov had came from the room in which Trotzky worked, a nucleus of order amid the confusion of this building. Trotzky declared over and over again that without a new and thoroughly disciplined army the country would break up into tens of thousands of centres of anarchy.

The new individual centres of force came into existence only during the actual progress of the Revolution.

Lenin was head of the Presidium in the Council of People's Commissars; each Minister was bent on making endless speeches. Now that the new lords of the country had writing desks, shorthand typists, and official motorcars at their service, they imagined that the golden age of rhetoric had begun again. The Prime Minister, however, had a stop-watch brought in, measured out the time allowance for each speaker, and after five or ten minutes would point with a threatening gesture to his watch.

After a few sittings the Ministers did not dare to perorate for longer than fifteen minutes.

The Council met daily, and discussed all questions as they came up, without formal agenda. Lenin, as the chairman, kept a sort of minute-book, and always recorded a brief summary of the conclusions reached in the debates. If he wanted any definite information, he would pass his questions to his colleagues on little slips of paper. The replies had to be written on these same slips. That was a lesson in brevity and discrimination!

These notes of the Premier's and his little slips of information were the basis of the legislative work of the Republic.

He himself acted on initiatives coming from below, but was able to control their effect on the summit of the pyramid that was now coming into existence. His work was like that of the commander of an army in the field. The position changed from day to day; every new development had at once to be dealt with. There could be no months of drafting of bills by permanent officials. The State was a camp, the Government a tent set up every day on a new and unknown terrain.

"Every sitting," writes Trotzky, "presented a scene of legislative improvisation. . . . Great matters were amazingly interspersed with small. . . . In spite of all this the Chairman was able to pilot the meeting through the right channels. . . . If there were many present at the sitting, including specialists or any unknown persons, Vladimir Ilyitch had recourse to a favourite gesture: he would spread out the fingers of his right hand over his forehead and look through the fingers at the speakers . . . observing them . . . keenly and attentively. . . . At a definite moment Lenin would then read out a draft resolution, which was always deliberately worded in a provocative, almost a schoolmasterly way . . . whereupon the debate either came abruptly to a close or entered the phase of practical proposals and amendments. The draft read out by Lenin then became the basis of a Governmental decree."

Amid this urgency Lenin sketched the Constitution and the Socialization decrees. The socialization of the means of production—which was his conception, as it is that of all the parties of the proletarian class struggle, of a new order of society—had little to do with economics, but a great deal to do with war. This socialization was a looting with a purpose: by the confiscation of their property the sections of the population hostile to the Revolution were deprived of the power of resistance.

And this man, who saw and gathered together all the scattered elements of the new order, was a fanatic over whom every Philistine seemed to be justified in pouring ridicule. Again and again he prophesied to his aston-

ished colleagues that Russia would "become the most powerful State in the world." When? In a hundred
years? No, in a few weeks. Before "the successful
achievement of Socialism in Russia" there must, wrote
the Dictator after a few days of power, elapse "a certain
interval of at least some months."

Out of the union of such opposites History forms the
tools with which she works. For such men the day is lit
by a wonderful sun of the future, and, for all its unreal-
ity, this light picks out with the utmost accuracy the next
steps to be taken.

He had, perhaps, at this moment not only to recognize
the various conflicting forces better than the rest, not
only to discover lines of march out of the entangled
thickets, but also, as the leader of a nation readily inclined
to faith, to bend the knee more devoutly than the rest
before the Idea. Amid the confused activity of Smolny,
Lenin lived as a hermit in the country of miracles.

Ulianov, who for three decades had thirsted for power
more than any of his contemporaries, until victory proved
to him the soundness of his theory, was confirmed by success in the conviction that he could perceive apocalyptic
signs of coming splendour. But for him the methods of
autocracy were too weak. He remembered how firmly
the Tsar had formerly been enthroned, and that made
him dissatisfied with the shifting nature of everything
around him. In the rooms next his office, where official
papers were already accumulating and where much futile
grumbling went on, he saw nothing but irresolution.
Again and again the Premier stormed: "Get things into
shape and buckle to work—that is our only alternative to
falling back into slavery. . . ."

Nothing seemed to Lenin more treasonable than easy-
going office methods. Those around him had not faith
enough in their mission to satisfy him. He wished they
had some of his own sternness. They in turn must be

more merciless. He ordered his underlings to cultivate authority.

Ulianov learned with horror of the abolition of the death penalty. This seemed to him a measure inspired by men in a dream. "It is madness," he writes; ". . . how do you think you will deal with all your enemies, once you disarm yourselves? What have you left to enforce State authority with? Imprisonment? Who bothers about that in time of civil war, when every party hopes for victory?"

In the first weeks of the new régime the Terror demanded no human lives. The murmur of captives was not yet to be heard in the dungeons of ancient Bastilles. The opposition Press was allowed to appear, and so spread the wildest of inventions about Smolny; about the orgies of the People's Commissars, the harem life of the new rulers, about the German officers who were alleged to be conducting all the military operations of the Bolsheviks. Lenin was furious at this tolerance, derided his chief officials, said again and again at sittings of the Soviet and in private talk: "What has become of the dictatorship? Show it to me! What we have is pap, not a dictatorship. . . . Where is there a sign of dictatorship? There's nothing but talk!"

In public he would say: ". . . To tolerate bourgeois newspapers is to cease being a Socialist. There can be no standing still in a Revolution; one must continue to get ahead or else fall back. . . . We shall . . . not permit . . . the bourgeoisie to monopolize printing-presses, paper and other material. All these things must be the property of the Soviet Government. . . ."

There was the most violent opposition even from the oldest of the Bolsheviks, who were horrified at the Master, and shuddered at the thought of the iron curtain which more and more cut off the Government from the Socialist Parties nearest to it, and was now beginning to be sprinkled with drops of blood. But the Premier secured the censorship which he had demanded.

Ulianov was unable to understand the opposition in his own camp. He might have given the opponents among his comrades the answer which Tsar Ivan the Terrible gave to the interpreter when the Dutch Minister asked why the lord of so mighty a realm must proceed with such ferocity: "Tell this foreign idiot that he doesn't know Russia, but I know it well: if I didn't hang my subjects they would hang me. . . ."

Lenin, however, was not thinking of the forefathers of the Romanovs, but of the leaders of past revolutions in Europe, of the civil and political strategy of the Jacobins. Like Marat, he saw the strength of the Republic *at the moment* not in the remains of the armies of the old régime, but in the armed ranks of the partisans through whom the driving power of their class must be expressed.

His friends of the Soldiers' Committee were obsessed by a purely abstract, theoretical, formal logic.

Ulianov knew that the majority of the army, which had helped him into power, had no intention of fighting further. The soldiers were determined to go home. Now, when the Government was inviting the peasant to make an end of the old conditions of landowning—where this had not already been done—the peasant soldier saw himself as a happy proprietor, not a fighter. The revolutionary leaders in the garrison imagined, as Kerensky had done before them, that they could command.

And when the first attack came against the new régime the garrisons did not stir.

On the second day of his rule Lenin inspected the general staff.

The new military leaders, who already regarded themselves as generals, looked askance at this carelessly dressed civilian; they were taken aback, and asked if this visit implied mistrust of them. The Head of the Government answered in the name of the supreme authority, spoke sharply, definitely, refused to enter into controversy: "No mistrust; the Government only wants to know what its forces are undertaking."

"Lenin," relates an officer, "asked us for explanations why this or the other point was not being protected, why one step was proposed to be taken in preference to others, why Kronstadt had not been invited to give aid, why this position had not been developed, why that passage had been closed."

Kerensky's troops were marching on St. Petersburg—a few more kilometres and they would be outside the Smolny Institute.

Lenin went straight to the office of the general staff, chose a desk, sat down and stayed there.

The regiments were busy discussing the situation; guns were nowhere to be found; commands issued from headquarters failed even to arouse interest.

If the victory of November 7 had been only a soldiers' *Putsch,* this would have been the end of the new régime.

From the military staff offices Lenin issued order after order. All the factory whistles blew; the workers were armed by the staff, trains armoured, the suburbs mobilized, all conveyances requisitioned. He sent for the Commissars from Smolny, placed them in charge of districts; telephoned to the aviation headquarters and to the headquarters of the propagandists of the Régime; ordered the military leaders to get at once into touch with the local Soviets, the trade union federations and the district Works Committee; asked the supreme command how the food supply was working, and sketched a fresh plan of distribution. After ten hours of work the haste of his instructions lost the appearance of casualness, and his essential aim took shape from the myriad details.

The staff officers felt injured; their commander came to Lenin's room to resign.

Blazing with wrath, the Head of the Government

shouted at him: "We shall have you shot; I order you to go on with your work and not disturb me at mine."

Kerensky and General Krasnov were driven back; the rising of the Cadets in St. Petersburg itself was suppressed.

In their advance the revolutionaries occupied the wireless station at Tsarskoye Selo.

Now the stream of words could begin. In spite of all their executive duties, there awoke in the Commissars their old journalistic instincts, and leading articles were wirelessed across the world. The first news sent was a song of victory:

"The whole country must now realize that the Soviet Government represents no mere passing phase, but the permanent, actual, ruling power. . . . There can be no return now to the past. . . ."

In a few days Tsarskoye Selo was to address its remarks to All, to send out polemics against All, to reply to all the Powers who imagined that they could treat Russia as they pleased.

A wireless message went out to the Paris Radio news agency of M. Clemenceau:

"The Paris Radio news agency is daily sending out defamatory reports about Russian political life and its leading personalities . . . in particular . . . Lenin . . . is continually referred to as an agent of the German Government. In this the Radio agency of the French Republic is placing itself in the service of backstairs propaganda. . . . The defamatory material is issued in Russian, apparently in order to find its way direct to the heart of the Russian people. . . . No one else would be so disposed to believe in the venality of a great revolutionary party as people like M. Clemenceau, who at one time was directly associated with the Panama affair. . . ."

Tsarskoye Selo was the only wheel in the Government machine that continued to turn.

Elsewhere, in every office of the bureaucracy, the blinds had been let down; the thousands of rooms in the Ministries were a yawning void. The general strike, so often longed for by Lenin as the leaping flame of rebellion, was but a farewell message of the dismissed officials, but it threatened the very walls of Smolny.

Not only, however, did the higher officials—the permanent secretaries, heads of departments, heads of sections—ridicule the new dictatorship; the countless small folk too—who all their lives had sat in unventilated rooms in government offices, wearing out their elbows at their desks, chewing penholders, shivering under inspection by their head, expert only in the art of cringing—resolutely declined to perform their duties. Engineers, doctors, all the food supply officials, station superintendents, railway officials, copyists, bookkeepers, telephone girls and shorthand typists declared that it was beneath their dignity to serve a Government of bandits.

All that these poor souls knew of life was their beds, their offices, their way to work and home again, Christmas trees, screaming children belonging to their neighbours or themselves, a rare joint on a Sunday, and an occasional vodka debauch. They consoled themselves, however, with the reflection that the Power that they served walked in purple. The palaces of their breadgivers, the Ministers' wives' jewels, the servants at the court of the Autocrat, the majestic sternness of goldbedizened porters made their own poor existence tolerable.

Now came the new Ministers—ordinary men without frock coats, wearing soft collars. They collected around themselves the army of officials, spoke to them, said that up to now they had been in the service of enemies of the people, but on November 7 the day of the underdog had dawned. On that day the Idea had been wedded to Power. The proletarians of town and country counted on the aid of the administrative staffs.

Horror seized the troglodytes of the offices.

The shorthand typist had a hungry life of it, but at any rate, was a lady. When she was not taking down a letter she manicured her finger-nails. Now, when the new authorities talked of the destruction of wealth, the poor girl shuddered. She slept in a single room with her mother and sister; but before going to sleep she enjoyed a peep into the houses of the best people; for she was reading a novel about an unhappy countess, whose sorrows she shared. The slave in the office had no overcoat, but for all that he was a member of the cultured class; for he wore a stiff, washable celluloid dickey over his cotton shirt—and the proletarian had only a blue smock. All these people refused to serve the People's Commissars, indignantly and with utter contempt.

A few aristocrats and senior officers, who had no more belief than the rest in the new régime, but had never worshipped the authorities, were readier than these others to keep at work.

Smolny was surrounded by a hostile, malevolent whispering. Even those who ordinarily would bow the knee before power in any form, who felt as happy in the waiting-rooms of Ministers as children trotting alongside marching soldiers, mocked and hissed.

Only now and then a few curious visitors would approach the People's Commissars, to photograph them or to pick up a memento of these queer monsters that would be disappearing in a day or two.

To Lenin this bloodless and yet dangerous attack, these passionate cries of the poorest of the people, came as a surprise. Their resistance did not cripple him, but it further strengthened his impression of being surrounded by malevolence, sowed in his mind those seeds of mistrust out of which terrorism shoots up. Was he to be deterred by the sabotage of mere Jacks-in-office from pursuing his deathless Ideal? And Ulianov, who knew nothing of the dreams and illusions of a telephone girl, now despised the creatures who did not share his own. He had little understanding of men and women who were ready to renounce the splendour of an ideal future for the sake of a few moments of pleasure in the present. This resistance showed him the myriad sources from which hostility might arise, and led the Dictator to the conclusion that danger would always threaten so long as any opponents stirred, even though apparently defeated, dejected and in hiding.

Suddenly he found opposition even from his nearest friends. A section of his own department, affected by the general state of mind, also struck work. Three of the People's Commissars resigned; Party members of long standing expressed agreement with the deserters.

The Mensheviks and the Right and Left Social Revolutionaries negotiated with the three ex-heads of Commissariats, declared their readiness to form a Coalition Ministry with the Bolsheviks, made only one condition: the resignation of Lenin and Trotzky.

Ulianov's reply was that the whole strength of the Revolution lay in its inflexible purpose: he mobilized the factories—as a few days before against Kerensky—against his own sabotaging party leaders, and wrote at once a manifesto to the whole country. He had this printed in millions of copies. The crisis in the Smolny was not to be allowed to remain a secret affair or an intrigue in the lobbies of the Cabinet. The retiring leaders were to be fought by the unknown and nameless multitude:

"The second All-Russian Congress of Soviets," said the manifesto, "gave a majority for the Bolshevik Party. A Soviet Government can therefore only be formed from the ranks of this Party. . . . Several members of the Central Executive Committee of our Party and of the Soviet of People's Commissars—Kamenev, Zinoviev, Nogin, Rykov and some others—yesterday . . . announced their withdrawal from the Central Committee of the Party. . . . Kamenev, Rykov, and Miliutin have resigned from the Soviet of the People's Commissars. These comrades have incurred the guilt of deserting from the colours. . . . We are firmly convinced that all . . . workers, soldiers in sympathy and peasants will agree with us in our condemnation of these deserters. Shame on these men of little faith, spiritless doubters who . . . allowed themselves to lose heart and to be cowed by irresponsible clamour!"

Below, among those who struggled in the slough, Lenin had allies. And not only among the unskilled factory workers. Every maidservant and manservant, every docker and droshky driver, all the apprentices, the soldiers, the improvers, the sailors, all the homeless tramps, all the poorest of the poor, were ready to tear the wreckers to pieces. Never had a Government such friends in rags. The drab suburbs watched and listened. Mass espionage defeated countless plots. A whole company of voluntary hangmen and police crept out from the miry underworld to save the régime. These people, wounds in the body of every society, who at other times hid their troubles in dark alleys, answered the call. The destitute acclaimed Lenin, and tens of thousands came into the meeting places. Here the Dictator told them about the desertion of comrades and sabotage of enemies.

After a few days the Commissars came back, begging for forgiveness, and Ulianov also broke the resistance of the educated classes and the semi-educated.

From placards put up on the walls of St. Petersburg the leader spoke to the masses. These manifestos were like bulletins reporting on the progress of a patient at the door of death, on the sufferings of Russia.

"The Soviet of the People's Commissars," runs one of Lenin's manifestos, "has received the following urgent telegram from the staff at the northern front:

" 'We can wait no longer. Do not let the army die

of hunger! The armies on the northern front have not received a crust of bread for several days. . . . A panic-stricken homeward stream of starving soldiers, weak from three years in the trenches, sick, shoeless and . . . driven almost insane with misery. . . .'

"The Revolutionary War Committee draws the attention . . . of the workers of Petrograd to this. While the situation . . . calls for the most urgent and decisive measures, the officials . . . in the government offices, banks, railways, postal and telegraph departments . . . are on strike and stultifying all our efforts. . . ."

In these *communiqués* from the Government its opponents saw only the weakness of Smolny. But the leader was intent on making all its difficulties publicly known; the masses must learn the needs of revolutionary government as he was learning them himself at his desk. The rage of the hungry people, after standing for long hours in vain outside the bakers' shops, must be directed not against him, but against those who were sabotaging the Government's work. From the universal collapse of the system there must arise new energy, passion, life, activity, resolution.

He defeated one by one every centre of resistance.

The officials of the State Bank refused to open its safes. Lenin ordered that every missing key was to be replaced by dynamite.

The Commander-in-Chief, General Dukhonnin, tried to thwart the peace negotiations. The Head of the Government had himself put through to him on the telephone. The general gave diplomatic replies. Ulianov broke off the conversation, dismissed the general from his post, appointed Krylenko, who was still a cadet, to be head of the army, and at the same time wrote an appeal to the community: ". . . Dukhonnin, who has refused to begin negotiations for an armistice, has been removed from his command. Soldiers! If you want to go on with the war, defend Dukhonnin; if you want peace, protect with all the power of your weapons the Soviet of the People's Commissars!"

The general was murdered shortly afterwards, bayoneted by sailors. The crews of the Baltic Fleet formed the palace guards of the Revolution, picked troops of the insurrection, the janissaries of Smolny.

Six telephone girls showed the sailors how to work hundreds of instruments; simple railway linesmen were appointed station superintendents.

And slowly, badly, irregularly, trains began to move again, the Government telephones began again to ring, and food supplies began to come in.

The leaders of counter-rebellion, beaten by Ulianov and driven back from the gates of St. Petersburg, the Cadets routed in the street fighting in Moscow, placed their hopes now in the Constituent Assembly. In Russia's first free Parliament, born of universal suffrage, the Dictator was to be called to account. Their finest orators saw themselves already speaking from the tribune in the Taurida Palace, where the Duma had once had its sessions and the new Parliament would speak in the name of the legislative power.

They smiled complacently at the thought of their speeches, heard already their resonant words. "I should not like to be in Lenin's shoes," thought each one of these coming Deputies; "this usurper will collapse like a pricked bubble; my evidence will be unsparing." "What a fine thing it is to have a clear conscience!" thought all the provincial lawyers as they noted down the points of an imaginary impeachment of Lenin.

"But suppose Ulianov dissolves Parliament?" asked some sceptics in the camp of his opponents. "He will not dare to," was the chorused answer. "Has not the Constituent Assembly been the dream of uncounted generations of Russians? Has not the thought of that day consoled thirty thousand revolutionaries on their way to the gallows? He cannot possibly do that." "No," thought Lenin's closest associates, "we cannot possibly do that. We have been calling for parliamentary government for thirty years past; we turned out Kerensky from fear that he would not introduce it."

Lenin had spoken on this question in one of the first sittings of the People's Commissars; quietly and unconcernedly he had said, to the horror of his colleagues: "Of course we shall have to break up the Constituent Assembly."

He had not yet, however, declared himself definitely against Parliamentary government. The Social Revolutionaries had split up into Right- and Left-wing parties, but both wings were united on this question. "We must," he said to Trotzky, "put off the elections . . . extend the suffrage to include youths of eighteen. We must give time for the polling-lists to be drawn up afresh. Our own lists are worthless: a crowd of intellectuals, when what we want is the workers and the peasants. We must deprive the Kornilov people and the Cadets of civic rights."

The People's Commissars replied to Ulianov that the provinces, just won over, would not understand a postponement of the elections.

The Premier gave way, but said: "It is a flagrant error: we have already obtained the mastery, and now we have brought ourselves into a situation which compels us to resort to military measures to obtain the mastery over again."

For him there was no possible question whether the Assembly should be dissolved; he was only disturbed by the idea of wasting time over the formality. He had not defeated the enemy merely to enter into a peaceful discussion with them, possibly ending in a majority resolution compelling him to resign. Lenin was not going peacefully to shake hands with a new Head of the Government, to gather the heads of departments around him and ask them to give loyal service to his Right Honourable successor. Was not he himself, in the formula of Louis XIV, the State? Had anyone peacefully handed the reins of government over to *him*? Was *he* the vanquished leader? The majority? The majority represented a thousand years of slavery, the majority was the outcome of the institutions that had been overthrown.

He spoke little, therefore, to his colleagues in the Government, but made minute preparations for the day of the opening of Parliament, appointed an officer in command of the Taurida Palace, ordered the dispatch "of one of the Latvian regiments, which consist almost entirely of workers, to Petrograd."

"In this business," he said, "the peasant might fail us."

On the morning of January 18, 1918, there were five thousand marines in St. Petersburg. They broke up all the crowds that collected, and cleaned the boulevards of humanity as an electric sweeper cleans a floor of dust.

Lenin conducted the operations from a window of the Taurida Palace. Again and again he called to the officers in charge of the various landing-parties: "Keep strict order in every street! Ruthlessly! If anyone fails to stop, shoot him down!" Thirteen years before this he had been fighting in Moscow against Dubassov, and he knew, therefore, how a rebellion is scotched: he was the most expert barricade building contractor and the ablest Commissioner of Police that Russia had ever had.

The Deputies assembled in the Chamber: 273 opponents, 140 friends.

His Party had gained nine million votes, those of the Social Revolutionaries twenty-two millions, those of the Bourgeois Democrats four millions. On the basis of the Bolshevik victories at the polls in the principal cities, he calculated what his Party's theoretical majority should be, and wrote: "We may define three conditions which have helped Bolshevism to victory: (1) a pronounced majority among the proletariat, (2) almost half of the votes of the army, (3) a preponderance at the critical moment at the critical points—namely, in the capitals and the sections of the front nearest the centre."

This was a majority of the active elements, and Lenin therefore considered himself entitled to wreck the Assembly.

He sent his group of Deputies at once to the factories and the barracks to explain the measures adopted for the dissolution.

The 273 members of the opposition to him suddenly took alarm. They were ready to talk in the name of the Holy Mother Russia, but had no idea what else to do. Suppose Lenin dissolved? That had not been foreseen! Stolypin had once, ten years before, packed the Duma off home—and the dismissed Deputies had appealed to the public conscience, had announced that they were very annoyed with the Government, had called on the citizens to refuse to pay any more taxes. Lenin had ridiculed them then, and he did so again now. "They brought candles with them," writes Trotzky, "in case the Bolsheviks should cut off the electric light, and huge quantities of sandwiches in case the kitchens should be ordered to supply no meals. So Democracy entered into battle with Dictatorship, armed to the teeth with sandwiches and candles."

Lenin left the Taurida Palace to speak at the Central Executive Committee elected by the Soviets. Here was assembled the supreme authority of the Republic—born on November 7—and it now declared war on the other supreme authority. The Premier was authorized to draft the decree of dissolution. He wrote it on the spot and with the greatest alacrity. He charged the Constituent Assembly with refusal to recognize the programme of the Soviets. "Through this attitude the Constituent Assembly has broken every bond between itself and Russia's Soviet Republic. . . . Outside the Constituent Assembly the parties composing its majority are carrying on an open struggle against the Soviet Government, are advocating its overthrow in their organs, and, regarded objectively, are so assisting the exploiters in their resistance, hindering the transfer of the landed estates and the factories into the hands of the actual workers. . . .

"Accordingly the Central Committee resolves: . . .

"That the Constituent Assembly shall be dissolved."

Lenin returned to the Parliament, sent for the officer in command, and wrote on a slip of paper: "The Constituent Assembly is not to be dissolved before the close of the present sitting." Verbally he added: "Now mind; from to-morrow onwards you will let no one come on any account into the Taurida Palace."

It was already 4 a.m., the sailors were tired out, the Deputies were holding all-night sittings, the officer in command of the palace wanted to wait no longer, but send the Assembly home at once. Lenin was delighted at this note of impatience, smiled, bade the officer a cheerful farewell, and went to the Smolny to rest.

The commandant entered the Chamber, went up to its President, Tchernov, patted him familiarly on the shoulder, explained that the Parliament had been dissolved, and asked the Deputies to leave the building as the sailors were tired.

And the members of that Assembly, which had been the object of aspiration for a hundred years, since the rising of the Decabrists, melted away, under protest, and took to their beds.

When Ulianov had dispersed Parliament with the aid of his young marines, and the Deputies had scattered like frightened sheep, the prophecies of all his revolutionary forerunners proved to be a transitory phantasmagoria. Yet he had the courage to propose to foretell not only Russia's future, but that of all Europe; he marshalled quotations from Marx and Engels, tried to show that the Socialist parties of the West must act as he had done, and put the finishing touches to his theory of the State. There could now be no "freedom." A temporary tyranny must be set up in defence against enemies within and without; this was only a state of transition on the way to an order of society in which there would be universal freedom and no class distinctions.

Out of Russia's defeated state, out of the dust and débris of overthrown idols, he built up the gilded domes of Theory, without which he could not live; for it was his Conscience.

PEASANT AS DICTATOR

In opposition Lenin had often advised retreat. The labyrinthine ways of insurrection had compelled him even "to sign the incredibly disgraceful tacit agreement with Stolypin." But during the long period of rebellion this conspirator had never spoken so openly or so urgently as now of necessary concessions. How he had abused Plekhanov, after the failure of December 1905, for his warnings of the hopelessness of street fighting! But the same considerations of dogmatic theory which had formerly led him to sound the attack, now compelled him to call a parley.

Until November 7 every venture had contained the possibility of injuring his opponents, even if only for a time. The enemy was bound, moreover, to have hammered into Lenin and his followers the necessary realization of their position. Now, however, there would be no opportunity of making up for lack of experience. One false step on the narrow path of power, and there would be no recovery from the fall, no chance to try again.

He imagined that if power slipped from his hands the result would be for the peoples of Russia and all other countries the beginning of wild orgies of suffering, the end of the revolutionary era but just begun. The conviction that never left him, the dæmon of his faith, gave him the strength not only to destroy all that withstood him with the inexorability of the passionate believer, but to make compromises that would have seemed abominable to him had any other leader entertained the idea of them.

His government's long series of capitulations have their resemblance to his outlawed life under the Tsardom, his thirty years of refugeedom. The dirge was no less important, no less characteristic an element in his rule than his songs of triumph. This man was at the head of the State when he said to a company of his friends: ". . . . If you do not know how to suit yourself to circumstances, if you cannot crawl in the mud if need be, you are not a revolutionary, but a mere phrase-maker."

Of the section of his most intimate circle with which he felt the closest ties, the men on the Left among the Bolsheviks, who were sunk in gloom by every retreat and in bliss by every attack, Lenin says: ". . . Their outlook on the world is that of the dying Pole who struck a fine attitude, held aloft his sword, and shouted: 'Peace is disgrace, war honour!' Their outlook on the world is that Pole's; but I go to work from the standpoint of the peasant."

In the first days after the seizure of power Ulianov summoned an All-Russian Peasant Congress to St. Petersburg. He was determined now to exclude all resort to force. The Premier must be able to persuade, to win over, must be gentle as a martyr, patient as a pilgrim, wily as a Don Juan.

On November 8 he read from the platform at the All-Russian Soviet Congress the Land Decree:

"I. All private ownership in land is abolished, without compensation, as from the date hereof.

"II. All private properties, all estates belonging to the Crown, the religious communities, and the Church, with the whole of their livestock and implements, buildings and accessories, are transferred, until the meeting of the Constituent Assembly, to the administrative authority of the district land committees and district Soviets of peasants' Delegates.

"III. Any injury to the confiscated properties, which belong henceforth to the whole people, is regarded as a serious crime and punished by the revolutionary tribunals."

The district Soviets were local land committees which had no more regard for the purple of Communism than had the landowners driven from their homes, and the provision that confiscated property must not be damaged remained a pious recommendation.

The country houses of the aristocracy had accumulated treasure through three centuries.

The art treasures of the heirs or assigns of those who had received serfs by the thousand as gifts from the Empress Elizabeth, the Empress Catherine or Tsar Paul for military, administrative or intimately personal services, seemed of no value to the peasants either for exchange or for food. The proletarians made linen shoes out of the tapestries on the walls, kitchen tables out of the pianos. Barefoot, dirty children thumbed eighteenth-century books, looking for pictures; and such of the rococo porcelain as was not too intricately made served for pickling cucumbers for the coming year.

The latest heirs and assigns had a peculiar realism of their own.

Ulianov was not horrified at this destruction. But the work of the land committees, which had created the new system of peasant proprietorship, must have seemed to him like the hideous spectre of capitalism disinterred.

Of Lenin's land reform Rosa Luxemburg, who in all other matters praises him, wrote that it "has planted on the soil a new and powerful social element of hostility to Socialism, an element which will put up a much more dangerous and tenacious resistance than was that of the aristocratic landowners."

But the Dictator's first care was for the frail seedling of power.

He knew that the liberated peasants, eighty per cent. of Russia's humanity, were not carrying out the Revolution according to his formulæ. Was he on that account merely to bewail the perversity of human nature like the Mensheviks, to go back to exile in Zurich, and there to turn over the pages of Marx, glancing at the Master's dicta like a mirror in which to see his own dogmatic purity?

Ulianov's reflections ended in a smile. He felt his mind released from a heavy incubus.

He thought he would be able to lure the peasantry to Communism with the siren song of self-interest. A new dream brought him illusory consolation.

Tens of thousands of tractors, hundreds of electric power stations, synthetic fertilizer works, the wealth of the towns, the economic planning of the revolution in Western Europe, would show the small farmers of the countryside the unprofitable nature of private ownership. Socialized industry would bring the peasants all the technical assistance they needed, and Communism would put new life into everything.

Whatever might have been said over and over again for decades past, Socialism might be a philosophy or a prophecy, a faith or a science, justice or necessity, probability or certainty, transition stage or final aim, simple logic or a matter of controversy, or all of these put together, or something quite different not here mentioned —as you will! Anyone might take his choice, with the single exception of the revolutionary who was in power— Lenin. For the first time, however, in history, Power was dictating *her* laws to a Socialist—not to a man in opposition, not to one of the oppressed, but to one who possessed

LENIN AFTER THE SEIZURE OF POWER

LENIN'S MAUSOLEUM, UNDER THE WALLS OF THE KREMLIN

her, who kissed the feet of this living goddess, humoured her every mood, was inseparable from her.

Lenin was ready to make any compromise whatever. Determined to win without resorting to force, he went to the All-Russian Congress.

The Bolsheviks had only one-fifth of the seats; the majority of the delegates were Left-wing Social Revolutionaries, and in their name a delegate from the provinces declared: "We refuse to recognize the so-called Workers' and Peasants' Government so long as the peasants are not represented in it. Up to now this Government has been nothing but a dictatorship of the industrial workers."

People's Commissars who tried to speak were howled down.

The assembly would not listen even to Lenin. When he ventured to speak the delegates shouted, "Sit down, you have nothing to tell us."

He did not sit down, but waited for a moment of calm:

"I am not speaking here as a member of the Soviet of People's Commissars," said the Head of the Ministry. "I am . . . a duly delegated member of this Congress. All the same, no one will deny that it was the Bolshevik Party which formed Russia's present Government." In the end he was being listened to with curiosity. He spoke for a long time and in outspoken language: "What is it exactly that you want? You have your farms—keep them. But if we no longer rule in the State everything will be taken away from you again. There are no differences of opinion dividing us; every path and every field for agreement is open. It is true that you could turn us out. But who would come after us—do you know? Alone you have not the power to rule; you are bound to rule in association with someone else."

The peasants looked at one another, puzzled. They had been told that the People's Commissars wanted to take their land away again, to restore the big estates and give them to the town workers. Many began to say: "He is not against us after all."

Lenin had broken off his speech and was energetically trying to calm his own followers. The Bolsheviks could not understand the Master; they were outraged and wanted to leave the Congress. Twenty marines, they urged, could clear the hall! Ulianov lost patience, shouted at his fraternity, ordered them to stay: "But don't let one of you," he added, "dare to speak!"

The Premier returned to the hall and resumed his speech: "The Party of the working class . . . must not let its advance be hindered by the lack of education among the average men and women of the masses. It must lead the masses . . . but in order to be able to lead the hesitant, our friends in the camp of the Left Social Revolutionary group must overcome their own indecision. . . . We accept the plan of the Land Committees . . . because we wish to carry out the will of the people . . in order to consolidate the union of all the elements that are fighting for the Social Revolution. . . . We invite the Left Social Revolutionaries to give their adhesion to this Union . . . and definitely to break with the compromisers. . . ."

When he had finished his speech Ulianov went to Smolny to carry on secret negotiations with the Left Social Revolutionaries, gave them seats in the Ministry, and encouraged them to complete their land programme themselves.

The Right Social Revolutionaries, who had been in power for months, had not had the courage to carry their own proposals into practice; they were now concluding alliances in every direction against the Republic. They charged Lenin with plagiarism, with confiscating their ideas. He replied that they were "aroused, indignant, outraged, crying out that the Bolsheviks had stolen their programme!" But they had only earned ridicule: "What a party, that one must beat and turn out of the Government in order . . . to put into practice all that there was of value in their programme!"

Lenin would not hear of an alliance with the Mensheviks, and now was he coming to a compromise with the Social Revolutionaries? But at the elections for the Constituent Assembly the moderate Socialists obtained only half a million votes and the official party of the peasants twenty millions.

Smolny was brightly lit up, in festal array for the first time since the dictatorship: the members of the Congress had been invited.

"Welcome, peasant comrades!" was Trotzky's greeting. "You are here not as guests, but as the lords of the country."

Lenin wrote his Thesis on the Constitution, had it placed before the Congress for acceptance at its final sitting, and sanctioned as from November 7 by the peasand majority. ". . . The Peasant Congress takes its stand on the principles of the Revolution. . . . The indispensable condition of victory . . . is the close union of the working peasants with the industrial workers. . . . The whole organization and administration in the Russian Republic from top to bottom must rest on this union."

The suffering of the country was greater than the validity of the ukases of Ulianov. Realities were unresponsive; they rarely returned tangible results however many eloquent manifestos the Government might send out.

"If we had supposed," declares Lenin, "that by issuing a hundred decrees we could entirely change the life of the countryside, we should have been first-class idiots. . . . These decrees, which in practice it was entirely impossible to put at once into full effect, played an important part as a form of propaganda."

The manifestos did at least harmonize with the popular demands; they were moral remedies, since their drafter told the masses through his prescriptions what they themselves wanted, voiced and formed their will.

Lenin's strength lay in his capacity to divine the changing moods of the nameless multitude; with no machinery of State, with no statistical staff, he was able to sense the desires of Russia's millions. Only in this sense was he Dictator, and only for this reason was he able to discipline and master his own fraternity.

Ulianov often secretly harboured purposes with which the majority was entirely out of sympathy. Often deep gulfs divided him from the ideals of his subjects. Those were moments of crisis, and at such moments the Dictator would try to make good the defective idealism of the masses by the sanguinary work of his own minority. After a few days or months a cold and cheerless morning would come to compel him to abandon these distant ideals for the sake of immediate constructive achievement.

In his eyes the end justified the compromise, any compromise. "Anyone who wants to solve the tremendous problem of getting rid of capitalism must be prepared to try out one method after another until he has discovered the one which is best suited to carry out his purpose."

He remained rooted in the countryside; in spite of all the influence of the humanitarian philosophy of the industrial West, he was only concerned to secure what the countryman wanted. Other aspirations he agreed might be more intelligent, more desirable of realization, but they were not realizable. He was rooted in the national spirit as the spreading forest and the running river.

It was impossible for the Russian bourgeoisie to lead the rural population. Of the irresolute bourgeois intellectuals the Dictator said that they beat their breast, wept and confessed: "I am bad, I am loathsome, but I am taking thought for my moral perfection; I am no longer eating meat and am living on rice cutlets."

What Ulianov says of Leo Tolstoy in writing to Gorky may be applied to Ulianov himself: "Tolstoy—what a rock, what a source! . . . The really magnificent thing about him is his peasant voice, his peasant way of thinking: he is a real peasant if there never was another. Before this Count the true peasant had never lived in literature."

Internationalist theory only freed Lenin from national particularism, from the local patriotism of the parish pump; it gave him his first insight into the meaning of nationalism. It was through the eyes of the urban proletariat that he saw the wide spaces outside Russia: the sea coasts and the land frontiers around which, mesh on mesh, an infinite web of potentialities of war is spun.

The Dictator liberated the forces on which he depended and gave them the opportunity of effectiveness; these forces were to finish the work of November 7. ". . . The local revolutionary garrisons," runs one of his ukases, "are to proceed with the utmost energy against the enemies of the people, without waiting for orders from higher quarters." The leader gave colour and direction to the passions of the mob, took pains to incite the enemy to violence in order to be able to destroy him, to clear the country of all that was working against it. "The Soviet of People's Commissars," he decreed, "declares the Cadet Party to be an organization . . . of insurrection. . . . The Soviet of People's Commissars pledges itself not to lay down . . . its arms. . . ."

After a few weeks he already had St. Petersburg, Moscow, Kiev, Nijni-Novgorod, Kharkov, Odessa, Ekaterinoslav, Samara, Saratov, Kazan, Rostov, Tashkent, Vladimir, Reval, Pskov, Minsk, Krasnoyarsk, Tobolsk, Serpukhov and Tsaritsyn in his power.

"Victory came," writes Lenin, "because the new political form had attained definiteness and finality, and we had nothing to do but to issue a few decrees bringing the Soviet Government out of the embryonic condition in which it existed in the first months of revolution into the officially recognized form of the Russian State, the Rus-

sian Soviet Republic. . . . The creative powers of the
nation itself, which had behind it the bitter experience
of 1905 . . . set up this form of proletarian power."

The storm which swept away the old deeds of ownership, broke up the lives of tens of thousands of innocent
families, carried the barricades to their very doors, gave
birth with equal wastefulness to feelings of success and
facts of misery, the storm which invaded every threshold,
had conquered power.

The disasters that followed were to establish it.

The next thing was to struggle for peace on all fronts.

For the Russian peasants the campaign had come successfully to its end. They went home in search of dreams
fulfilled, and, as Lenin discovered, sold "our guns to
the Germans for a few pence." The enemy, however,
remained the enemy; he was not conquered; not in flight
like the great landowners of Muscovy, not in captivity
like Nicholas II, not deprived of his all like the bourgeoisie of St. Petersburg. Before the enemy there lay
the open road into Russia, whose strength was only to be
gathered up in the course of a long, slow process.

If Lenin had been in the situation of the German general staff he would have demanded of his partners in the
negotiations, if not territory, certainly their own heads,
and would have sent a troop of hangmen to complete the
deal.

The victor along the front was not only strong, but
hungry, was living on *Ersatz,* and imagined that he saw
in front of him unending golden cornfields; he dreamed
of eggs, butter, fat cows, of coal and oil.

"In the first days of June," writes General von Kuhl,
"Austria had reached her worst period of food shortage;
Vienna was nearly starving. Help came from a chance
accident. Stocks of maize were passing through from
Rumania for Germany. . . . General Landwehr, a
member of the Food Council . . . had them dis-

charged in Vienna. . . . General Landwehr said to Windischgrätz: 'I know it was highway robbery, but I had no alternative. Now they have food in Vienna for at least a fortnight. . . .' "

And were the leaders of Austria's neighbour country, who had to pay on this scale for the maintenance of their alliance with her, likely to be convinced by the Russian evangel? Could Ulianov, who had been writing about imperialism for thirty years past and had called Kerensky the agent of the wealthy firm of England, France and Co., suppose that the enemy, who was now in occupation of the richest provinces of the Republic, would succumb to the lure of the anarchy in St. Petersburg as the boatman of the song to the strains of the Lorelei?

"Well, have we all gone mad, then?" he asks. "Not in the slightest! The non-Bolshevist officers declare . . . that the army could not possibly go on with the war, could not be kept at the front even a few weeks longer . . . the thing could be kept up artificially, one might copy Kerensky's tricks and so delay the end for a few weeks. . . . The army is now the diseased part of the Russian State organism. The more quickly we demobilize it . . . the sooner the country can be ready to face the severe trials to come. . . . The more quickly it is de-mobilized, the more rapidly will the healing process throughout the whole national organism begin. . . ."

The country could only gather up new strength in the mild air of peace. The soldiers, too, could only recover at the plough, in the factories, at their office desks. As an exhausted man can overcome his weariness for a few hours with the aid of drugs, but cannot by any such means do away with it, so the *mujik* was no longer to be kept indefinitely at the front by any enthusiastic speech-making. As a persecuted fugitive gains fresh life from sleep, is restored by food and drink and joy, so a war-weary nation can regain the faculty of resistance only through a breathing space. Lenin found his impotence in face of this disaster unendurable. He bowed his head and yielded to the inevitable: the seven million soldiers dissolved into the mass of the hundred million Russians. The healing strength of the earth, the everyday scene, would lift their spirit out of its dull numbness. In these tortured hours his own thought was the peasant's: All back to their homes! All of them back to their homes! Capitulate, make any compromise, sign anything! This lover of power, who lived for it, had patience, was ready to wait in order, later, to consolidate it afresh.

"I will give up territory," said Lenin, "to gain time."

"I recalled the history of Prussia. Many people have the childish idea that once a treaty is signed one is sold to Satan and received into hell. That is simply nonsense; history shows us quite clearly that the signature of a treaty in defeat is a means of regathering strength. . . ."

His comrades counted on revolution in Germany and Austria to ease the international situation of the Republic. Had they been smashing the statues of the Tsar only to be charged with helping to crown a bevy of Hohenzollern princes in Reval, Riga, Finland and Poland? The negotiations in the German fortress at Brest Litovsk must be drawn out as long as possible, in order to show the peoples of the world that the Russian Government was not in the pay of Berlin.

Lenin agreed as to the necessity of shilly-shallying. Peace had certainly arrived: the fighters were to be seen everywhere with the one important exception of the front. The Russian Deputies were profuse with their indignation, supposing, no doubt, that if there were no guns left their words would serve just as well to bombard the trenches on all fronts.

In Brest Litovsk the representatives of the Republic and those of the allied monarchs stood on an equal and opposite footing. Each side hated the other, each was out to destroy the system of the other country. As, however, they were unable to do so—Ludendorff had no soldiers to spare, Lenin no soldiers at all—there must for the present be peace.

"We entered on the peace negotiations," writes Trotzky, "in the hope of rousing the working masses not only of Germany and Austria-Hungary, but also of the Entente countries."

"Certainly," wrote Count Czernin, the Austrian delegate, "this Russian Bolshevism is a European peril, and if we had the power . . . it would be right to refuse altogether to negotiate with these people, to march to St. Petersburg and to restore order."

At this moment Lenin no longer had hope of deliverance through the World Revolution. The speeches at Brest were no more for him than a necessary formality.

This man who for thirty years had been talking of the sacred vessels in which the drops of revolt must be collected, to rise up and foam over one glorious day, this man who apparently had only seized power on the assumption that a European insurrection was approaching, this man to whom at other times no adventure seemed too daring, became, when arrived at the pinnacle of power, and faced with the realities in Russia, a supremely cautious tactician.

"I made no bones about proposing to sign the peace," writes Lenin. "There was no possibility of our getting peace on any better terms than the Brest terms."

Ulianov came to a compromise with his supporters which took into consideration the possibility of a revolution in Germany, without in any way placing peace in jeopardy. His delegates were to drag out the negotiations, but were to capitulate at once when the German ultimatum was delivered.

Trotzky, however, shrank in horror from the acceptance of the enemy's conditions. Yet on his journey to the place of the negotiations he had seen nothing but soldiers in flight. Here and there an isolated sentry still did duty; except for this the earth seemed to show only the exhaustion of three years of combat. The head of the Russian delegation accordingly invented the formula: "For us the war is at an end; but we refuse to sign this peace."

The German legal expert hunted for precedents. After exhaustive research he informed the Conference that the last similar case had occurred a good many centuries before, after a clash between Greeks and Scythians.

Ulianov, who knew his own situation as well as that of the enemies, waited for an advance.

Trotzky, returned from the negotiations, was actually in Lenin's room when the telegram came reporting the advance. The Premier jumped up and cried, "There is no time to lose now!"

He wanted to sign at once, but could not venture to do so without the assent of the Soviet institutions; for they might have refused to ratify the peace.

The Executive met in the Taurida Palace. The Chamber which had lived through so many orgies of revolutionary rejoicing, now witnessed scenes of impotent rage. The delegates could hear already in imagination the march of the enemy regiments. The factories and the Kronstadt sailors sent delegates to demand the renewal of the struggle. One speaker after another stood up and called for resistance, hoping still that European insurrection would hasten to the assistance of the revolutionary war. The memory of the overthrown power of the Romanovs, of the easy victories within the country, came to the aid of their wild rhetoric.

All longed for a wave of saving destiny, even if it should carry them away as its victims.

When Lenin came into the Chamber, old friends received him with shouts of "Traitor!"

Like the applause of so many other occasions, this upbraiding in defeat left him unmoved. But he knew that all was lost if to-day the force of his conviction could not move his comrades. He looked long and gloomily down the Chamber:

"Let us beware," he began, "of becoming slaves of our

own phrases. . . . In our day wars are not to be won merely by enthusiasm, but by technical superiority, by the condition of the railways. . . . The axis on which the World War is turning to-day is the rivalry between British and German high finance. It is this struggle that the Revolution has to turn to its own service."

He asked the army commanders to speak, and they told how all along the line there was nothing left to command.

And the World Revolution?

After the debate Ulianov replied:

". . . When we took the power into our sole hands as the Bolshevik Party, we did so with the conviction that the Revolution was ripening into fruition in every country, and in the end—in the end, not at the very beginning—would come. . . . We are proceeding from the basis of absolutely abstract truth, but in doing so we must take care that in course of time it does not degenerate into a mere phrase. . . . Yes, we shall see the international World Revolution, but meanwhile it is just a very good fairy-tale, a very pretty fairy-tale. . . . Every fairy-tale contains an element of truth; if you were to tell the children a fairy-tale in which the cock and the cat did not talk in ordinary human speech, true to life, they would not be interested. . . . You are proposing to stake everything on a single card. . . . If you do, the people will say to you: 'You have been acting like egoists . . . you have shown yourselves unserviceable.' . . . The attempt . . . to apply the tactics of the period of triumph, . . . with nothing but imagination to support them, to the whole course of a revolution has never in history succeeded. . . . The last flicker of the war has given the Russian people a bitter and painful but important lesson, and compelled it . . . to learn to obey. . . . Bring discipline into play yourselves, the strictest discipline.

"Learn from the German *his* discipline; otherwise we are a lost people and shall lie for ever in the dust of slavery. . . . There must be no mere talking in fine phrases. . . . I repeat, I am ready, and regard it as my duty, to sign a peace twenty times, a hundred times, more humiliating. . . . I am for national defence . . . I am for renewing the army, even from the remotest depths of the country. . . . We shall . . . oppose the enemy army with our own army when that revulsion in the mind of the people has come which is now ripening . . . when the masses of the people saw something different from what they are saying now. . . . Our only watchword is this: . . . learn the practice of war . . . then, in spite of defeat, we shall be able to say with *absolute* certainty that the victory will be ours."

Bent beneath the terrible national disaster, the bankruptcy of the Idea, the malevolence of the enemy, the burden of responsibility; amid utter solitude in defeat his soul still sang; for he had faith in ultimate success.

"If necessity compels," said Ulianov, "we must retire yet farther eastwards, beyond the Urals, even to Kamtchatka; but somewhere we shall come to a halt. The international situation will change a dozen times over, we shall . . . once more extend our frontiers, and come back to Moscow and St. Petersburg. . . ."

Lenin did not appeal to nationalism, but held none the less that only where it existed did independent Muscovy exist, and acted in the spirit of the national traditions. The "Gathering in of the Russian lands" around a central nucleus had gone on in former times for a period of centuries under the Tsars. Now, under the Revolution, the territories of the realm would unite within no more than a few months.

The destruction which Lenin had wanted, which his theory demanded, was much more than realized; not only the State hierarchy, but the provinces of the realm fell apart, to come together again through their common suffering.

THE REVOLUTION IN ISOLATION

Moscow had long since lost its peace-time aspect. Its roads used to look like those of a huge and wealthy village. In its quiet side-streets there were villas whose gardens protected the owners from the dust of the roadside. Only here and there a modern many-storeyed building disturbed the general air of old-time comfort. The palaces of the landed gentry and the merchants were filled with treasures.

Abruptly, close alongside the rich districts, there began the poor quarters; not tenement barracks, but tiny cottages. Here, too, the similarity with a village remained, but a village of beggars. Now all the city seemed tense like a listening, persecuted victim.

The glory of the day, which, after all, is born of the soul of man, had gone, its light was extinguished, and in the gloom all men were tortured, in the spell of a deep apprehension.

All stood in fear of one another, and all were hungry.

The homes of the well-to-do looked now like secondhand dealers' shops. No one was allowed more than one room. As the poor man behind with his rent used to be turned out, so now everyone was evicted from the rooms not actually used to sleep in. The dictatorship was a stern bailiff's man. It distrained on the rich, and already as much as a spare pair of trousers was reckoned as riches.

The Revolution had not only plastered every wall with its placards, it had taken every door off its hinges, picked every lock. Moscow had become one great casual ward.

But hunger remained.

The Republic distributed a disgusting loaf, with sand and straw mixed into the flour. For most people the ration of thin potato soup or preserved fish was only to be had by begging; for there was only work for few. Only the munition factories were still at work. In the long corridors of the government departments pale women sat sewing overcoats for the soldiers, speaking not a word.

"The Republic," declared Saint-Just, his country's chief defender, in hungering Paris a century and a quarter ago, "is not a Senate, but righteousness."

"Righteousness in action," shouted Robespierre.

In Moscow, too, the bread was made day after day of more mysterious materials. Everything disappeared except revolutionary virtue. A pin, a reel of cotton, a piece of soap, a shirt, or a pair of stockings had become the rarest of jewels. People tried to soften the heart of the illicit dealer with books, vases, carpets, pictures.

Was this, after all, the Social Paradise? At least everyone was almost as naked as the dwellers in Eden, and found raw apples a luxury.

In Moscow now all wore the same cloak of poverty. Destitution had levelled all like a plane. Tears washed off every artificiality, every traditional distinction, every asset of intelligence and knowledge and training, till the naked stood over against the naked.

In this city of the poor, rats and beggars crept out from every corner. The professional "askers" had always dragged out a precarious existence; now it was made worse by the competition of colleagues who could talk French or English. Until a little while ago the new bundles of rags had imagined no worse terrors of bankruptcy than to have to manage on two villas or mistresses instead of three. Their present deficit was beyond anything provided for in their insurance policies. Former independent gentlemen, staff officers, bank directors went into the streets to sell newspapers or cigarettes.

The disaster crippled the will of the golden youths of a month before. They sat on the kerbstones, bored and melancholy, as formerly in their club settees.

No one can get used to an empty stomach. But the men and women of the poor suburbs were better able to stand hunger than the dispossessed rich, felt the torture of these days less than the bourgeoisie. For the influence of the Idea had raised up the living dust of the suburbs like a wind. The common people of the old régime were *not yet* made apathetic by the pinch of want.

"Everything loved," says Novalis, "is the centre of a Paradise."

The more they starved, the more they hated the well-fed of yesterday, the supremely unfortunate of to-day.

Long processions of armed workmen and women marched in drill in the centre of the city, singing and listening to speeches; riders galloped through the streets; motor-cars rushed at top speed to and fro; motor-lorries passed by with loads of "suspects."

The movements of the vindictive populace were directed from a terraced hill rising forty yards above the Moskva, from the most famous fortress of Russian history, the Kremlin. This centre of the capital is surrounded by a wall over a mile long, with nineteen towers. For eight centuries section after section of the city had been built at the foot of the fortress. Behind its ramparts each succeeding age had left its chiselled image. Crowded together as in a badly arranged museum, there had risen up monasteries alongside palaces, churches next to arsenals, towers and barracks, chapels and mews. Here the Tsars had their prisons, their fortifications, their seraglio and their tomb. The laughter, the wit, the clarity of Rome and Athens had never stirred hearts here; here only the most frightful tyranny had ruled; an extraordinary mixture of learned orthodoxy and barbarism had always governed men's minds here, and governed them still.

Perhaps this holy place of Russia has some resemblance to the Tartar city of Peking, that pearl of cities.

All the art of Persia and of Byzantium, the Renaissance, Gothic, Lombard art that had formed the Kremlin could not give nobility to the gilded tawdriness of the Tsar's many apartments.

Now Ulianov went to and fro in them, with soft collar and ill-fitting coat, his hands deep in his trouser-pockets.

From beneath the pinnacles of a tower the lord of this palace could see the starving city below him. The conqueror of another revolution, the one who became Emperor, the once semi-Communist Lieutenant Bonaparte, had looked out from the red staircase of the Kremlin on a similar picture of misery: the burning earth beneath a flaming sky.

Lenin did not inherit Napoleon's love of grandeur: triumph brought him personally not even a new suit. He went up and down the shining parquet floor with old hobnailed boots, and his trousers dated from Zurich times. The bare walls of his bed-sitting-room had not depressed him in exile, and the Oriental magnificence of the painted corridors in the Kremlin found this intruder equally unconcerned. He held that this was the obvious place from which to govern; for the Kremlin was important strategically and symbolized power.

Here the leader pitched his tent. "His private apartments," writes one who visited him after he had been three years Dictator, "were of the simplest and most unassuming character. I saw more than one workman's home that was much more richly furnished than the dwelling of the all-powerful Dictator of Muscovy. I found Lenin's wife and sister at supper . . . it was as modest a meal as that of any average Soviet official at the time: tea, black bread, butter, cheese. Later in the evening his sister was asked to look and see if there were any sort of sweet to offer, and she managed to unearth a little glass jar of preserved fruit."

Lenin went from this room to one in which unwashed, driven, hoarse men sat at silver tables. They wore black leather jackets and had pistols in their belts.

The Revolution was isolated.

The countryside was abandoning it, and even in the towns some of its enthusiastic supporters were beginning to lose faith and complain.

"It is a fact," said the leader, "that very many of the representatives of the working masses are falling into despair . . . under the pressure of the exceptional difficulties. We are not afraid of this. Never has there been a revolution in which some of its supporters have not been seized with despair. . . . We shall continue to rely on the industrial working-class elements who helped us to victory last October. . . ."

The stuff of which the Revolution was made had achieved miracles which astonished its victorious leaders no less than the vanquished. Not only had the insurrection destroyed in a day the petrified institutions of the past, but in a few months it had altered the balance of the whole social structure. But the current which had flowed from the people towards the Kremlin, carrying the leaders of the Bolsheviks into office on a flood-tide, threatened now to ebb away from their seat of power.

These days were far more critical than the first weeks of the Revolution. Then only the types familiar for centuries past had opposed the new régime; the rich, the politicians, poets, philosophers, journalists, fanatical fine ladies and their set. The depths had longed for change, only the surface foam had splashed and hissed against it. ". . . In October 1917," writes Lenin, "we seized power with the support of the whole of the peasantry. That was a bourgeois revolution, for the class struggle had scarcely yet begun in the rural districts. Only in the summer of 1918 did the real proletarian revolution begin in the countryside."

Perhaps all history is illusion; perhaps on the world stage where great events run their course there is merely a constant repetition, as elsewhere, of the classic situation of a pair of lovers, who imagine that they are working out their own destiny while in reality they are serving other purposes beyond their ken.

Ulianov would not have regarded it as part of his task to set in motion this sanguinary struggle in the villages, this "proletarian revolution in the countryside." He had to do it, however, in order to fill the empty stomachs of the towns, to maintain the grain monopoly, to feed the Republic's armies, to protect the peasants, who were now in revolt against him, from the landowners, who were placing themselves at the head of hostile armies.

"If we wait," said Trotzky to the Dictator, "until the peasant comes to his senses, it may then be too late."

The Communist Lenin had, from the pinacle of power, to fight for the private property of twenty million peasants or go to the wall.

For the countryman the Revolution was over.

The looter of yesterday had no further interest in the world outside his little holding, wanted to live a regular life, to enjoy his gains, to have an easy time, and to give up to the State nothing at all. "Was there not a rising and were we not the victors? Are we now to pay taxes as if nothing had happened?" The State was unable to supply manufactured goods, was fixing maximum prices for grain, and paying with bits of coloured paper which it called money. The peasant crept out of sight like a snail, reduced his sowings to a minimum, and manufactured legends about Moscow. Ulianov puts it very clearly. "The peasants are saying, 'Long live the Soviet Government, but down with the "Communy." '" The Soviets, thought Ivan, are our friends, they say all the things we do about the old landowners; but "Communy" wants to get our grain. He would best have liked a joint guarantee of his loot from Lenin and Tsar Nicholas. The story went round in many Siberian villages that the new lord of the Kremlin had been appointed by the Tsar to be Prime Minister and Crown Prince.

Expropriation had been followed by the distribution of

the soil in equal holdings. But after a few months there were once more rich, middling and landless peasants in every village—some with six cows and others with only two. The rich joined forces with the middling peasant in defence of their property against the new pariahs.

In the honeymoon of their power the Bolsheviks had ruled by virtue of the countryman's hopes fulfilled; they now inaugurated a campaign of terrorism against him. The Government set out to organize the poor peasants against the rich ones, formed an alliance with the hungry. Lenin called these tactics "the struggle for bread."

"We are faced now, in this summer of 1918," he said, "with the fundamental essential problem of all life in human society—how to achieve victory over hunger, or at least over the pangs of actual present hunger. . . . We must turn the statistical surplus of grain into actual reality. . . . *To arms for the bread crusade!* For the crusade against the speculators, against the usurers. . . . It is . . . necessary for . . . propagandists of the Soviet power to carry into the villages the gospel of the distinction between poor and rich. . . . Against the usurers, the criminals who are torturing the people with hunger, who are inflicting suffering on tens of millions— against these persons we shall muster all the forces of the State. To the poor of the villages we shall give every sort of assistance. . . ."

There began in the countryside a new war.

"In Tver, Tula and Ryazan," writes Mr. Philips Price, "pitched battles were fought and parts of villages wrecked. Spurred on by hunger and by desperation, caused by the oncoming counter-revolution, the urban workmen and the 'Committees' (of the poor peasants) regarded the 'middle peasants' as traitors, who were stabbing them in the back."

Every phase of feeling among the rural population, its resolution and its impotence, its fighting spirit and its desertion of the colours, was reflected in the organization of the Social Revolutionaries. That was why their Party was so vague and indeterminate. No one knew which way it was moving; its decisions were always a mystery. There were Social Revolutionaries at the head of armies marching against Lenin, and Social Revolutionaries filling the highest posts under the Republic. They disapproved of the Terror, and yet they presided over revolutionary tribunals and had the majority in the fifth Soviet Congress, which was then sitting in Moscow.

After Brest Litovsk, the Left Social Revolutionaries had resigned from the Government; but they had not taken up any position of active hostility to the Bolsheviks; they had simply formed a loyal Opposition.

Although the peasants were against war with Germany, the Social Revolutionaries were for tearing up the Treaty. Did they really want the struggle along the front to begin over again? They did not even know their own minds on this question.

They merely went about praising the tradition of insurrection, building up a revolutionary hagiology, prophesying symbolic stormings, telling the peasants that now they were free they would find happiness in the free commune, declaiming against any sort of central administration, jeering at every attempt at organization, hymning an eternally static November 7, and pointing to the guerilla war of the rural population in the Ukraine against the Germans as an all-saving miracle; they were the idolaters of insurrection.

Lenin, however, argued: ". . . the Revolution has . . . broken . . . the oldest, strongest, and heaviest chains. That was yesterday. To-day, however, this same Revolution demands . . . the disciplined subordination of the masses to the united will of the leaders of the economic campaign."

A whole universe divided the Social Revolutionaries from this conception.

The Premier thought that production could be revitalized through the organized workers of the towns. The proletariat understands the necessities of discipline, as it sees and acquires the regularity and orderliness of the factories. The works were to be centres of reconstruction, stilling the unrest of Russia, stemming the boundless tide of destruction, fighting the mighty forces of confusion.

"Among the small peasants of the countryside," declared the Prime Minister, "there has naturally remained not a little of the pure anarchism, the increased brutalization and savagery that accompany every long-continued reactionary war; there have, too, been not a few who have become full of despair and purposeless rage . . . and the elements of dissolution are bound to show themselves in the increase of crime, in hooliganism, in corruption, in speculation, and in every sort of atrocity. To master these requires time and an *iron hand*. . . . Here and there, there has sprung up among the Left wing of the Social Revolutionaries a regular call to hooliganism, an agitation which appealed to evil instincts and to the efforts of the men of small means to 'make money somehow.' "

But for the very reason that the Social Revolutionaries were calling for a renewal of the war with Germany, that he was aware of their anger at the shooting of Ukrainian peasants by the German occupation authorities, Lenin counted on these men of the Left assisting him in the restoration of the country's productivity. For the problem of work was also the problem of defence.

Yet when the fifth All-Russian Soviet Congress was opened in July and the Head of the Government entered the hall, the Left Social Revolutionaries roared: "Paid pro-Germans! Traitors! Lenin has sold the Revolution!"

Ulianov listened in mute patience to the speeches of the Social Revolutionaries, who protested against any sort of organized work, as though they wanted the war to be carried on with pitchforks. One of their women leaders, Spiridonova, said: "Lenin is reintroducing the death penalty, giving the law immense powers, instead of leaving it to the revolutionary enthusiasm of the masses to punish traitors in critical times. Worst of all, he is coquetting with foreign imperialism. The German murderer-ambassador, Count Mirbach, has his permission to stay in our revolutionary capital. He talks of stemming the hostilities of Allied imperialists by throwing forest and railway concessions as a sop to them. He has betrayed the Revolution, and on his head lies the whole burden of responsibility. . . ."

Before the Congress met, Lenin had sketched the "next tasks of the Soviet Power": ". . . We won the victory through the method of repression; we shall find out how to win also through the method of administration. . . . Without bringing in experts . . . there can be no transition to Socialism. . . . In the same measure as administration supersedes military repression as the chief problem of power, the typical means of repression and compulsion will cease to be summary shooting, which will be replaced by the procedure of the courts . . . the courts, the instrument of training in discipline. . . . The whole difficulty of grasping the situation in which we are living, for many who regard themselves as Socialists, lies in the fact that these people had become accustomed merely to opposing Socialism to Capitalism . . . more than that simple notion the majority of the so-called Socialists, who have read of Socialism in books, cannot get into their heads. . . . Try and compare the ordinary, facile conception of a revolutionary with the qualities called for by the special needs of the moment through which we are passing: to know how to take a zigzag course, to retreat, to be patient, to build slowly, brick by brick, to tighten up control ruthlessly, to enforce a stricter discipline, to sweep away all that is easy-going. . . . Is it surprising that some 'revolutionaries,' when they hear of all this, are seized with a noble indignation and begin . . . to thunder at us charges of forgetting our traditions . . . of coming to terms with bourgeois experts . . . of Reformism? . . . We do not want a hysterical effervescence; we want the measured march of the iron battalions of the proletariat."

Lenin saw that expropriated factories produce no goods until muscle and brain have got to work in them. He called the form of reconstruction which he desired "Socialism."

It may be that no idea is ever realized. The ideal works as a ferment, but when the dough has shaped itself no prophet could recognize the result.

The men and women of the factories had to pass in and out of countless meetings in hall and square before they could return to the machines and, under the caresses of the Idea, reconcile themselves to the mercilessness of life. Communism paid worse wages even than those of Romanov times; but the sufferers were comforted by the thought that they were building a house in which they would some day themselves live. As yet they were only putting up the scaffolding.

Hunger and the Tsar would also have compelled the masses to produce; now, however, the poor people were forced into discipline by the public opinion just born into the world and by a new power, not, indeed, arising from their midst, but created with their help. The novel feature in this economic process was that a Government was issuing orders in the name of the hungry themselves, was brightening the gloomy present with evangelistic phrases of a class mission, and was saying to man, woman and child: "To desire days of happiness here and now is to be a bad citizen: the community must work for the promise of a social paradise if it is not to go under."

In these speeches, against the Social Revolutionaries and against anarchy, was not Lenin at issue also with his own past?

He was now a man metamorphosed by the changed situation; that was why he was able himself to complete the task performed in every other revolution either by two opponents or by two separate and successive leaders.

Without the destruction of the *ancien régime* Napoleon's work of civil reconstruction and administration would have been impossible. If on July 14, 1789, ten thousand men and women in Paris had not killed a dozen army pensioners in the courtyard of the Bastille, and if this easy storming had not been trumpeted as a heroism, France would have met a similar fate to that of Spain—prolonged impotence. Napoleon himself saw the necessity of his Jacobin predecessors; he said in front of astonished field-marshals and dumbfounded duchesses: "There can be no social revolution without terrorism. . . . How can those who have the whole administration in their hands, who hold all offices, enjoy all advantages, simply be told to pack themselves off? They must be beaten down by Terror, driven to flight, and that is what the *lanternes* and the popular tribunals are for. . . . The masses only really grasped the Revolution when the Terror began."

The Emperor was fortunate, however, in not having to do this work himself; his fame rested on the echoes of the tocsin which Jean Paul Marat sounded to summon the mob to the murder of people who had had the misfortune not to be born in tenement buildings.

The forces which Marat called up from the depths lived also, under other conditions, in Russia. But History has so rich a wardrobe that she never puts the same dress on twice. The forces of rebellion could not now be evoked from the slums in the name of a Napoleonic eagle.

Lenin feared that the forces of the countryside, which had come to his aid on the threshold of November 7, would be unable to crown the edifice of power; the flames of rebellion were threatening now to reduce the Kremlin itself to ashes.

He was forced to part ways with the Social Revolutionaries. But in a revolution two parties do not separate without trouble. Revolution not only, in the name of freedom, prohibits—freedom: it also restricts the field of choice, of initiative. Rebellion, the over-toppling of a great wave of accumulated causes, produces entirely clear situations, which every illiterate may read. Insurrection loves simple issues, continually asks the same questions, hates every nuance, every fine distinction.

The Social Revolutionaries were intent on a struggle against Lenin, on an immediate return to the barricades for their own ideal. But the earth was satiated with crises. Ulianov held, therefore, that if the plans of the Social Revolutionaries were not baulked the field would be clear for the return of Tsarism. Yet these friends of yesterday and enemies of to-day had the majority in the Soviets which he himself had extolled.

It was impossible for him openly to flout legality. He needed the Soviets as the foundation of his own constitutionalism. The Premier accordingly refrained from dissolving the Fifth Soviet Congress in the same way as he had dissolved Parliament; he merely juggled with the franchise.

A conference of landless peasants' committees which had been convened in St. Petersburg sent delegates to the Soviet Congress in Moscow, and so altered its composition; the Bolsheviks had then a majority.

The Social Revolutionaries made up their minds at the eleventh hour to open hostilities against Lenin. They contrived the assassination of Count Mirbach, the German Ambassador, in order to compel a resumption of fighting with the enemy armies, and also fomented a revolt in Moscow against the Soviet Government.

The revolt was suppressed in a few hours; but the successful assassination of Germany's representative brought a fresh danger. Lenin feared military intervention. "There is ample occasion for it," he declared.

The President of the People's Commissars prepared to go to the grief-stricken Embassy, to tender apologies.

"What must one say to them?" he asked Trotzky. ". . . I should have liked to express real sympathy, but I suppose one must keep to formal phrases of regret."

"Lenin laughed wryly, put his coat on, and then said firmly to Sverdlov, 'Let us go.' His face changed and became stony and grey. The visit to the Imperial German Embassy was a bitter pill for him; probably one of the most trying personal experiences of his whole life."

The failure of their *coup* was the end of the Social Revolutionaries' existence.

"In future," declared the Dictator, "we Bolsheviks must bear the burden of the Revolution alone."

The last freedoms disappeared.

In the Soviets there were no Right and Left wings, no stormy debates, no more votes of no confidence. These popular institutions continued, however, to take their share in administration. The Government still found in the Soviets competent leaders who were not members of its party.

The bureaucracy of the Kremlin had to keep watch over the thousands in charge of Russia's administration, and was responsible for their actions to Lenin's all-powerful Cabinet. The whole of the work was apportioned in the Political Bureau of the Communist Party, of which Lenin, employing diplomatic inventiveness, said that it "synthesizes the activities of all the Soviets, of every organization . . . and endeavours . . . to deal with all the problems of international Socialism and of home and foreign policy."

On the benches of the Soviets there sat the grown-up children who were learning the A B C of Bolshevism and of politics. The pupils were free to ask questions—for the central administration wanted to know the feeling of the country, and with this knowledge to test the accuracy of its own course. Here the leaders spoke to the masses; here they sought only to show strength, not to use it; here those who had the power strove to work through persuasion; these were the conciliation courts of the régime, in which the myriad threads from town and country were woven together.

The Soviets had been tireless in drawing strength from the depths, had spread countless fables and slogans, and had covered the country with a ghostly fear. Their dictatorship, Lenin's victory, was also the end of their efflorescence. The Autocrat made an end of bourgeois "freedom" because it refused to revolve around his truth, because it was incomplete. He also made an end of proletarian, peasant and petty bourgeois "freedom"; he made an end of every sort of freedom; freedom was now dead and could make no more mistakes.

THE REPUBLIC'S STRUGGLE FOR LIFE

In Lenin's big office all was in scrupulous order. He had no staff of secretaries, very rarely dictated anything, wrote with his own hand the most important and the most trivial advice and instructions. His attaché case contained the whole policy of the State. Responsibility was an ever-present inspiration to him.

The Dictator's brain was Russia's Parliament, there only was debate free and unrestrained.

He insisted on having a hand in the appointment of every divisional commander, went into every strategic decision, had full reports sent to him of the meetings of numbers of village Soviets, looked through the new school books, made himself censor of instructional films.

His innate seriousness prevented Ulianov from taking any interest in outward appearances. He hated half-knowledge. This hardest-worked of men was constantly warning the most radical revolutionaries: "You have a lot to learn. No amount of theory can make up for lack of experience."

The day's problems were for him exciting chapters in a book which he believed he knew had a happy ending.

His teachers of Western European philosophy could not solve his problems for him. For his task there was no precedent in the past that could be consulted; no one has yet laid down the theoretical basis of the building up of a State or of the winning of wars. "In our discussions of present-day problems," he said, "we are finding nothing written in the past about Communism of any relevance; for to-day's story is bound up with the everyday task, with all its ramifications into every field of activity."

To this most matter-of-fact of men, the attitude of the artist who builds up a world tragedy out of his own unproductivity and unclear thinking, and sees in all power symbols of the eternal, could only seem ridiculous. The artists daubed over all the walls, painted mass meetings of rebel goddesses, out-Bolshevized Olympus. They wanted a new sun and moon, wanted to change the names of the months and days and rivers, to revolutionize procreation in the animal world and among mankind through class consciousness. The cafés were unfortunately closed, but idlers always find a meeting-place; and nowhere are poets, painters, writers and other geniuses more abundant than among the loungers. All of them tried to get into the Kremlin, showed their proletarian pedigree, talked of visions of insurrection, were effusively loyal to the system.

Lenin took refuge behind a pretence of diffidence; declared that he had no competence to discuss these questions.

The Dictator hoped, however, for help from another quarter. This idolater of science, with his dreams of technical advance on the American model, wanted as supreme ruler to meet the starving scholars who in the worst years of the Republic, without forming Soviets and without swearing eternal loyalty to Bolshevism, had quietly and peaceably gone on with their work. Lenin tried to comfort these unfortunates; at the end of a meeting devoted to the reorganization of the scientific institutions of St. Petersburg, he said of some of the professors: "One can see at once that these people know what they want. One can work with people of that sort; it is a pleasure. . . ."

Gorky asked Lenin: "Is it only my imagination, or do you really feel pity for people?"

"For the intelligent ones," he answered, "I am sorry. We have not many intelligent people. We are a gifted people in many ways, but lazy-minded."

Did he stand in fear of the hot, infectious breath of the plague that makes it easy for people to kill and to die themselves?

This man was an ascetic of the purest type; he loved the silver gleam of southern seas, the haze over the meadows, loved every valley of his homeland, envied the leisurely traveller in the countryside; declared to his friends: "I know so little of Russia! Simbirsk, Kazan, St. Petersburg, exile—that is all!"

Perhaps he was afraid that the spirit of joy would tell him that the red lips of a dairymaid, laughter by the riverside, all that tempts by its peace is more wonderful than the distant visions of a better world.

One evening he said to Gorky: ". . . Very often I am unable to listen to music, it affects one's nerves too painfully. It makes one want to talk nonsense and stroke people's heads . . . but nowadays one cannot stroke anybody's head for fear of having one's hand bitten off. One has to hit out hard and unmercifully at these poor little heads, though ideally we would have nothing to do with force. . . ."

Reformers who send many to the gallows comfort

themselves with the idea that some day they will put an end to all compulsion. Robespierre himself devoted his first speech to the abolition of the death penalty.

Ulianov had no time to go on dreaming of the old and yet perpetually new legend of a humanity at peace. He had to mobilize every man, after every defeat to proceed more resolutely with the defence of the territory of the Republic.

Russia was growing smaller and smaller. Victory seemed impossible; yet the leader declared that it was certain.

The overthrown enemies within the country beat their drums abroad. For all who charged the Bolsheviks with betraying their country there was only one problem: should they appeal to German, British, French, Japanese or American bayonets? Most of these gentlemen were Liberals, and accordingly they decided to leave it to each one to make his own choice, and to find blessedness in the shelter of whatever guns seemed to him the safest.

Ex-deputies and landowners who for three years had been spreading the tale that the Sunday amusement of the Prussian Guards was to go straight from church to set fire to an enemy village, begged for help in Berlin. Princes and manufacturers, "popes" and fugitive officials, Social Revolutionaries and past owners of racing studs, having now no property in Russia, were able to assure their new friends that Russia herself no longer existed. And every European Power became a knight-errant and set out to save the Russian dame who had fallen into deep water. Or was it her purse that seemed to be floating alluringly on the surface?

As on a winter night the snow piles itself up into white mountains, so in a few weeks, north and south, east and west, there sprang up out of small roving bands the fronts of enemy armies. Britain began a blockade, and all the peoples of the earth tried their luck against the Kremlin: Frenchmen, Austrians, Germans, Poles, Finns,

Czechoslovaks, Americans, Japanese, Esthonians, Lithuanians, Serbs.

The lands to be shared out had suddenly expanded; there had come into view out of unknown seas a real fairy gift—an unarmed continent: Russia. None were more keenly anxious to get there than the Britons. As a poor man who suddenly learns that gold has been discovered in the next village is torn with fear that someone else may get there before him, so His Majesty's Ministers were on thorns with impatient expectancy.

The British representatives in Murmansk, Vladivostok and Archangel had British or other troops landed and the local Soviet leaders shot. Yet they brought a gracious message of liberation. "Peoples of Russia," wrote the manifesto from London, "your Allies have not forgotten you . . . we come as friends to help you. . . . Gather round the banner of freedom and independence which we . . . have raised in your midst . . . our only desire is to see Russia strong and free and then to withdraw. . . ."

The Japanese drew up in Vladivostok a yet more marvellous self-denying document. The French armed the 100,000 Czechoslovaks who had fled from the Austrian army into Russian territory, and published a moving appeal, worthy of the Académie.

And the Russian peasants were unwilling to fight. Ammunition dumps exploded in the towns, railway bridges were destroyed, the Liberators' International conquered province after province.

And in Moscow itself a shot rang out.

At a meeting of workers a small, dark, lean Jewess came up to Lenin, gave him a slip of paper to read, shot, and hit; he sank to the ground, gravely wounded. The leader was carried into the Kremlin.

In the dismal gloom there arose pæans of joy. The blessed magic of the news spread like pollen in the air, and all the enemies of the régime spoke out. "My lands, my dividends, my diocese," cried the Russians; "Our loans, our rights, our spheres of influence," cried the foreigners.

But the Republic was not prepared to die. The Red regiments, who for months had been retreating, halted. On the Volga front the dispirited revolutionary armies hardened and stood firm. The way to Moscow was blocked; the critical engagement came; the struggle, as so often in past wars, had reached a point which was either end or beginning—and it was the beginning.

Perhaps it had been necessary for despair to give birth to resolution.

"They will come and hang us!" Rather than freeze on the gallows they made a stand.

On one section of the front the enemies made a successful encircling movement.

"The divisional commander present," writes Mme. Reissner, one of the women fighting at the front, "mobilized the whole of the train staff, the clerks, telephone attendants, ambulance men and escorts . . . in short, everyone capable of holding a rifle . . . the offices of the Staff were completely empty—there was no longer a 'base' behind us. . . ."

Next day the commanding officer determined to show that the death penalty was not a privilege of the enemy only. He had two dozen party members shot without trial for running away from the front. They had consoled themselves in the guard-room—"I remember the O.C. in Paris—often used to have a coffee with him in the Café du Dôme; sometimes I used to pay for his."

The Bolsheviks first employed terrorism against their own people; all the more mercilessly did they then extend it to their opponents and the indifferent.

"Order of the Chairman of the . . . War Council. I declare: . . . it has been proved that there are Soviet representatives who at the first approach of danger make haste to run away, imagining that their first duty is to save their own lives. Such creatures . . . who abandon their posts . . . are traitors . . . and will be punished with death."

"Secret order. I declare: Once for all the idea must be stamped out that offences against military duty—whether of single persons or of large bodies—can be allowed to go unpunished. . . . For deserters who are caught there can be only one punishment—shooting. . . . In isolated cases in which the court . . . returns to their units . . . men suspected of desertion from the colours . . . such men must wear black collars for identification. . . ."

This "I" was Trotzky. As at Brest Litovsk he had had closer experience than anyone else of the impotence to which his country had been reduced, Lenin had entrusted him with the organization of the army. They agreed in resolving to make use of military experts. Until now officers had been murdered. Now the dictators declared that the Revolution needed some live generals. A ukase was issued which contained the statement that: ". . . Enmity to all and every ex-officer is . . . no part of the policy . . . of the Soviet Government."

To make it dangerous for the old regular officers to go over to the enemy a decree was issued:

"The renegades are betraying the Russian workers and peasants to the British and French, Japanese and American brigands and murderers. The renegades must learn that at the same time they are also betraying their own families, fathers, mothers, sisters, brothers, wives and children. . . . I order . . . that the families of the renegades and traitors shall be arrested."

Not until Lenin's four weeks' incapacitation—until the attempt on his life—did the Terror of which he had been talking since November 7, 1917, begin to display all the dire consequences of civil war.

Only now, some months after the Revolution and in face of its threatened collapse, did the party of the Bolsheviks begin in its turn to be a determined tyranny. It was carrying on a desperate struggle against chaos. Lenin's organization grew through war, became in the eyes of some a monster and of others a deity. It lived as a many-eyed, many-armed monstrosity. His political followers were inquisitors and Red aristocrats, who led armies, methodically squeezed the taxpayers, repaired bridges, registered births, conducted schools, protected railways, administered provinces, extracted coal from the mines, set factories running again, expelled foreign intruders.

Their leader rapidly recovered. For three weeks he rested in the solitude of a village near Moscow. His wife tended him: only the closest friends and the peasant children in the village were allowed to visit him. For the first time for months he had time to read. One day he enthusiastically asked his friend Balabanova, who was staying with him: "Have you read Barbusse's *Le Feu?* Do you know, he too is for the abolition of private property, for Socialism?"

The Dictator who exercised authority over a hundred million souls, who looked in menace and in dream towards Asia and towards Western Europe to command, convince or allure with the evangel of his theory, rejoiced to find that a writer had arrived at the same conclusions as himself. So uncertain seemed all things in this world, even to the prophet! Doubt was growing, and no Terror can root up that weed.

His judges, however, made the attempt.

These servants of the established order sat at their desks; six centuries of autocracy seemed to be prompting them. Those of them who had principles murdered on principle; those who were weaklings or venal murdered for fear of their superiors or out of their own degeneracy. The Terror was like a giant whip that would allow no one to dance out of turn. It raged against peasants, workers, bourgeois, aristocrats, Socialists and Bolsheviks.

Its only law was that of all States—Lenin's decree ran:

"Any person who renders aid to the foreign military authorities, whether directly or indirectly, shall be regarded as a traitor to the country and shall be tried by court-martial and executed."

Part of the nation, however, was allied with Russia's enemies.

The courts received instructions from Lenin: "Our Socialist fatherland is in danger! . . . The Soviet Government must protect its rear, and to this end the bourgeoisie must be brought under control and mass terrorism instituted. The universal watchwords must be: Death or victory! Mass expeditions for bread! Mass instruction in military defence! Mass arming! . . ."

Special suspicion attached to the moderates in the Government camp. Not long before, the Bolsheviks had sat with them hatching conspiracies in the same secluded hiding-places. Lenin feared their knowledge of underground methods. Grand dukes and bankers had not the ability of these ex-allies quickly and efficiently to disguise themselves as fishermen, dockers, or peasants, whispering against the régime and throwing bombs. The attempts on the lives of the Soviet leaders were carried out by the Social Revolutionaries.

The Russian provinces in which Ulianov's opponents held sway—Siberia, where Admiral Koltchak ruled for months; the Crimea, where General Denikin was king —offered the same picture in different colours. At first the moderate Socialists tried to govern in the name of the Constituent Assembly which Lenin had dispersed. But the admiral was no friend of Assemblies, and promptly arrested the lot. "What I want," he declared, "is underclothing for my armies, not Parliaments."

Britain recognized him, praised him and wished him luck. No blockade threatened *him*. The dreadnoughts brought him gifts: munitions and tanks, doctors and medical stores, cloth and gold. His staff quarters and offices were not filled with ragged illiterates; he was surrounded by experts, scholars, professors, Russians and foreigners skilled in military science. Denikin and his army came within a few days' march of Moscow, Koltchak crossed the Urals, Judenitch even came in sight of St. Petersburg.

Liberated from casemates and cellars, from misery and the expectation of death, the rich felt yet richer, the gilded youth yet younger, the loveliest women yet lovelier.

Generals without commands, landowners without estates, "popes" without altars, Ministers without dispatch-boxes were on thorns for the moment of revenge for the humiliations that they had suffered, saw in every peasant and worker a Lenin.

"What the Red Kremlin can do," they declared, "we can do even better." Everyone turned judge. and everyone had a sword.

In the territory they had won it was not long before the mass of the population, which at first had received them gladly or with indifference, stood in fear of the cheerful, resolute victors who went from house to house to find men and booty. Bloody spectres danced in broad daylight. The streets seemed the long wards of a giant prison; from the houses there came the lamentations of the victims. The very poorest were afraid to open their mouths, for if they made a sound its echo might take the form of an officer's patrol.

The Soviet Government had commandeered the grain, but the new lords threatened to take the very land from them. The White army commanders were not Communists, but landowners in the old uniforms of the World War. Now the countryman rose up again. Countless partisan bands grew up like threatening cloudlets beneath the blue, white and red sky of the Counter-revolution.

To these persecuted people the distant Kremlin seemed the Promised Land. The name of Lenin shone like a miracle-working ikon. Bands fought on their own initiative in his name. To them he stood for Moscow, Russia, the great resource against the great peril.

Wedged between two minorities—Bolsheviks and Whites—every home and every little market town suffered from the vengeance of alternating victors, from looting at the hands of vanquished fugitives. Every town and village of Russia had a thousand and one tales to tell of the sorrows of tragic days and nights.

In the morning, when the Tsarist anthem or the Internationale announced fresh terrors, men would ask: "What is all this killing and torturing for? Whither are we all going?"

The good citizens of the United Kingdom little dreamed that Whites and Reds alike were casting the blame on them. They would have been shocked at the idea of the *bona fides* of their foreign policy being doubted. When the Allies' gamble had failed, the British Foreign Office returned to the strict letter of the Gospel, and Lord Curzon, prompted by truly religious benevolence, wired to the conquering Ulianov:[1]

"I have for some time past realized . . . that the military struggle . . . cannot be continued indefinitely . . . and have brought all my influence to bear on General Denikin to induce him to abandon this struggle. . . . Our country is particularly interested in the fate of the Denikin army . . . and we therefore regard ourselves as in honour bound to give them assistance to the end. Now that they have suffered defeat we must . . . protect them from disaster and annihilation. . . . We await here the early arrival of the Soviet delegates. . . ."

To Lenin this tone of Anglican piety had the genuine ring of the hypocrisy of European civilization. The noble Lord had spoken very differently a few weeks before. The Dictator was moved to a wry smile.

---

[1] Re-translated.

Ulianov could not carry scepticism to undue lengths; but he was compelled by events to examine everything doubtingly. After the dearly won victory he was deeply concerned with the critical, and at the same time unprecedented nature of his problems. "One has to proceed with the utmost caution; our policy calls more than ever for careful handling. At the moment it is more difficult than ever to find the right line, as no one knows the track on which the train is standing. The enemy himself does not know what he will do next." Even during the actual civil war Lenin recognized that Terror by itself could only deal with the difficulties of the moment. The enemy, too, had used all-destroying violence, and still he had come to grief. Compulsion must have a policy behind it. It was not enough to murder as resolutely as Koltchak had done; victory called for more discernment.

The eighty per cent. of Russia's humanity—those it was who counted. Now they were looking towards the Kremlin, tilling their fields and saying to themselves: "Moscow has freed us." Lenin drew on this attitude. He reminded himself that the peasant was incapable of grasping abstract ideas; he would simply compare Reds and Whites and ask, "Who is giving more and asking less?"

And with the same decision with which a few months before Lenin had been calling for a crusade against the richer peasants, he now condemned terrorism in the village altogether. "We shall not permit the resort to force in any shape against the middling peasantry, and even against the rich peasants we do not say 'Expropriate' as decidedly as against the bourgeoisie. . . . It is clear that we must come to the aid of the middling peasantry."

A Communist organization in the district of Nijni-Novgorod, supposing that the words which the Master had spoken a few months before still belonged to the text of the Evangel, had issued instructions that "the decree on . . . taxation must . . . fall with its whole weight on the shoulders of the rich men of the village, the speculators." Lenin declared that this order of his friends was either a collection of printers' errors or a dangerous, premature, ill-considered, counter-revolutionary measure.

At the Party Congress he asked his supporters to set their faces against all use of force, all experimenting; he repeated his request, so that his pupils might thoroughly understand him, that they might leave the hall with the impression that he had always taken this line; that his view really hardly called for expression, that they, his hearers, of course understood the problem better than he himself. ". . . To work through violent means is to spoil everything. . . . The peasant, not only in our country but all over the world, is a practical man and a realist; we have to show him concrete results. . . . Nothing can be more foolish than for people who have not the faintest idea of the special needs of agriculture . . . to set themselves up as teachers of the peasants on everything under the sun. . . . Here the task before us stops short of expropriation . . . and even of talking learnedly! That is the rule which we have set before ourselves. . . .

"First give assistance, then demand confidence. . . . We must . . . offer advice. That does not mean the command of one in authority, but the advice of a comrade. . . ."

The Communists' Congress came to an end with songs and cheers for the speaker. No one asked whether the armed bands of Reds, who a few months before had been burning villages by his orders, had been industrious agricultural experts and comrades of the peasants. Lenin was working as the brain of the country, the members of the Congress as its limbs.

PEACE, WAR AND WORLD
REVOLUTION

The British world teachers had to abandon their peda-
gogic method of Blockade. They tried next to train
the Russians to be democratic gentlemen, using an Upper
and Lower Chamber as gentlemen should, by means of
a system of oil deals. The madness of civil war had been
cured. The nation was coming to its senses as after a
long debauch.

The soil of Russia oozed with the sweat of the six
years' anguish of a people. Impassable roads, wrecked
railway lines, stations shot into splinters, graves in main
streets, villages reduced to desolation produced the hideous effect of the day after an orgy: the remains of Russia's wealth.

Lenin could feel this dawn of peace. The fortress of
the Tsars was no *oubliette* for him; he was not shut off
from the world, slept no enchanted sleep on a golden
throne amid the scent of roses, kept no flagellant's watch
in a dark cell of the palace. This man of endless activities went hunting, like the junker heroes of his favourite
novelist Pushkin, and saw that the time had come when
men must laugh.

His asceticism was a jealousy of Time. He felt the
great clock of the Kremlin to be the ally of his Idea
and the enemy of his life. He pressed on because even
the second-hand counted the days of the all-powerful;
for Lenin wanted to live to see the first flowers of the
earthly paradise in which he firmly believed.

After the two years' wandering in the wilderness,
Ulianov believed that he could see in the valley the fount
of peace. It might perhaps have been more in accordance
with theory not to be lulled by thoughts for his own
country, but to go in search of the invisible kingdom of

the Idea at the head of revolutionary armies in a war
with neighbouring countries. Lenin, however, was too
well aware of the weakness of his country. With the same
boldness and confidence with which he had created an
army of millions of men out of a few ragged bands, the
leader of the country called now for collective work for
reconstruction. Like every one of his messages, this one
was repeated innumerable times; he himself seemed to
hear it echoing from all around. After his enormous work of destruction he saw houses, roads and
squares beginning to show again like buds that open in
a night.

He called this movement, the fruit of his will and his
aspiration, "the Great Initiative," for the work must be
done voluntarily, as he understood voluntariness.

The Bolshevik Party was to create a public opinion
which should make the country work by the force of persuasion. Every idler, he held, would have to be as
ashamed to be seen in the streets as a naked man. To
Russia's true men and demigods, the supporters of his
faith, the task fell, in his view, of mobilizing the country.
As during the war the secret police had kept the population in a state of perpetual alarm, so the Communists
must now be the turgid orators of reconstruction. The
construction work must not, however, be freely decided
on, through elections or Soviet congresses or time-wasting
debates: shrill sergeants' shouts must reverberate through
Russia, short and sharp as forked lightning. "The will
of hundreds, of tens of thousands," said Ulianov, "can be
incorporated in a single person. . . . More discipline,
more scope, more dictatorship, are needed."

Now, however, when the worst of the pressure was
over, townsmen and peasants were hoping at last to be
able to stretch their limbs.

But, for Lenin, peace was struggle in another form:
". . . A new war is now beginning," he proclaimed,
"a war without bloodshed. March now to victory over

famine and cold, over typhus and economic collapse, over ignorance and devastation."

But the people were well content with a period of rest. "The ruins," they said, "will gradually disappear even if we lie another hour in bed. After a hard time it is natural to have a thirst." The leader, harassed with endless tasks, heard in these murmurs only the voice of the past. ". . . We find," he complained, "that the old bourgeois inertia is gaining the upper hand: it is stronger than we are, we must admit that at once." In spite of victory he could detect the tread of the silent millions for whom Communism was only the official language of the Kremlin.

Ulianov had no thought, however, of having gallows set up. The enemy majority as he saw it, the masses swayed by their personal interest, must be won over by the prestige of the Party, must be disarmed by the "moral authority . . . of the men and women who sacrificed themselves for the victory of Socialism."

He held that the Bolshevik organization had many unworthy members. Had not many adopted the badge and password of Socialism for no better reason than that the delectable privilege of command was to be enjoyed only within the ranks of the official party? The Great Initiative would winnow out the chaff from the grain. Every revolutionary must be prepared to fell timber, carry stones, drain marshes without special remuneration. If the Party lost three hundred thousand members out of its half million—so much the better! There would remain two hundred thousand Bolsheviks and four million workers organized in the trade unions. The Bolsheviks would set the proletarians in motion, the proletarians the poor peasants, the poor peasants the "middle" ones, the middling ones the rich—and this machine, built up of men, would function like a gigantic workshop for Socialism. Dictatorship was the leather belting that would link up the wheels and keep them in motion.

Force lurked in the background, ready to strike at any moment. For the moment nothing more should be heard than the factory sirens. *Lenin even issued a decree abolishing the death penalty*. This was partly diplomacy—it was a demonstration to foreign countries of the security of the Régime—but it was none the less in line with the intention of the leader who for years had been in favour of terrorism. So long as Europe left Russia in peace, even the hangmen should turn navvies.

Lenin was ready to make any compromise to secure peace along the frontiers. He was never a kilometre patriot, and much too good a nationalist to see in the loss of a few square miles of territory the downfall of a nation. There were threats from the new States invented by the victors in the World War—that favourite dodge of Entente strategy. (If the German general staff had been strong enough to carry out their plans there would by now have been a "liberated" Flemish State, a Basque, a Breton, and one of San Marino.)

Poland, the big link in Germany's fetters, was no more than a creature of Britain and France; but she was an animal that had cost a great deal, and must be kept in a good humour lest she should sulk and die. The British Cabinet would have preferred peace with Russia. But the collection of feudal, aristocratic anarchists on the Vistula were solidly determined to be received in the Kremlin with the bread and salt of the victors, and the lords of Versailles gave way.

To complete the spoils they had accumulated, the Entente rulers and their field-marshals felt that one corpse more was wanted: Russia's. Perhaps the Poles would bring the body back. "We are not risking anything. Whatever happens, this war will make the weak weaker and ourselves stronger."

Lenin still remained in the spell of his vision of reconstruction, was convinced that through hard work, authority, stern supervision and careful planning, life could be endowed with a finely woven Socialist magic carpet. The peoples of foreign countries would then admire the wonderful creations of the happy Communist State. If the brethren in the Faith, if the dispossessed of all countries asked it, a future Muscovite army could hurry to their aid, with recruits from Bashkiristan, Turkestan, Vladivostok, carrying Hegel's *Phenomenology of the Mind* in their knapsacks, and discussing, in between the fighting, dialectics or economic rent or Beethoven.

The present time, however, needed peace at any price.

The past three years had deeply furrowed his brow. The thought of coming disasters had made him an old man; his shoulders gradually bent like an iron framework that can no longer bear its burden. Lenin lost the calm application of the recent weeks of constructive work. He carried his new nervousness into his diplomacy. He wired *fifteen offers of peace,* communicated them all to Paris and London, reminded Curzon of the tears that Britain had wept over Denikin. Now the compassionate peer armed in the Crimea a successor to the defeated general: Wrangel.

Poland interpreted Ulianov's readiness for compromise as mere weakness. Pilsudsky's white eagle spread its wings and went in search of prey. The bird saw boundless fertile territories: the Ukraine, the Caucasus, Galicia, White Russia, the Don territory. All defenceless were the glittering domes, the shining fields, the rippling streams. Warsaw was to become the capital of uncounted buffer and vassal States.

The Republic of the silent Soviets became once more a theatre of war. Polish muskets found easy work. The country knew these flaming messengers of want; for six years it had heard the hymns of many crusaders and had seen their work. Men, women and crockery, windows and babies, dogs and orchards, fowls and grandfathers, were one enemy mass in the eyes of the conquerors, one

weed to root out. The trees received no more consideration than the men hanged on them.

Out of the Russian wilderness there arose a new spirit
of stubborn endurance, resistance, aggression. It showed
that everything in the world, even exhaustion, may be
deceptive. There is no relying even on the weakness of
the weak. Men seem to have more patient tenacity in
the stranglehold of war than in their peaceful pursuits.
Ragged and hungry, the Muscovites forgot their old skill
at dying. The Kremlin received unexpected aid from the
exiled and the oppressed. Engineers, specialists, staff
officers, doctors, professors, technicians in all fields, who
but a few weeks before had been fighting under Denikin
and Koltchak, saw in Lenin no longer the enemy but the
deliverer. Robbed and ruined aristocrats, men from
whom Revolution, with her greasy, dirty hands, had torn
the very shirt off their bodies, volunteered for service.
The one general who had survived the war with the Germans—Brussilov—wrote to Ulianov that the Poles were
threatening "Orthodox" territory, and begged permission to lead an army against the enemy.

Lenin accepted all the help that was offered.

Put opponents of the system to defend the country?
Yes, even that. Certainly things were much simpler in
those leading articles from Zurich. Then it was easy to
show on paper how to do all things in national and social
life; thoughts never got entangled unless the blotting-
paper was lost and by some accident the hand swept across
the wet ink.

Had not all his rule since November 7 been the rebellion of a poor country, a semi-colony, against cosmopolitan
bankers?

He did not loosen the reins. His office remained the
centre of everything. He threw his appeals for the Great
Initiative, for voluntary work, into the corner, and issued
orders for a general mobilization.

The dream of peace was gone. All thought of it would

now be a weakness. The first need of all was to be armed
—there was no other way to win through. All over
Europe it was being declared that force was Lenin's god.
And he had never denied that his rule from the Kremlin
had been built up on iron discipline. Yet at the very
moment when peace was dawning in Russia, when her
ruler, full of the thought of her poverty and need, had
begun to seek other means than force for attaining his
purposes, there came preachers of peace who armed
mercenaries, lest Russia's peace should last for ever. How
often were foreign foes to break in through the gates of
his homeland? When would it all end? If once more
he defeated them, who would come next? The sources
of this blood lust were inexhaustible. Lenin remembered
his allies (not that he ever forgot them), the wage-earners
of the West. Only they could help and protect the hundred millions of Russia from aggression. *World Revolution?* Had he not, on November 7, 1917, expected it on
the 10th of that same month; yet had not Ludendorff
carried out his offensive; had not the World War ended
in the Versailles "settlement"; had not the German
workers, even after the collapse of their empire's resistance, declared that they were not patriots of the Russian
type?

"Superficially," he wrote in answer to these voices of
despondency, "that is true. But why did the Entente
troops have to evacuate Odessa and Archangel? Because
their soldiers . . . objected more and more to fighting
us the more they penetrated into Soviet Russia. Thus
one of our great hopes of victory lies in the fact that we
can only be fought with large forces, while a big army can
only be made up from workers and peasants, and they
. . . refuse to fight us."

But between refusing to attack and actively helping
there was a great difference.

His faith helped him again in this hour, in which new
and bold resolves were called for, army commanders were

waiting in his ante-room and munition factories were once more working day and night.

"Every time a few issues of European or American Socialist papers come into our hands they are a great pleasure to see. They prove . . . that . . . the interest in the Soviet Power is increasing enormously everywhere, and that everywhere the revolutionary ferment is spreading."

Lenin could not, however, give utterance to all that he hoped.

The army was an army of peasants; if they were to leave their fields and march against the Poles, his propagandists must not sound the trumpet for the beginning of World Revolution, must not say to the sons of the soil: "We are off to London and Berlin to restore order there; we are going to send the theoreticians who have been concealing their opportunism beneath talk of Mach and Kant to the galleys, much as the Bourbon Louis XIV sentenced all his subjects who had written against Aristotle to convict labour."

After the peasant had repulsed first the Bolshevik bands and then the Whites, Lenin respected his determination. He never forgot the lesson, and constantly repeated that the *mujik* was a practical man and would have nothing to do with mere theory.

Would the countryside answer the call to mobilization?

In a few days the Kremlin had the answer it wanted.

The recruits came forward as in 1914; the recruiting-halls overflowed. For the first time for years the peasant again felt the strong arm of the State, and bowed before the central power. Its inexorable rule seemed to have regained the old solidity and to have lost the indecision and impermanence of the first year of the Revolution. In the villages, military bands played; the young men were once more soldiers, drinking the prohibited, badly distilled vodka, looking forward once more to their stripes. Death came now to other words and another rhythm;

no longer those of the national anthem of Tsarist days, but of the Internationale: "Refuse to serve, ye soldiers. . . ."

But in spite of the invitation in their official marching-song the soldiers did not refuse to serve; they were dreaming of the decoration of the new order which had replaced that of St. George.

Once more, like the Tsar before him, Lenin had his soldiers, countless as the saplings in a forest. But once more, as in 1914, there was shortage of munitions.

The wild fires of enemy invasion were put out. The Russians invaded Polish soil and took eye for eye, tooth for tooth. "Our soldiers," Ulianov confessed, "have had to requisition bread and other indispensable things from the Polish peasants and shopkeepers. And these saw in the men of the Red Army enemies instead of brothers and liberators."

The man at the head of the millions of this conquering army, Leo Trotzky, the genius for organization, tried to train the *mujiks*. He threatened them: "When we make Polish workers or peasants our prisoners, anyone who lifts his hand against an unarmed captive, a sick or wounded man, deserves to have it cut off."

On this day of victory the pride of Western civilization was humbled. The radiant palaces of power in Paris and London became dusky as Gothic cathedrals; Versailles, after leaving only its friends with guns, was horrified to see that not all enemy forces were yet disposed of. Every worthy citizen of London tried his door before he went to sleep, to see that it was well bolted. "Is civilization going under," he asked—"this decent six-roomed flat, these shares in Indian cotton mills, the tennis matches, afternoon tea, the rule of the waves, *Jus Britannicum* in China and Egypt?"

Conservative politicians had been foolish enough to suppose that the Soviet enthusiasts were guided by more stupid and brutal motives than persons of other political views. Up to a few months before, it had still been believed that the Kremlin was in the hands of maniacs, that passers-by were shot down from its towers, that the Muscovites flavoured their soups with the fingers cut off their enemies' hands, and that rape was the favourite method of Communist procreation. Now Europe bowed politely to Russia.

Germany's Foreign Minister, Dr. Simons, said of the Bolsheviks: "A really enormous work of reconstruction has been achieved, which we might well take as a model in many respects."

Lord Curzon's feelings were particularly stirred. As the responsible shepherd of many peoples he wired to Lenin:[1]

"The British Government . . . earnestly desiring . . . the restoration of peace, proposes that an armistice should be agreed to between Poland and Soviet Russia . . . a Conference should then . . . be summoned . . . as soon as possible in London . . . the British Government would be glad to receive an immediate reply. . . . The British Government has undertaken not to support Poland in any hostile action against Russia, but it is bound, on the other hand, through the League of Nations . . . to defend . . . the inviolacy . . . of Poland."

The general staff and the headquarters of the Red Army in Poland urged Ulianov to conclude peace; the army supplies were running short, and Wrangel was threatening from the Crimea.

Lenin, however, refused to listen to any warning. By virtue of his own supreme power, after a short Communist Crown Council, he ordered the march on Warsaw to be renewed.

Ulianov, who had been for "capitulation at any price" at Brest, and only a few weeks before had been striving for opportunities of peaceful construction work, now called on his armies to march.

[1] Re-translated.

In two years he had brought to a successful conclusion such labours as no statesman before him had ever performed.

On March 3, 1918, Lenin had had to abandon the Ukraine, Finland, Courland, Batoum and Kars, and the islands at the mouth of the Gulf of Riga, and to hand over many gold ingots. He did it "because the peasant was voting against further fighting, and that not with his hands but his feet—he was running away." Ulianov had said in reply to his friends' urgent protests: "When the revulsion in popular feeling has come which is now ripening; when the mass of the people say something different to what they are now saying," then it would be possible to take up the sword again.

Now, in July 1920, the men in war paint whom he had foreseen were in the field. Prophecy had become reality.

To hundreds of thousands of armed soldiers his rule had already become a matter of course; they were waiting patiently in camp, at the front and in the barracks. It was a peasant army fighting in defence of their fields, determined never again to endure the miseries of enemy invasions.

But Russia's national defence, this million army of small proprietors under Lenin's leadership, was at the same time the barrier against Lenin's Communism. That was why the leader was now for the advance. "Once Poland," he thought, "is governed from a room in the Kremlin and the Red Army stands on the borders of Germany and Hungary, Western Capitalism will no longer have a bolt on its door. Before long there will be allied Soviet Governments in Berlin and Paris; and they will free me from the burden of the twenty millions of petty bourgeois in my own country, from all the pressure of compromises. In the diadem of World Communism Russia will glitter as its noblest gem! Now the die must be cast. Otherwise Britain will soon order a march against us once more." Victory on a European scale was possible. "The risk," writes Trotzky of Lenin's plan, "was great, but the end pursued was yet greater. The plan might fail, but that would not endanger the existence of the Soviet Government, but only weaken it."

To-day his supreme hour seemed to have come, and a thousand voices whispered of the foundering of the enemy world. A wave had lifted him high above the ordinary level of existence; his eyes saw what it was given to few mortals to see; he almost feared the dazzling radiance.

Lenin did not, like the wiser Cæsar on the Thames and the Rhine, voluntarily retire; he too, like Napoleon in Moscow and Alexander on the Hypanis, had to endure the slings of Fate.

"Impossible," said a few of his friends. Why should it be? Had not the last years witnessed a great deal; had he not left a Zurich restaurant for the respectable poor, to enter the Kremlin as its lord; had he not for many months balanced his Government on the narrowest of knife-edges, and was there not now in being an army of millions ready for battle? Was not Europe a potsherd, and did not a big section of humanity call for deliverance?

"Push on! Push on!" shouted supporters from all countries, assembled in the Kremlin for the second World Congress of Communists, and adoring in the victorious army and in Lenin the sanctity of Socialism.

The first sitting of the new International, which Ulianov had wanted to found as far back as Zimmerwald, had taken place in March 1919. At that time Denikin and Koltchak were advancing on Russian soil. The sitting was to remain the buried treasure of the Idea if the enemy generals handed over Lenin to their judges. Europe was still blockading the Kremlin. Proudly Ulianov had written then: ". . . The most advanced and 'democratic' countries, armed to the teeth . . . controlling the whole world, are in deadly fear of the infection of the ideas of a ruined, starving, backward country, a country which they declare to be semi-savage."

Now he could announce: "We are still hampered by old prejudices . . . but every hour these are fading. *More and more effectually we now defend and represent seventy per cent. of the population of the earth. . . . If* our international comrades help us . . . no defects can prevent the success of our mission. This mission is to bring to triumph the cause of the . . . World Revolution, to create the Soviet Republic of the World."

The Russian Revolution had on the mass of the populations of Europe, Asia and Africa the effect of an unceasing clarion call. They envisaged a great tribunal of Red judges. Looking beyond the familiar scenes of their own poverty, they seemed to see arms stretched out to help them.

From India, Egypt, Siam, South Africa there came pilgrims to Moscow; and they lost nothing of their devotion when they found themselves before the walls of the Kremlin.

The economic consequences of the World War made of the words of Communist slogans drums and cymbals which sounded in every public place and at the gates of every palace.

Why had the work begun by the Bolsheviks gripped the imagination of the wage-earners of the West and the populations of Colonial territories? Not because St. Petersburg's 7th of November proved, in Lenin's view, a Marxian thesis, not because his tactics were the "only right tactics" of Socialism, not because the victory of the Smolny had presented the school of Western European philosophy with a Tsar's crown and the looted treasure of a bourgeoisie; what the masses saw in Moscow was the proof that a power hostile to the existing social system can conquer and endure. A real kingdom had come out of the land of dreams; fortunately for the Faith, they could only see it in outline and not in detail. In Europe the workers

had for decades heard talk of Socialism. But the policeman at the street corner and their own Party organization
were both warnings against haste and excess. The proletarian realized the strength of the existing order, and
was used to the domination of traditional institutions. To
talk to him of rebellion was to conjure up a vision of a
precarious triumph with gallows to follow.

Now Russia's rebels had under their control not only the
Tsar, but all the owners of economic power. This
example was bound to tear down the veil before all the
mysteries of domination, and so the sin of the war threatened to be expiated through insurrection.

When the workers in Western European factories were
told how much better they lived than the Russians under
Communism, they pointed in reply to the difficulties that
had been made for Moscow. The more dreadful the distress grew in the country of the Soviets, the brighter
shone Bolshevism and its incorporated spirit—Lenin.

Ulianov had come to be regarded as a panacea for the
sufferings of this world, and all that he did was greeted
with delight. The Dictator became the spiritual head
of countless communities; his success raised him high
above the local apostles. Out of such love grew the
saints in the Middle Ages, the saints whose feet, according to legend, lions licked in the amphitheatre.

The incense did not turn his head. He remained cool
and matter-of-fact in conversation with foreign delegates
as with everyone else. Amid the business of State he carefully read the Communist sheets from the West, looked
out for deviations from the Theory, wrote articles himself, watched the course of every strike movement, wrote
letters to various comrades. During the offensive against
Poland he dictated orders to the commanding officers and
at the same time would discuss at length a resolution sent
in by a meeting of some works council or suburban branch
in Paris or Berlin.

His wife relates that in talk with him his followers

would grow romantic about their work. Lenin would search for the actual truth, and from time to time would turn and rend the exaggerations of enthusiastic supporters; he wrote a pamphlet against them: *"Left Wing" Communism: an Infantile Disorder*. Even at the second Congress this man of caution uttered a warning against the attempts to prove that there was no way out of the crisis for Capitalism. "That is an error; no situation is absolutely hopeless."

When, however, Lenin was talking with Socialists from abroad he became the old Bolshevik of Zurich and London, concerned as few others for the revolutionary movement, but seeing everything from the standpoint of the Russian cleavage. He was Russian in every fibre of his being, as when he had led the guerilla warfare of 1905 or given direction to the lootings by the partisan bands; spiritual offspring of the terrorists, king of the illiterate, Tsar of serfs just freed.

How he had once attacked August Bebel when the leader of the German movement had tried to play the schoolmaster, how he had protested against any outside intervention in Russian party business! Now, one of his admiring supporters said, following his lead: "It will be quite the best thing for the Communist Parties of all countries if they stand a little in awe of the International. We must always have a mirror in which they can see themselves."

Ulianov remained Dictator also—perhaps against his will—among the international Communists. He did not want his portrait to be hung up in every room; but he did want every word of his thought to dominate everywhere.

Most of the pilgrims who came to him were people in the poorest circumstances. The ruler of a State received them, regiments filed past them, banners were lowered to them. Revolutionaries are not as a rule worse than other men, but they imagine (naturally, for every preacher of a new idea has something of megalomania in him) that they are better. The pilgrims found the splendour of the power that greeted them irresistible, and little was more contemptible in their eyes, more abominable, than any ideas that came from elsewhere than the Kremlin. All of them had the same arguments, the same evidences, the same way of thinking; all prostrated themselves before the same symbols, sacred and profane. To take thought for national needs, to think independently at all, was mortal sin; one more reason why the Communist International was unable to create anything permanent out of this current of deep enthusiasm. Its error was not its revolutionism but its scholasticism. All the virtues of the realism which Lenin showed in Russia became weaknesses in his foreign Socialist policy. Help from the conquering foreign fraternities was to free him from compromises and to bring the triumph of the pure faith, as in the Christian religion Eve's fall is effaced by the idealized Virgin Mary.

Lenin prescribed compromises also for his European friends, but the world Labour movement was to be drilled and inspired only by the teachings of the text-book of Bolshevist victory, only according to the letter and the spirit of *Where to Begin?*

The seventy per cent. of humanity on whom he relied failed to reach the gates of Warsaw to lighten the task of the Red Army. It was a much easier matter for a trainload or two of sergeant-majors and general staff officers to be sent thither from Paris.

"So the . . . army," writes the Russian commander-in-chief, S. Kamenev, "undertook a hazardous enterprise . . . even if every task before it was successfully performed, the operation had to be carried out without any sort of lines of communication . . . after all the destruction it was quite impossible for these to be so quickly restored. . . . Robbed of the opportunity of bringing up reinforcements, our forces melted away daily, their armed strength and stocks of munitions diminished day by day up to the crucial moment; the front continually extended. . . . Now came the moment at which the working classes in Poland . . . might have given aid . . . but their support . . . failed to be offered. . . . On August 14 the enemy began the attack. Below Warsaw there were bitter struggles until August 17 over a few villages. . . ."

Lenin always won when he was relying on Russian forces, human and material, within Russia's frontiers; usually he lost when he speculated with men and things outside Russia.

In its effort against Warsaw the army was beaten.

It could have gone on fighting. Lenin resolved, however, on negotiation—the course which many experts, especially after the collapse of 1918, considered would have been the best for Germany after the defeat on the Marne. Ulianov ordered immediate withdrawal and offered an armistice.

The critical engagement had been fought to a decision, and the industrial workers of Europe had not moved in his support. He would pursue no mirage, no fiery cross on the horizon.

If he had failed to secure a splendid victory he had given proof of Russia's strength. Poland had had to pay for fleeting moments of invasion and looting with devastation of her own territories. There was strong resistance to the idea of peace in the Bolshevik camp.

"I was faced," said Lenin, "with the most violent opposition. Almost all of our experts declared . . . that there had been a fair prospect of complete victory. . . . I think myself that we were not compelled . . . to conclude peace. . . . But I considered it to be politically more prudent to come to terms with the enemy. . . . The pacifist slogans are, of course, humbug, nothing but humbug. We shall make good use of our peace with Poland. . . . After all the years of the imperialist war and the civil war, could we face another winter of war, with millions starving, freezing, dying off in dumb despair? . . . The workers were complaining, the peasants growing restive. . . . No . . . we had to conclude peace."

The battle fought out at the gates of Warsaw was not an incident in any ordinary campaign.

A thousand years before, during the Crusades, the world had offered a similar picture. Every section of society had been filled with hatred and rage. Emperor was fighting archbishop, prince fighting prince, bishop fighting bishop, pope fighting pope. An unwashed hermit on a lame ass rode through Europe, adding fuel to the flames of infuriated fanaticism. Now, six years after August 4, 1914, the Continent seemed to be in labour with new crusading hosts of a new faith.

KRONSTADT AND THE SEQUEL

For a moment Lenin had looked at the sun of World Revolution. Its rays blinded him.

There was no more help to come from abroad. No rescuing hand was lifted. Now that the proletariat remained unresponsive, would the Western bourgeoisie help? Instead of a Continental rebellion, were gold credits to be had?

"For seven years," he declared, "blows have been rained down on Russia, and we may thank God if we can still move on crutches. . . . To suppose that we could do without crutches is to show a complete failure to realize the situation. . . . To come safely out of this situation . . . is well worth the hundreds of millions, even milliards, which we must draw from our boundless national wealth, our abundant natural resources, in order to secure the assistance of the world's accumulated capital."

It was impossible to put off any longer the solution of the problems of reconstruction with which Lenin had been concerned before the march on Warsaw. The peril of the unstable equilibrium which the years of war had left behind them in all countries was not less ominous in Muscovy because the country's ruler was a devotee of the Communist manifesto and still an advocate of its doctrines. The shocks sustained by imperialism, which had brought Tsarism low, had thrown open the gates of power to Lenin. He had now been fighting for three years himself in the defence of his country. Would not a fresh tremor of the earth throw him from the scaffolding of power like his Romanov predecessor, destroy him as a glass shaken from a table?

Lenin realized the danger at once; his answers, moreover, no longer had the directness of the past year. The Great Initiative seemed to him now not enough; he wanted to investigate and ascertain the precise relationship between the various productive elements of society, and he was anxious, as always, to learn what the countryman was saying.

To gather the opinions of the peasants he officially granted them some crumbs of the much-despised liberty. A newspaper called *Poverty* was full of complaints from the villages. He wrote to its editor: "Would you tell me very briefly (two or three sheets at most) how many letters *Poverty* actually receives from the peasants? Could you also send me a report twice a month (the next one on March 15)?"

When the editor came to the Dictator with a bundle of these protests he was overwhelmed with questions; of every letter Lenin wanted to know, "Who wrote this? A rich peasant, one of the middling peasants, or a poor one?" "Here is one," said the editor, "complaining that the Soviet régime is worse than the Tsar's."

"Worse than the Tsar's!" repeated Lenin, and laughed, looking at him out of half-closed eyes. "Who wrote that?"

He glanced through hundreds of these complaints,

went out to the villages, talked with the men of the fields, called for statistics, in which he placed no faith when he got them, made a comparative study of the whole facts; then at last he made his speeches on the problems of land-ownership.

Even if at the moment the Dictatorship of the Proletariat had enjoyed the enthusiastic support of all the industrial workers, would it not still be like a palace in the midst of a malevolent jungle? The countryman had defended his holding from the return of the old régime; now the *mujik* no longer stood in fear of a Restoration; with Lenin's sword he had conquered. Why should he go on bearing the burden of the Red Kremlin, which only sent out demands and never gifts?

"If we fail to plan out . . . the future development of our Russian industrial system," wrote the Dictator, "correctly to the last detail, so as to be able in good time to supply the peasant with goods in return for his grain, he will say: 'You are a splendid fellow, you have defended our country and that is why we have done what you asked of us. But now get out of the road, if you cannot manage the country's industries!' You may be sure that that is what the peasant will say."

Was Ulianov really acting in the spirit of his teacher Marx when he summoned the Bolsheviks to sole leadership? Who can say?

His hand was forced by the situation, not the doctrine. Theory is only a map for a mountaineer. Life is constantly disclosing fresh peaks, fresh inviting paths, fresh glaciers threatening destruction. No chart with plotted routes can remove the need for attentive observation. The books of theory told him what statesmen had already learnt broadly from Karl Marx: that social strata are guided by self-interest, that hunger remains hunger, no sophistry and no promises can change half a loaf into a whole one.

"Classes," declares Lenin, "cannot be deceived. . . .

Our fundamental principles and . . . our experience . . .
alike make it a duty to deal with every problem openly
and without reservations. . . . We . . . have . . . openly
to admit that the peasantry are not content with the
form of social relationship which has developed among
us, that they will have nothing to do with this form and
refuse to countenance its perpetuation. . . . We are suf-
ficiently practical politicians to say openly: 'This has
to be looked into and amended.' "

Lenin felt as if he were walking through a field full
of nettles, but thought that with care it would be possible
to avoid getting stung.

All sections of the population were voicing their aspirations, but nowhere was the tune of the Internationale to
be heard—or at most in barracks, police guard-rooms,
Communist Party palaces, at official receptions of foreign
friends and guests. He seemed to have won his difficult
victory after three years' struggle on every front, only to
have now to abandon power. *The Government was again
becoming isolated.*

In such a situation, Dictatorship in its traditional sense
only becomes more sanguinary. Ulianov, however, was
concerned to unravel the tangle of opposing forces by
new devices of policy.

Speaking from the pulpit of Theory, he had once
announced in the Smolny that it would take some months
to consolidate the victory; later, in the Kremlin, he had
spoken of two to three years; now the leader declared:
". . . But you will easily realize that to procure steam
ploughs and machinery and electric power for so immense
a country will be a task of nothing short of decades."

During the long intermediate period of lean years it
seemed to him to be his duty to maintain his Party in
power by combining force with compromise. Compromises were dangerous? So was the struggle with Koltchak and Denikin!

The postponement of final success mattered little to

Lenin. The day was bound now to come sooner or later when Communism would throw wide the gates of blessedness; impatience had only plagued him during the thirty years of opposition. Now, in power, he was filled with the gamester's passion, hoping for the winning card, unable to leave the green table.

The men and women whose country had become a wilderness could not show his endurance. He saw the distress of the population, and admitted that their complaints were just; but even that filled no hungry stomachs.

When Lenin first began to make his fresh compromises, enemy shells were bursting at the gates of St. Petersburg; Kronstadt was up in arms.

No Entente army was fighting here, nor any Wrangel or Denikin, but soldiers and sailors of the very fortress in whose surrounding waters Ulianov's sails had first been filled by the breeze. The rebels were no longer the old crews, the palace guards of the Bolsheviks, for the friends of the past in this island had paid dearly and uncomplainingly for their devotion to the insurrection. The new men of Kronstadt were peasants from the shores of the Black Sea.

Lenin received the news of the revolt while his Party was actually assembled in congress. "I have not yet the latest news," he said, "but I have no doubt that this rising . . . will be liquidated within a few days. . . . *We must, however, carefully study the political and economic conclusions to be drawn from this incident. . . .*"

But first of all the defiance from the fortress had to be broken. Its wireless station must no longer operate, awakening hopes among the great mass of the impatient. Kronstadt was the gateway into St. Petersburg. Already all the beaten generals were looking at the cabin plans of ships sailing for Finland and Scandinavia; Britain proposed shortly to send the Fleet for manœuvres in the Baltic. The shrewdest among the million émigrés concealed their true purpose, said nothing more of

Restoration, and adopted all the slogans of the mutinous sailors.

Lenin proposed to crush the crews. Was the town in insurrection also a town in the right? If so, the greater the danger!

"What would a successful rising mean?" he asked his assembled friends. "The transfer of political power from the hands of the Bolsheviks into those of a . . . union of the most diverse elements, standing, it might be, a little to the Right or even a little to the Left of the Bolsheviks. So uncertain is the net total of the various groups who have tried in Kronstadt to seize power."

The thing that Kronstadt wants, the abandonment of Communist experiments, only I myself can effect, thought the Dictator; and he refused to enter into any sort of negotiations.

The Régime had now stood for years, and had its own military students, and units that were its own creation and devoted to it. In 1917, by Lenin's order, officers' training colleges were set up. Their cadets were called *Kursanty*. On orders from Ulianov they would have shot with equal readiness Tsar Nicholas II or Karl Marx. He would not wait for the estuary of the Neva to be freed from ice between St. Petersburg and Kronstadt. The soldiers marched across the ice, under their young, scarcely finished officers, against the formidably defended fortress. They could not use artillery, for the crust of ice was too thin. Silently and rapidly they advanced. In perfect discipline, as though roped together, they halted before the fortress.

The gleaming, level desert of ice was a cruel battleground: not a wall, a tree, a trench for shelter! Kronstadt could shoot down its attackers as a huntsman so many hares.

Often the ice gave way. Then the water would shoot up high, and long lines of the storming parties would disappear in the gaps. A fresh onset would begin from the shore, until at last the silent devotees of the Régime had reduced the mutinous fort.

Their success was more bitterly felt by the victors than by the vanquished. It had wiped out whole battalions of the best troops of the Kremlin. The booty consisted of sailors who had shouted, "Soviets without the communists, new Soviet elections!" and sons of peasants who had demanded freedom to trade.

Lenin took the slogan "Freedom to trade" as his trophy, and said that this demand must be carried out.

Up to now the Communists had consoled themselves with the thought that though the peasant was now a proprietor the land was still the State's; for the fruits of the work on the land were being commandeered by the Kremlin for the whole nation; a State monopoly had been declared, and maximum prices instituted.

The countryman knew nothing of his being only a leaseholder, took little notice of what Moscow's theses called him; he was lord in his poor home, and grumbled bitterly at intolerable requisitions. Now Lenin threw away the last crumbs of Theory and wrote: "The peasant must have the certainty that he has no more than a definite quantity of grain to supply, and may use the balance for his own purpose of petty exchange. . . . It is of the utmost importance to ourselves that we should allow the peasant the opportunity of a certain freedom of local exchange, should replace compulsory supplies by a tax, so that the small owner may be better able to calculate . . . to offer the small producer the best conditions for the development of his productivity. . . ."

"Freedom to buy and sell means freedom to trade. But freedom to trade means the return to capitalism. Freedom to buy and sell and freedom to trade mean the exchange of goods between small agriculturists. . . ."

Lenin confirmed by legislation the inviolability of ownership of land; by legislation he prohibited the attempts at communistic collective farming.

The white breakers of small ownership had inundated the Kremlin. The peasants had beaten Lenin under Lenin's own leadership. Trade and industry were no longer to be carried on as a charitable institution for the needy, but by strict bookkeeping; new capital was to accumulate and the revived market distribute goods. Even this was not enough for Ulianov. So long as it was impossible to give any practical assistance to the countryman, all these regulations were but scraps of paper.

"How can one speak of freedom to buy and sell," he asked, "when there is nothing to buy or sell; or of freedom to trade when there is nothing to trade in?"

Goods were even scarcer than soldiers at the front had been in the days of Brest Litovsk.

In the first weeks of rule the victor had already been aware of most of his difficulties. But, in spite of all, he too had been intoxicated with enthusiasm and faith in rapid success. Can explorers who set out to discover remotest countries begin their journey without the inspiration of an unconscious excess of optimism? Lenin too thought he saw lagoons of good fortune, joys which irradiated this earth with the impartial glamour which the moon on a clear night throws over roofs and mating cats. On November 21, 1917, he had issued this order: "Comrades . . . take the land, the grain, the factories, the machinery and goods, the transport system, and protect them all as the apple of your eye—all these will henceforth be your common property in the fullest measure. Gradually, with the assent and approval of the majority of the peasants, after the lessons of their own practical experience and that of the workers—gradually but steadily and inflexibly we shall proceed to the victory of Socialism."

The results, even where the means of production had actually been socialized, were appalling.

"Touch was lost," writes Trotzky, "with reality; that is, it was no longer known whether a factory was working well or badly, whether it was using its coal economically or not; for there was only a pretty doubtful central statistical organization, and no businesslike commercial costing at all in the separate works. . . ."

As early as 1917 Lenin was already talking of State Socialism, holding that it represented a step in advance in comparison with the existing chaos.

State Socialism, which required the most careful planning of production, the most accurate distribution of the product, was a far cry from the activities of many of the proletarians, who had taken possession of the factories in the same way as the peasants had seized the land. Everywhere there was muddle and discord, and the only constructive work had been the chance product of needs and instincts, folly, madness, self-sacrifice and barbarism. Now men needed new shirts on their backs and new spades to dig with, the towns needed more lighting, more railways, more canal communication. The foreign capitalism that was still hurling menaces at Russia, and the internal capital now beginning to develop, must, Lenin held, together provide these necessaries. In his eyes the old system of wage labour was the Beast. He hoped, however, by main force to tame and domesticate the young tiger before it grew up.

Ulianov declared his readiness even to lease factories. But would not the splendour of private profit shine in contrast to Russia's poverty, would not the system force its way into the control of the State and disintegrate it? The principal industries and the country's foreign trade must remain in the hands of the Government; they would give proof of the strength of the Idea and sweep away the mountainous ruins.

Scholiasts of insurrection wrote, as in 1905, countless articles discussing the nature of the Revolution—whether it was a bourgeois one, providing capitalism with its first opportunity of unrestricted development, or whether it was abolishing class and so making, not indeed suffering itself, but at all events material want, a thing no longer known, a memory of an evil past.

Lenin answered on the fourth anniversary of his rule: ". . . The first and immediate task of the Revolution in Russia was a bourgeois-democratic one, to remove the last traces of mediævalism . . . and we are entitled to be proud of having carried out this purging . . . more resolutely, more rapidly, more boldly, with more widespread and deep-seated success than the great French Revolution of a century and a quarter ago. . . . Lifted up by the waves of enthusiasm . . . we calculated on being able to achieve at once . . . equally great economic advances . . . or, perhaps it is more correct to say, we proposed without sufficient calculation to set going State production and Communist methods of distribution. Experience has shown us our errors . . . not directly . . . but through the impact of personal interestedness, with the aid of economic calculation. First let us build a solid bridge which . . . shall lead to Socialism."

Bourgeois and proletarian progressives like to maintain that the past was wretched, that the present already looks a bit better, and that the future will be radiant and wonderful. Optimists, whether they call themselves economic or religious thinkers, project their favourite systems and ideas as with a magic lantern on the white sheets of distant decades. If one shares this faith one must admit that Lenin's methods were probably right. Moderate Socialists who aimed at less, who had better prescience of the limits of the possible than Lenin had, actually had their turn in power in St. Petersburg, but failed to uproot the past. Lenin did it, and so worked for the coming day, even if there seems little to choose between the morrow and the day before. The Dictator enriched the earth with the fruits of his brain more than any other man has done. To those who, during the process, died of hunger or cold, were shot or lynched, this is no more comfort than are the laws which govern the cruel winds to seamen who perish in a storm. Lenin, however, did not produce the catastrophe, but was born of it, and had the courage to create.

Now his one anxiety was to avoid isolation; for even the class in whose name he was ruling was discontented. His own organization began to long either for accentuated terrorism or for peace. Ulianov was not surprised at this; he declared that it was intelligible "that our Party, which counts more than half a million members . . . should be influenced here and there by what is going on outside its ranks."

He saw the limits of force, and sought for means of conciliating public opinion. Lenin held that the only way was through education. But as Dictator he never abandoned the idea of force. Freedom, thought this man of conviction, was bound to be harmful until the ideal State brought contentment to all, until happiness was as all-pervading and intoxicating as the perfume of a lemon grove. Now that the heroic period was ended, that the wounded no longer came back in trainloads from the front, that the times no longer called for that hysteria which passes into heroism, he closed the path to original effort and new thought. The choice between "Yes" or "No" would have given vitality to the masses and so to his own institutions. Error or irrelevance can only be discovered by the people with their own eyes, felt in their own persons; they cannot learn as children at school, but only as adults in their daily life. Every result, every action arises from the play of opposing forces. Even St. Peter in his eternal garden needs an Opposition, and the Lord God invented the Devil to save Himself from the eternal monotony of the song of angels.

Lenin was not afraid of criticism, but he hated critics for their scepticism *of the work itself*. "Let all the dogs and swine of the dying bourgeoisie"—whose co-operation in national reconstruction he was inviting even while he cursed—"and the petty bourgeois democracy that apes them heap their anathemas and derision on us for our failures and mistakes. . . ."

This Dictator and specialist in abuse, who wanted to do everything through the fraternity of his Party, considered himself entitled to claim the monopoly of opposition for the Bolsheviks, cast himself for the rôle of the "free and independent Press" in his régime, and accordingly said for himself all that anyone could allege against the Soviet State.

This he did with the same thoroughness with which he did everything else.

"The peasant or worker," said Ulianov, "who has no notion what sort of a thing Communism is, knows at all events that capitalism was able to provide for his needs. . . . The peasant's reply to us is: 'You Communists are splendid folk, but you are not equal to the economic task you have taken on. . . . You paint the noblest of ideal pictures, you are saints and ought to be taken up alive into Heaven. Only—the work of the capitalists is more than you . . . can do.' The man who says that is right. . . . The Communists, however, don't see it, and imagine only the 'uneducated common people' have such ideas. . . . The time for programmes . . . is over. . . . The merchant or his traveller goes to the peasant and offers his services, not for a gossip about Communism, but to build him something or get him something. . . . Our Communist pride is preventing us from recognizing this. The people who . . . never feared death and carried through the greatest revolution in world history . . . are unwilling to admit to themselves that they are not good business people, don't know how to manage a business and carry on trade, and have a lot to learn from any average shop assistant who has spent ten years behind a counter and knows what's what. . . . We have all the resources of power, but we do not know enough. . . . Don't imagine that we are short of political power; we have even a bit more than would have been absolutely necessary. . . . We have poets who have written that formerly" (during the civil war), "in spite of hunger and cold, everything was nice and clean in Moscow, but that now the ugly faces of the dealers and speculators are to be seen again. . . . Let the versifiers go on with their versifying, but let the rest of you put off . . . theatricalities, learn to see things coolly and to deal with them practically, prove that you do not manage worse than the capitalist. . . . Our governing body of Communists is still without culture of any sort . . . ninety per cent. of our people in responsible positions still imagine that to conquer the enemy and render him harmless is to finish their job. The Communists are but drops in the ocean of the people. . . . What is wanted now is no longer politics, but the most prosaic of detail work. . . . For this the people will be grateful, and only if we realize what the people want shall we be able to rule."

The Dictator was sure that his system could bear these disclosures. As no one else was allowed to criticize, he felt bound to do it as publicly as possible himself. The new system, he declared, was functioning as badly as the first steam engine; nowadays, however, people travelled to very good purpose in express trains. This immense openness was intended to remove the necessity for hostile groupings. "The enemy," said the leader to himself, "knows our weaknesses; we must know them ourselves if we are to go on ruling."

"If our opponents," he said, ". . . point out that Lenin himself recognizes that the Bolsheviks have done an enormous number of stupid things, my answer is: Very well; but there are stupidities and stupidities . . . if the Bolsheviks do something silly it is of the order of 'twice two makes five.' If their opponents do something silly it is of the order of 'twice two makes stearine candles.' That is not difficult to show. Take, for example, the treaty with Koltchak, the treaty made by America, Britain, France and Japan. I ask you, Are there more highly

educated and powerful States in the world? And what
came of it? . . . It was a fiasco which seems to me beyond
human comprehension. Or take another example: . . .
the Treaty of Versailles. I ask you, what sort of job did
the 'glorious' Powers make of that?"

For all the practical obstacles to it, Communism
remained, in Lenin's view and in that of his disciples,
impregnable. The unattained never loses anything of its
perfection as it is never seen in the concrete, and consequently no one can prove that it has shortcomings. Ideals
can always find excuses—the weather, the times, their
murdered enemies, their martyred victims; all else may
be at fault, but not themselves. Every historical process
that failed of realization can say: "*I* should have saved
the world and given birth to pure happiness."

THE LONG AGONY

Lenin, who in all his life as an émigré rarely felt the
temptation to indulge in irony, who saw nothing then but
the overwhelming power of the enemy, could now, in his
fourth year in the Kremlin, survey the boundaries of
repressive and constructive power, compare great gestures with the results of practical work.

The Dictator did not start back in horror; he merely
smiled. At the fourth Congress of the eloquent Communists of all countries he spoke of Russian and European
necessities: ". . . The foreigners too have to learn. Not
in the sense in which we have to learn, of reading, writing
and understanding what we read . . . It is a moot question whether these are the elements of proletarian or of
bourgeois culture—I leave that question open. What is
certain in any case is that we have to learn . . . to read
. . . write . . . and . . . understand."

His own daily detail work, his effort to see clearly
every difficulty of the moment, was also a mirror in

which he could see his own friends. Ulianov used to say
that the Bolsheviks were like a man who one night in a
dream sees a vision of the universe and thenceforward
is in love with the creations of his own fantasy. That
was, of course, a very necessary process; how else, in such
a country, could anyone have formed the conception of a
Socialist Revolution? Now, however, the all-too-sacred
groves must be abandoned. The clouded skies in this
springtime of the Theory compelled him also to give
advice in regard to the aims of world Communism of a
sort which he would never have given in earlier years.
The lord of the Kremlin poked a little fun at the length
of the thesis in which past international Congresses had
expounded the Communist programme. "The resolution," he said on one occasion, "is admirable. But the
resolution is almost expressly confined to Russian conditions. . . . That has its good points. . . . But it has
also the weakness . . . that no foreigner . . . will be
able to read it; it is too long, fifty paragraphs or more.
Foreigners cannot read that sort of thing. Secondly, if
they do read it, no foreigner will be able to understand
it. . . . Thirdly, even if a foreigner here or there, by
way of exception, does understand it, he cannot put it into
practice. . . ."

Lenin did not live the life of an official. His keenness
and energy and definiteness of initiative left him no room
amid all his activity for the quiet of a bureaucrat's
existence. When official business was done, the signed
papers on their way to the authorities concerned, Ulianov's active interest in men and things was not ended.
His nature had nothing in it of the official element. Urged
on by responsibility, his thoughts continued uninterruptedly at work, like a mill-wheel driven by a stream.

After the long years of war he felt that he could once
more see men as individuals. They had no longer to be
thrown like fuel into the flame of national defence. The
leader knew that men had not raged for the Revolution,

but the Revolution for men. In the cottages of town and village in which exhausted men sat at unspread tables, on whose hard beds and broad stoves children played and wrinkled old women fell asleep, there still throbbed the unending, tired murmur of the suffering. To bring contentment into these homes was the one great task. He had never forgotten it; and instinctively the great mass of people began to feel this love. All the scholarly literature of the theoreticians left him still close in spirit to the dumb and dismal homes over which poverty, barbarism and pain threw their shadow in every continent. At the summit of power, more and more securely established, he lost nothing of the inexorable rigidity of the Theory; but he ignored the marble magnificence of its palaces in his constant effort to bring immediate mitigation to those who suffered.

The Seeker often expressed his ideas only in tentative form, often wrote them down on slips of paper which he passed to his friends: "Private. Draft. Not for publication! I may change my mind once or twice yet."

Lenin's brain was afire; and the victim of the fire was he himself.

The world of men as he saw it was a murmuring, stirring, swishing, foaming sea; and in the lighthouse— his own reason—one little flame after another went out.

The eye grew more and more exhausted, but no sleep would come. Apprehensively, he sought to tear away the veils that were folding over things. Their flapping edges eluded him; an evil, unknown nightmare pressed the life out of him.

When the leader sat down at his desk, the work would go well for the first half-hour; but the deeper he delved into the material the more his thoughts would wander. After a short time interest flagged and failed; the applied energy was dissipated in clouds.

His head seemed to be in the grip of a cold, unfriendly hand.

He shuddered, resisted, tried to keep himself in hand. One day the current carried him away. The sick man wanted to rise and could not; to move his hand, and the muscles would not answer; to speak, and found himself dumb.

He was taken, breathing with difficulty, away from the Kremlin to a country villa. At the edge of the forest, near Moscow, in the village of Gorky, rest was to lull him, sleep to hover round him and join up again the torn threads of his life.

The doctors found that the brain had suffered organic injury. He lost the power of speech, and the right foot was crippled.

For three months he remained so. Gradually then suffering grew less. After some weeks he was able once more slowly to move his hand, to speak, cautiously and with difficulty to walk.

Patiently Lenin lay in the wheeled chair, looking like a soldier with a slight wound, making no complaint. Nature had made a terrible gash in him. But she seemed, like the surgeon in an operating theatre, to have dulled the senses of the sufferer, to be stroking the sick man's forehead and his hair, to be throwing a protective cover over his consciousness.

Once more the leaves in the forest at Gorky began to throw their shadows, the bees to hum and labour; the sky was blue; rare wandering clouds passed quickly by. It was the summer of 1922. In the sunshine Lenin's malady melted away. His pallor disappeared. By slow degrees life returned.

In September the sick man believed himself well again, and told his friends that his song was not yet sung. He had no time for dying. And if he was after all near his end, there was a long road which must be traversed in all haste, a work to be completed.

The leader had launched the New Economic Policy. It was the fruit of his own thought and initiative, as the seizure of power had been. Awkwardly his friends had stumbled along, losing the track. Weakened by his sickness, but throwing aside all thought of rest, he left Gorky and sketched in his room in the Kremlin the new plans, asked a hundred times: "Why are we doing stupid things? The answer is clear. First, we are a backward country. Secondly, our technical efficiency is next to nothing. Thirdly, we are unaided. No civilized country is helping us; on the contrary, they are all working against us. Fourthly, because of our machinery of Government. . . ."

Lenin felt, however, that his strength was ebbing. The memories of the tortures from which he had just recovered warned him. He could not evade these ghostly attendants. The rhythmic call of creative work was overborne by the dull drumming of sickness. The Dictator determined to set narrow limits to his activities, reduced the field of his labour, resolved to devote himself only to economic problems.

He noted the improvement in the economic situation, declared that the new goal must be the stabilization of the rouble and the restoration of the heavy industries: "Our salvation . . . lies not only in a good harvest . . . nor only in good conditions in the light industries . . . we still need the heavy industries. If we are without those we are doomed as a civilized country."

In a few weeks' time the fifth year of rule would be completed. He surveyed the past once more. Rarely had the outlook been entirely promising, but now there seemed already to be flowing from the fountain-head of November 7 a broad stream which daily grew more placid. From month to month it rose, sometimes following an underground course, but reappearing, flooding a great deal of the countryside, devastating many a town, destroying many of his own dreams for ever. Perhaps in the next five years the moist soil would bring forth a rich harvest. Ulianov went to the celebrations of the

fifth anniversary. "I will follow all the prescriptions of
the doctors—I will work less. The pains still shoot now
and then—but I just won't think about them!"

The pale man entered the hall of the Moscow Soviet.
Russia's frontiers were now freed from the enemy. *He
handed over a united realm, one great Republic, to his
friends.* "You know what great sacrifices our achievement has demanded. You know how long the civil war
lasted; you know how greatly it crippled our strength.
Now the occupation of Vladivostok—Vladivostok is
far off, but it is ours . . . has decided the universal
struggle . . . in our favour. This struggle has freed
us both from our enemies in the civil war and from our
external enemies. . . . You see all this before your eyes!
Our machinery has remained as of old, and our task now
is to make the needed developments. . . . These are . . .
difficulties facing us. . . . Now, especially, when we are
pursuing a business policy and are not approaching
Socialism as though it were a brightly painted ikon . . .
it is necessary . . . that the masses . . . the whole population should observe our path and should be able to say:
'Yes, that is better than the old régime. . . . Your praises
are not self-praise but praise from us; we say . . . that
no one is dreaming of a return to the old system.' *We
have not yet got as far as that.* Let me close with the
expression of my conviction that we shall achieve the
solution of this problem, however . . . novel it may be
in comparison with our past ones."

Amid grateful acclamations he returned to the Kremlin.
It was a rainy, cold November. The warm room looked
out on the grey colour and tone of the first beginnings of
winter.

He sat down before piled statistics, made notes, discussed plans with the Knights of the "Order of the Civil
War," who were now administrators and captains of
industry. After all, the disciples had learnt something.
But it was difficult for them to unlearn the delectable

habit of command. Would their new labours really succeed in bringing conviction to the "whole population"? A hard task, more laborious than all the rest. The Dictatorship remained, still held the country together, as the hoop the cask; but within there was fermentation.

Arbitrary rule must be made endurable for the willing workers. But many would only be made willing by economic results and by propaganda. And the Muscovites must be brought to believe, without any sort of inquisition, what the inquisitors wanted them to believe.

This Dictatorship was distinguished in theory from all others by its effort to become unnecessary.

Four months passed. Ulianov no longer had the old alertness, easily became tired, but said to himself: "One must not give way to moods."

One morning in March, when Lenin tried to get out of bed, he was unable to move. He was alarmed, in a fever, declared that it was no more than a *sequela* of past nights of pain. The days had once more shown him the active life of the streets, his room, his work, his task. Now it was all passing away.

White and emaciated, he was carried to Gorky. Once more Lenin lay in the wheeled chair—which he had hoped never again to see. His eye saw and yet was as though sightless.

"Is it true that Martov too is dying?" Lenin asked his wife, before the power of speech left him for ever.

Through the long hours of the summer and autumn of 1923 he rested in the villa at Gorky, searching for pictures of forgotten life. Slowly, languidly, they came and vanished again. Scenes appeared in golden framing— Siberia . . . Geneva . . . London . . . the Kremlin. The sick man vividly remembered a room, saw the sheets of his first article, smiled as at a recovered jewel. Then he thought he was standing in a Finnish railway station, or sitting at his desk in the Smolny, or summoning the crusade for bread. Why did these scenes of past activities float by; what did they mean? They could not save him, had only the quality of fragments of a melody which never returns.

The last flicker of his life was soft and peaceful. He looked into the garden, saw the gate, noticed the guards, recognized a sailor.

The days fell to earth indifferently as a garment.

As though touched by a magician's wand, his body acquired fresh life. Lenin was able to get up again, walked unaided across the room, learned to speak. There still glimmered a last spark in his brain to light up everything. The sufferer was content even with so little of life—his hand was only able to move tremblingly and with difficulty; he tried to write, but was unable to hold the pen.

The first snow fell in Gorky. The trees had forgotten their leaves as men their work, and seemed to rejoice in their new dress. The earth glistened as though it were covered with floss silk.

The convalescent went out for a sleigh ride, muffled up in fur and rugs, so much better that he was able to take a sporting rifle with him. He stroked its cold barrel; it was pleasant to touch the steel; one could feel it—and that proved that one was still alive. He was in his fifty-fourth year.

In the stillness Lenin heard the white flakes fall from the boughs. He returned, came up the ice-covered steps of the villa; outside the door the sick man turned to look once more.

On January 21, 1924, in the evening, the wind of death blew which for three years had been circling round him, destroying one nerve after another. Muscular paroxysms passed over him; his breath came in quick, laboured gasps; he was choking. For an hour he was in delirium, hearing, seeing, feeling nothing more.

Then the last breath left Vladimir Ilyitch Ulianov.

INDEX